MW01055892

GREENBERG'S® GUIDE TO

TOOTSIETOYS®

1945 - 1969

Raymond R. Klein

Edited by
Steve Butler and Janice Smith

A GREENBERG PUBLICATION

Greenberg Book Division
Kalmbach Publishing Company
21027 Crossroads Circle
Waukesha, Wisconsin 53187
(414) 796-8776

First Edition

Manufactured in the United States of America

ISBN 0-89778-195-3

Library of Congress Cataloging-in-Publication Data

Klein, Raymond, R. (Raymond Robert), 1940 –
Greenberg's guide to Tootsietoys, 1945-1969 / by Raymond R. Klein.
p. cm.
Includes bilbiographical references (p.) and index.
ISBN 0-89778-195-3
1. Strombecker Corporation. 2. Vehicles--Models. 3. Metal toys-
-United States. I. Greenberg Publishing Company. II. Title.
III. Title: Guide to Tootsietoys, 1945-1969.
NK9509.65.U64S765 1992
629.04'6'0228--dc20 92-34034
CIP

Contents

Acknowledgments

The time and effort required to develop this guide was greatly enhanced by the knowledge, help, and encouragement of a number of special people. At the very beginning of this project, **Charlie Jones** and **Henry Van Curler** gave unselfishly of their time and treasures to help me begin documenting the many delightful postwar Tootsietoys; their suggestions helped develop the nucleus of this publication. **Henry Timmes** and **Edward Poole** also provided valuable information in those early stages. I would be remiss, however, if I did not give a very special thanks to **my wife, Trudy,** who, in addition to her constant support, performed an unbelievable amount of typing long before the text made its way to computer disk. Thanks also to **Barbara Festge** for the days she spent at the Library of Congress in Washington, D. C., going through many publications to find advertisements and articles on Tootsietoys.

I must express my heartfelt gratitude to the people at the Strombecker Corporation for their assistance, including an unforgettable visit to their factory and archives: to **Daniel Shure,** President, for arranging the visit; to **Myron Shure,** former President and current Chairman of the Board as well as our gracious host, for spending a most memorable afternoon with us reminiscing on the history of the company and for providing my publisher with so many articles and contacts for further information (many long-standing, unanswered questions were put to rest because of the access to catalogues, archives, and employees made possible by this most knowledgeable, wise, and generous man), and to his secretary, **Pat Lawlor;** to **Elliot Rossen,** Vice President of Marketing, who took time from his busy schedule to guide and assist us while we were there, and who seemed to thoroughly appreciate the treasures we uncovered; to his secretary, **Lucy Santiago,** for her warmth and attention to our needs; to **Joseph O'Brien,** Vice President of Manufacturing, whose tenure with the company helped explain many of the manufacturing decisions detailed in this volume; to **James Fink,** Vice President of Sales, **Alan Brouilette** and **John Schutz,** Executive Vice Presidents, **Joseph Gorecki**, Vice President and General Manager of the Esquire Novelty Corporation division, and **Harlin Monks** of Durant Plastics. **Harry Brown,** who was Vice President of Product Development until retiring in 1991, provided information on the changes taking place during the late sixties and early seventies. To all these I extend my sincerest hope that this volume reflects your individual dedication and commitment to making the best, basic toys so many collectors have come to love.

I want to sincerely thank the following collectors for providing their toys, their knowledge, and their exuberance: **Ken Jestes, Ed Bruening, Robert Straub, Roger Johnson, Charlie Breslow, Doug Campbell, Trip Riley, Perry Eichor, James Arrasate, John Scinicariello, Robert Day, I. Davis, G. Blankenship, Elmer Cruts,** and **Roger Bartelt.** Many of these also reviewed the manuscript and added information on values.

Special thanks go out to two gentlemen who provided a great deal of assistance in the home stretch: **John Gibson** for loaning a few unusual items to photograph as well as for helping to verify some of the oft-discrepant historical information; and **Steve Butler** for his hospitality in letting us invade his inner sanctuary to photograph his outstanding, pristine postwar collection, and for providing a final edit with important information on values, colors, and variations.

Finally, I give special thanks to the staff at Greenberg Publishing Company: to **Linda and Bruce Greenberg** for their help and support; to **Jan Smith,** my inhouse editor, for her insight, understanding, and patience as well as her research persistence and writing skills; to **Rick Gloth** and **Jackie Leister**, the graphic artists, for making this book so attractive and easy to look through; to **Alan Fiterman**, the photographer, and **Bill Wantz** and **Kevin Stansbury,** darkroom technicians, for all the great photographs; to **Barbara Frank, Marsha Davis, Carol Hall, Richard M. Watson,** and **Donna Price** for their editorial support; and to **Maureen Crum** and **Norm Myers** for the cover design. This book is testimony to the quality of their involvement.

Raymond R. Klein

Introduction

Welcome to the newest publication on Tootsietoys—a collector's guide to the many delightful vehicles, airplanes, boats, and toys produced from 1945 through 1969. Providing accurate information on all the toys marketed during that twenty-five year period has been a challenge which required over five years of research. This book has been organized to help the collector easily find the particular toy(s) of interest. It presents the most popular series first—the 6-inch, 4-inch, and 3-inch series—followed by the tractor trailers, military toys, airplanes, ships, miscellaneous series, the rare and beautiful boxed sets, and toys of the late sixties.

Dowst Brothers Company of Chicago, Illinois, the original manufacturer of these toys, is often referred to as the oldest toy company in America and as the first of the most successful makers of die-cast toys. As far back as the early 1900s, the company introduced die-cast metal vehicles with turning wheels. A general history of the manufacturer—from the conclusion of World War II when metal Tootsietoys could again roll off production lines, to the late sixties when a shift to plastic was more evident, and even to the present—will be outlined in the first chapter.

The Listings

The listings in Chapters 2 through 13 have been developed from careful examination of many Tootsietoys and company catalogues, as well as a visit to the factory's archives in 1992 and feedback from various collectors and employees of the company. Most of the toys are listed either by catalogue number and name (if known) or by the prototype's model year and common name, followed by the years of production (in parentheses) based on the listings in the catalogues. Where the lengths of the vehicles vary within a chapter, length is given next, followed by a description of the body, tire information, any cast-in details or designations, and any known variations. Cast-in information or decoration has been noted in SMALL CAPITAL LETTERS. The final cast-in notation in each listing or variation will describe any information on the underside of the vehicle.

Toys that are generic models or that have uncertain prototype model years will list a probable model name and year first. For instance, while many collectors identify one of the Tootsietoy trailer trucks as an International truck, research does not support this designation; the vehicle is listed here as a 1947 Diamond T Truck. An explanation of this choice has been provided in the chapter on trailer trucks. Boxed sets and blister packaged toys will be listed by the catalogue order number first (if known), followed by the catalogue name of the item, a listing of its contents, etc.

Readers who have information that is not included in the listings are invited to send comments to the Greenberg Books editor at Kalmbach Publishing for future editions.

Production Years. After the identification information for each item, the listing gives the year or years of known production for that toy based on its inclusion in the company's dealer catalogues. Neither Dowst nor Strombecker maintained production records, so verification is limited to catalogues and advertisements. The term "production" must therefore be a general one. Actual production may have either extended beyond the dates shown or have actually ceased prior to catalogue issue. The success of certain products often meant that the company continued to produce them to fill orders even after a new catalogue was printed that did not show those items. It is also true that certain toys were pictured in the catalogue because of the level of inventory remaining even though they were no longer coming off the line. Some pre-production units pictured in the catalogues appear to be different from the actual pieces issued; minor adjustments were often made to molds in the process.

As is the case with most major toy companies, advance orders from dealers or special buyers usually dictated the length of the first production run. Public reaction then translated to additional production runs. The company used top sellers as the mainstay for the popular lines for many years. There is evidence that in years where the demand for certain units far exceeded peak production runs, the company placed advertisements of their stated policy of "equitable allocation." In addition, any overruns were probably used in sets.

Body Features and Colors. A listing of all known paint colors used on each piece is included with its description. The most common colors are listed first, followed by the more unusual colors, in order of availability. The company generally used uniform colors (and shades) of red, green, blue, yellow, orange, silver, and gray on most of its toys. One or more of these were selected as the standard color for a specific issue, such as red or blue for the 1949 4-inch Mercury. While this practice continued in the sixties, the company developed several new colors and shades, but tended to offer fewer variations for an individual toy. Except for Tootsietoys of uncommon color, the color of an item generally does not affect its value. Two-tone units with painted features are in greater demand in some areas, and will therefore go for higher prices. The list of colors for each item has been compiled through collector comments, observation, and research since the catalogues did not list color variations. Therefore, additional colors may be found which are not listed.

However, caution should be exercised when considering a Tootsietoy of uncommon color, especially if it is not documented here. Many individuals have developed extremely proficient painting skills but will not necessarily inform a buyer that a toy has been repainted. In addition, if a vehicle is found in unusual colors such as pink or purple, it may have been made in Mexico. A Mexican company used "retired" toy molds from Strombecker to produce their own "tutsitoys." The molds were not changed; consequently, markings on the underside of these toys will still say "TOOTSIETOY MADE IN U.S.A." or "TOOTSIETOY CHICAGO 24 U.S.A." Chapter 13 has more information on how to distinguish Mexican Tootsietoys products from their American forerunners.

Throughout the listings there are several generic descriptions of features for the various vehicles. Some are described as having *painted features,* which usually include the front and rear bumpers, the front grille, headlights, and taillights. On almost all models, these features have been painted silver with an overspray. Other toys are described as having *body and features same color.* This means exactly what it says: the car or truck body and all of the features listed above are painted one color. Still others may be described as having *two-tone paint,* where the vehicle body is painted with two different colors and usually includes painted features, unless otherwise noted in the text.

Moving Parts. Besides being more costly to manufacture, vehicles with moving parts are the most likely to be found incomplete. The moving parts were easily broken off in play and lost. While none of the 3-inch, 4-inch, and 6-inch series toys have operating doors, hoods, or trunks, these features were included on a select number of vehicles from other series. The original 3-inch series vehicles, including several reissued prewar pieces, do not have any moving parts beyond the axles and wheels. The 4-inch series includes a Fire Truck with removable ladders, a Futuristic Wagon, two Field Cannons, a Searchlight Trailer, and an Armored Car, all with movable features. The 6-inch series contains the largest number of toys with some sort of a moving or removable part, including the 1947 Diamond T Dump Truck; 1947 Mack Dump Truck; 1947 Mack Fire Pumper with removable ladder and hoses; 1947 Mack Tow Truck; 1947 Mack Stakeside Truck with removable tin top; 1955 Mack Cement Truck; 1956 Ford Stakeside Truck with removable tin top, radar, searchlight, and anti-aircraft gun; 1956 Caterpillar Scraper; 1956 Caterpillar Dozer; 1960 El Camino with Camper Top and Boat; Farm Tractor with Scoop; Farm Equipment; and the Jeep with Shovel. In the tractor trailer series, the auto transport, the rocket trailer, the van trailer, the fire trailer, and the stakeside trailer have movable or removable pieces. All airplanes other than jets have rotating propellers.

Types of Tires and Axles. Information on types of tires used within the various series is included in each chapter. A general overview of the changes in tires is included in Chapter 2. From 1947 to around 1951, the 6-inch series used smooth black rubber undersized tires on the sedans and wagons, the 1946 and 1949 tanker trucks, and the 1947 GMC Bus. This type of tire did not wear very well. The World War II Willys-style Army Jeep was the one exception; it was given large rubber wheels. Around 1951, the company began to use larger, denser rubber tires to provide a tighter axle hole and reduce wear on the tire caused when the axle assembly turned with the tire. This resulted in a more-to-scale appearance. The 4-inch series vehicles have similar tire wear problems; however, because of their smaller size and lighter weight, evidence of tire wear did not occur until after many years of use. By 1956, the 4-inch series had undergone additional axle design changes; by 1958 this series finally featured the company's new treaded or patterned tires. The 3-inch series did not adopt the patterned tires until 1959, which significantly improved the looks of the vehicles.

In 1947, the company advertised the "Rol-Ezy" wheel assembly, an unusual but effective method it developed to mount rubber tires to the body casting or frames of the Jumbo Series, the 6-inch and 4-inch series, the tractor trucks, and the airplanes. An axle spacer (bushing), consisting of a hollow metal cast tube through which connecting pins were inserted for each tire and was almost as long as the axle, was incorporated into the assembly design. On vehicles with closed wheel wells, the ends of the pins fit through holes in the body sides. After the pin was inserted through one of the holes from the outside, a tire was placed on it; then the pin was pressed into the tapered opening of the spacer to secure it. This was repeated for each of the tires. On toys with open wheel wells, the pin was passed through the vehicle frame or through mounting struts protruding down from the body casting; then the struts or frame were crimped to hold the pin.

The axle spacer prevented the tire from moving out of position. However, after some use the tires would rotate around the pin without turning the axle assembly, which caused excessive tire wear around the opening and resulted in wobbling. Because the pins have been pressed or driven into the axle spacers, removing these pins to replace worn tires can be extremely difficult and may result in a broken axle spacer. This system was not used in the 3-inch series. As more vehicles were developed with open wheels, a one-piece solid axle replaced the spacer and pin in general production.

By 1964 all tires were made of a vinyl-type of plastic, and they remained unchanged through 1969, except for the unusually wide black tires used on the Hitch-Ups. The design for the tires on this series was new. For the first time, the tire rim was not part of the tire casting; it was made of plastic and fit on a very large axle.

Note: If a listing refers to "Tootsietoy tires," it signifies that "TOOTSIETOY" is cast in the tire on both the inside and outside. This feature eliminated extra steps on the assembly line since it did not matter which side was facing out.

Cast-in Identification. Dowst and Strombecker usually included the word "TOOTSIETOY", the registered trademark symbol, and a variety of information including model name and patent number in the casting on the bottom or underside of the main body. The quality of this cast-in information varies from crisp to very poor and sometimes incomplete, but this does not affect the value of the piece. To aid the collector in identifying their toys, this casting information is provided in small capital letters at the end of each listing. (Any decal information or cast-in lettering on the outside of a toy is also noted in small capital letters.)

Determining Value and Condition

While there are a number of publications written about these toys, only some contain values. For the most part, these publications are either outdated or contain only a partial listing of the items produced, which has made it difficult for the collector to ascertain the value of individual items in his or her collection. Values are provided based on responses from various collectors and dealers who have reviewed this book, and on prices realized at auctions and toy shows.

It should be stressed that the value of any one Tootsietoy, like the value of any collectible, will vary for any number of reasons. The major reasons are the quality, detail, and condition of an individual toy, the number produced, and its availability. The price realized for any one toy will depend on the knowledge of both the buyer and the seller, and on the amount buyers are willing to pay for it. Of course, supply and demand for a particular piece will account for the variation in prices seen at shows; and geographical location plays a major role in both the supply to be found and the market price. As collectors know, the largest supply of collectible toys and trains, as well as the greatest number of toy and train shows, can be found on the East Coast. Train shows are excellent places to find Tootsietoy vehicles as well as sets of the late forties and the fifties—when the toy train hobby was at its height and many Tootsietoys were played with on layouts, then stored with those trains in garages, basements, or attics. It is not at all unusual for someone to purchase a box of old trains and discover among the contents some Tootsietoy vehicles. Consequently, many Tootsietoys have been acquired by dealers and collectors at very reasonable prices, and eventually resold at higher prices. In each case that I have come across, the prices asked for each item have been noted as well as the prices realized. Then these have been compared to information received from other collectors, and an average value for each condition has been entered in the listing.

For any individual collectible, there are eight recognized categories of possible condition and equivalent value which are independent of the presence or condition of packaging: poor, fair, good, very good, excellent, like new, mint, and restored. Only three categories of condition have been given for the individual toys listed here that are not boxed or in sealed packages or blister packs: Good **(G)**, Excellent **(E)**, and Like New **(LN)**.

For the special boxed sets and blister packs, only a *price range* may be provided, since these items are usually considered mint when unopened. A range in price is provided as a guide for those boxed sets or blister packs that may contain a mint item but the box or container is not in Mint or Like New condition. Explanations of ratings and values for boxed and sealed items have been included in Chapter 11 and Chapter 12.

The following definitions of possible conditions are provided to assist in rating a piece already owned or one under consideration for purchase. They are based on well-established standards developed for the train collecting hobby but adapted for Tootsietoys.

(M) Mint: New and unused.

(LN) Like New: Paint finish totally intact, no wheel wear, no axle rust, appears mint but has been handled.

(E) Excellent: Very small isolated paint nicks or chips, no apparent wheel wear, very minor axle rust.

(VG) Very Good: Minor scratches, paint nicks and chips, some wheel wear and axle rust.

(G) Good: Paint scratches, flaking, nicks, chips, or discoloration up to 5 percent of painted surface, wheel wear, axle rust, and minor axle deformity.

(F) Fair: Paint scratches, flaking, nicks, chips, or discoloration exceeding 5 percent of painted areas, major wheel wear, and rusted or bent axles.

(P) Poor: Extensive paint loss, broken or missing parts, cracks in body casting, extensive wheel wear, tire cracks and/or chips, extensive axle rust or deformity, non-professionally repainted or modified casting.

(R) Restored: Originally rated as good to fair but with minor wheel wear and professionally restored paint finish; all rust removed from axles.

If **NRS** appears in the value column, it means that there have not been any reported sales to accurately gauge the relative price of the piece or set. It does not necessarily mean to imply that the toy or set is rare or even highly valuable. In some cases. these items were advertised by the company, but examples have not yet come to light.

Exercise discretion when you are thinking about buying a particular item. Extensive dirt or grime on the painted surface may be masking a piece in excellent or very good condition. It is up to each buyer to decide whether the dirt may also be masking nicks and scratches in the paint. There will be many variations in prices seen at shows and flea markets. Some sellers price their pieces higher regardless of the condition, and some well below. Being informed is the best way to make any purchase!

One final note which might be of interest to collectors or potential collectors should be pointed out. According to officials at Strombecker, some Tootsietoys were produced and marketed in Mexico after their appeal diminished here in the States. The original dies were sent to Mexico, and were used exclusively for the Mexican market as late as 1987. Though the paint, tires, and packaging of these toys may differ from their earlier counterparts in the States, the actual quality of the casting should be the same. Chapter 13 has more information.

I sincerely hope you will find this collector's guide interesting, especially the history that is detailed in the first chapter. Many of the questions posed by collectors over the years can be answered by understanding the management decisions over the years. I hope in many ways this book proves enlightening and beneficial, whether you are a beginner or a serious collector!

CHAPTER 1

From Collar Buttons To Bubbles

The Making of a Toy Titan

Tootsietoys . . . simply saying the word can usher back a time when childhood was filled with hours of make-believe, when little cars became real Fords and Chevys and raced around living rooms and layouts. While most collectors may know that Tootsietoys are still being made in Chicago by the Strombecker Corporation, few realize that they are the descendants of the first die-cast metal toys ever made—including a highly successful Model T Ford—which were created by the Dowst Brothers Company in Chicago. The history of Tootsietoys is indeed an interesting one. It covers more than a century of production, and it speaks of more than five- and ten-cent toys. Within the story, the developments of both the die-cast metal and toy industries in America are documented; in it is reflected the wisdom and ingenuity of a succession of businessmen who kept the company profitable through wars, depressions, recessions, and various material shortages. It is the story of a company that has been successful because of its products and because it has never—over those hundred years—lost its original focus to produce the best basic toys for children. It is continuing proof that a small company can develop into a time-tested titan of its trade.

Dowst Brothers Company was established in 1876 by Samuel and Charles O. Dowst to publish the *National Laundry Journal*. From this modest beginning, the company expanded, producing collar buttons and other supplies for the laundry trade. However, an encounter with a new machine in 1893 would quickly change not only this company, but the toy world as well. While visiting the World's Columbian Exposition in Chicago that year, one of the Dowst brothers[1] saw a display of the innovative Mergenthaler Linotype machine which produced a die-cast letter of the alphabet each time a key was pressed. It was obviously designed for the printing industry, yet this Dowst brother clearly recognized its potential to help the company inexpensively mass-produce die-cast collar buttons in various metals. Soon after bringing the machine into the factory, however, Dowst Brothers began offering more than collar buttons. Custom-ordered die-cast trinkets to be used as promotional items by various companies were in great demand. The company made a flat iron for the Flat Iron Laundry Company, an old shoe for a maker of shoe polish, and a miniature skillet for a company that produced frying grease. The line of trinkets and charms grew, and many were sold to the candy industry for use as prizes in penny candy packages.

In 1910, a No. 4482 Bleriot Aeroplane was issued in three sizes—from a watch charm size to 67 mm. Then, in 1911, a generic-looking 2-inch toy car, the No. 4528 Limousine with working wheels, was produced as part of an effort to upgrade the line and sell larger items for five and ten cents. In 1914, the realistic Model T Ford toy was introduced as the No. 4570 Model T Touring Car;[2] it was so successful (over fifty million were sold) that it launched Dowst Brothers into the big business of making highly detailed vehicles. In fact, Dowst's success with this one toy has been cited by many writers over the years as the official start of the wide-ranging die-cast industry. (An interesting note about this toy is that various literature, from company catalogues to newspaper articles, has noted its year of introduction as 1906.[3] According to the *World Book Encyclopedia,* the first real Model T Ford was built in 1909, and even with the best designers on staff, it is highly doubtful that Dowst could have introduced its model three years before Henry Ford issued the real car!)

Dowst began manufacturing doll furniture in 1922, and registered the "Tootsietoy" name in 1924 for its doll furniture and dollhouse line. It was adopted from "Tootsie," the name (or perhaps the nickname) of a granddaughter of Charles O. Dowst. Information published in the 1976 anniversary catalogue explained that the toy trade liked the name so much that, before long, the company used it on all their toys. Though some may wonder why a "girl's" name was chosen for the vehicle line, the company has in fact always tried to appeal to both boys and girls in its product line, according to Myron Shure, current Chairman of the Board of Strombecker. The catalogue covers from 1932 to 1935 picture both a boy and a girl in Victorian clothing; and the box cover of the 1950 No. 7000 Playtime Set, perhaps the most popular box set among Tootsietoy collectors, has the silhouettes of a girl flying a toy airplane beside a boy pushing a toy car.

The production of dollhouse furniture continued until 1942, when World War II mandated major changes in production. The last year dollhouse furniture appears in the catalogues was 1941. Production was not revived after the war.

In 1926, Dowst merged with the Cosmo Manufacturing Company, a competitor in novelties and white metal trinkets established in 1888 by the highly successful businessman, Nathan Shure, grandfather of Myron Shure. Cosmo imported and distributed novelties on a much larger scale than did Dowst; the production of their own novelties to sell to candy companies for use as prizes had begun in 1892. One of their biggest customers, the Cracker Jack Company in Chicago, included trinkets from Cosmo, the N. Shure Co., and Dowst, in its boxes of candied popcorn for fifty years, until it switched to using paper and plastic novelties. According to Myron Shure, the N. Shure Co. bought Dowst Brothers when Dowst was struggling. There is little written to clarify the circumstances of the merger; perhaps the Dowst brothers wanted to sell their business, or perhaps competition from other companies was such that sales were indeed suffering. Little can be found about the original Dowst brothers since then. Louis Hertz, in *The Complete Book of Building and Collecting Model Automobiles,* mentions that a Theodore Samuel Dowst stayed on as president and was very involved in the design and development of the Tootsietoy line during the twenties and thirties.[4] He retired in 1945.

After the merger, the Dowst company became Dowst Manufacturing Company, Incorporated, keeping its toy business separate from the large trinket and metal accessory business continuing at Cosmo and the N. Shure Co. While their products were generally different, some trinkets like the flat iron were being produced concurrently by both companies for different market applications. The N. Shure Co. and Cosmo trinkets were sold in much greater quantities for lower prices per item than Dowst's. However, both Dowst and Cosmo supplied trinkets to well-known customers. Parker Brothers used the flat iron in its successful Monopoly game and several items in Clue, and Avalon Hill used the miniature battleships and related items in its war games. (In a meeting with the author in 1992, Myron Shure said that they could always tell how Monopoly was selling by the orders they would get for the irons!) National Cash Register bought mini cash registers; various advertising specialty groups ordered souvenirs like watch fobs and heads for walking canes for the World's Fair, and clickers and novelties for presidential elections. Two miniature cars were even featured in the Stanford-Binet IQ test box.

Dowst continued to sell trinkets even into the fifties. The 1950 Miniature Toys Price List offered at least 225 miniature trinkets and charms with a "silver flash plating" finish or a "tumbled lacquer" finish in red, green, blue, black, or aluminum. (The colors white, cream, yellow, and orange were not available, though other colors could be obtained by special order.) All these miniatures were sold in lots per thousand, with the silver-finished trinkets selling for a slightly higher price. Today, collectors have reported buying individual trinkets for five to ten dollars. A dozen trinkets in a blister pack can command ten to fifteen dollars depending on the condition of the packaging.

Dowst's toy business, however, proved so successful that after the merger in 1926 it moved to a new four-story facility on Fulton Street constructed next to the old Cosmo manufacturing building. Myron Shure explained that the proximity of the two companies was often used to their mutual advantage: frequently, inventory from one could be stored at the other during peak production periods. The line of Tootsietoys was expanded during this era to include more models of the cars and trucks then on the road, the dollhouses, farm sets, train sets, and airplanes. Many patents on the toy designs were obtained, and the patent number was added to the casting to prevent infringement from competitors.[5] In the thirties, companies like the makers of Mack trucks and Graham automobiles subsidized the creation of Tootsietoy models of their vehicles and used them as promotional items to increase sales of the real vehicles. All in all, the inexpensive Tootsietoy vehicles were so popular that the company was able to succeed even during the Depression.

Before World War II, the company began exporting small vehicles to test the foreign market; the *Christian Science Monitor* reported in 1958 that, by the time the war had started, exports accounted for about 10 percent of total production.[6] The inexpensive, highly detailed Tootsietoys proved quite competitive with foreign toys, even though overseas companies took advantage of cheaper labor and tariff barriers. Constant improvements to production-line automation meant a more efficient, less costly process and, consequently, very desirable Tootsietoys.

With the coming of the war, the way the company was doing business changed dramatically. The War Production Board halted the manufacture of metal products on June 30, 1942;[7] regular metals were no longer available for use outside of military requirements. The company's participation in the war effort was to produce small die-cast detonators for hand grenades and mines, as well as parachute and military belt buckles. Employees were generally shifted around during the war between Dowst and N. Shure to fulfill the government contracts. Records indicate that Adolph Radnitzer may have been president of the Dowst company during the war.

After the war, the company tooled up to produce Tootsietoys again, making sure that they continued to be affordable yet highly detailed and of exceptional quality. Some of the items that were made before the war, like the 6-inch Jumbo Greyhound Bus and Jumbo Convertible and the 4-inch No. 4634 Armored Car, were reissued with black tires. While the company diversified somewhat by producing die-cast zinc parts for electronics companies like General Electric, Sunbeam, and Motorola, toy production nevertheless accounted for 90 percent of production.[8] New manufacturing methods including improved methods of automation, casting machines, painting methods, and drying procedures were continually invented and perfected. The Dowst Manufacturing Company was doing so well that by 1954 another facility with over 80,000 square feet of floor space was constructed on North Pulaski Road to keep up with production demands. By this time, sales offices were located in New York, Dallas, and San Francisco.

Probably the most popular and successful toy made after World War II was the Auto Transport Trailer Truck. A letter to Dowst in 1949 was typical of the reception the Auto Transport received. Mr. Elmer A. Tilden, Jr., from Canton, Ohio, wrote:

> Gentlemen:
>
> My wife purchased two sets of your Model No. 207 Tootsietoy Auto Transports for our two boys for their Easter

baskets. They were both delighted with their new Auto Transports.

I was very happy to find at last the name of the firm that manufactures "TOOTSIETOY." It strikes me that I was about 8 or 9 years old when I received my first Tootsietoy and I still have some of them today – the old Bulldog Mack, Model T Ford Pick-up and a few others.

I have made a hobby of securing quality toys for my boys. It is a source of real satisfaction to see a company such as yours continue to produce such wonderful toys, keeping up to date on design, bucking the higher prices of today and maintaining the QUALITY even better than it was 23 or 24 years ago.

I remember that in the old days you published a catalog which was a must with every Tootsietoy fan. If you have anything like it today I would sincerely appreciate receiving one.

I would like to make one suggestion and that is the placing of dual wheels at the rear of your larger trucks. It might be of interest to you to know that years ago we took some of the old-timers, cut the rear axles and put duals on – using the small metal wheels of that time. I think that today it would be the finishing touch to your most excellent detailed models.

Thanking you for reading the above letter, filling the above request, and for the privilege of corresponding with you, I remain

Sincerely yours,
Elmer A. Tilden, Jr.

The following spring, Dowst reproduced this letter in its February 1950 *Playthings* full-page advertisement with the banner "Good idea, Mr. Tilden! (and thanks for writing us about it)." Dual wheels appeared in 1954.

The sales force and management were often able to develop cooperative relationships with automotive and truck manufacturers; these companies would give their final designs for a new car model to Dowst before the actual cars were off the assembly line! Mold makers at Dowst were then instructed to develop a model which closely resembled the real car or truck yet could be produced economically. Sometimes, according to Joseph O'Brien, currently vice president of manufacturing, this meant simple design changes like leaving wheel wells open or having solid windows. The Tootsietoy models of newly released automobiles were often ready for distribution as soon as the actual automobile premiered. As D. K. Jaffe said in an article in the *Christian Science Monitor* on August 16, 1958, this kind of arrangement allowed both the Boeing 707 jet and "its Lilliputian copy" to be introduced at the same time. In addition to the distinct advantage this gave Dowst over other toy companies, these relationships helped Dowst develop the popular promotional toys for companies such as Pan American Airways, Ford Tractor, Caterpillar, Mack Truck, and Greyhound Bus. Meanwhile, the company's products were being used in other unusual ways that attracted the public's attention—as instructional items in classes taught by safety schools and the military, and as examples of traffic accidents in court cases![9]

By 1958, the company employed over four hundred people on two shifts to meet sales both domestically and overseas. Both the *Christian Science Monitor*[10] and the *Chicago Daily News*[11] that year reported sales in Australia, Canada, England, Holland, Italy, South Africa, and Sweden. Production was so prolific that Jaffe claimed "The Chicago firm outproduces Detroit's...(by making) more automobiles than all the United States automotive concerns combined" with over "25,000,000 cars, trucks, and trailers rolling out each year on 100,000,000 diminutive tires." Reporters from both newspapers interviewed Joseph Shure, Nathan Shure's son who was then president of the company; he credited the success of the business on the company's continued attention to keeping detail high and cost low.

In September 1958, Myron Shure, who was then in charge of sales, told the *Chicago Daily News* that the Auto Transport was their most popular item over the years; he estimated that they had sold over ten million of them. This article also mentioned that the toys, once painted, were baked for five minutes at 325 degrees in automated ovens.[12]

The sixties brought many changes to the company, including the purchase of the hobby division by the Strombeck-Becker Company of Moline, Illinois, in 1961.[13] The forerunner of this company, the Strombeck Company, was founded in 1911 by John F. Strombeck to manufacture wooden handles and knobs from scraps discarded by different manufacturing plants. The first facility was located in a run-down shed behind the John Deere facility, and it utilized much of the scrap wood from that plant. John's brother George, an engineer, who joined the company when business picked up, was responsible for developing better lathes and manufacturing processes to meet the demand. By 1920, the success of the business meant moving to a larger building and, by 1922, management saw a need to diversify. A line of wooden toys was begun in 1930 to keep the company from financial trouble should any of their products become less desirable. R. D. Becker joined the firm as plant superintendent, and the company name was changed to Strombeck-Becker Manufacturing Company. The first wooden model kits included a China Clipper airplane and the DeWitt Clinton locomotive. That same year, George Strombeck invented the first slot car track. In the forties, the company expanded the line of wooden kits to include ships, military equipment, and automobiles, and produced many wooden items for the war effort.

According to a 1981 article in the *Quad City Times,* "By this time, Strombeck-Becker was the acknowledged leader in the production of wooden toys,"[14] which included the famous Duncan Yo-Yo for the Duncan Toys Co. By 1960, the company was heavily involved with the development and production of all types of hobby items and road racing sets and equipment. They are credited in a 1966 article in the *Chicago Sun-Times* with introducing the first remotely controlled, electrically operated miniature car racing set in this country in 1960.[15] Yet according to the article in the *Quad City Times,* foreign toy competition made toy manufacturing unprofitable, so the company soon chose to abandon that end of its business. In 1961, the Becker hobby division was sold to Dowst Manufacturing, and the Strombeck-Becker name was changed to reflect this; the wooden products company reverted back to "Strombeck Manufacturing Co." and continued to market products on its own.

A few years after the purchase of the Becker hobby division in 1961, "Dowst Manufacturing Company" was changed to

The Tootsietoys sign on top of the present Strombecker plant on North Pulaski Road in Chicago, Illinois. This facility was constructed in 1954 to provide over 80,000 square feet of floor space to keep up with production demands.

"Strombecker Corporation"—the name still in use today—to take full advantage of the familiarity and respect for the Strombeck-Becker name in the hobby field. At that time, the Shure family believed that both the road racing sets and slot car racing business would continue to grow in popularity. They were not disappointed, since by 1966 the hobby had become a $200 million industry (according to the article in the *Sun-Times*); but competition proved tremendously fierce, and the hobby was to die out very quickly. By 1973, sales of the road racing sets had dropped to several hundred thousand dollars.[16]

About this time, the company decided to fall back on the popularity of the die-cast Tootsietoy vehicles. New automated machinery was brought in to increase productivity. One of these machines was capable of putting wheels on axles and attaching each new wheel assembly to a vehicle. Another allowed the vehicles to be painted electrostatically, and ended the long era of hand-painting Tootsietoys. A number of new die-cast vehicle lines were introduced. Some were developed as a result of ever-increasing costs in the price of zinc, while others were the result of new market ventures. The Midget series, a line of economical die-cast vehicles, required much less zinc than their predecessors because of their diminutive size. This series was very successful and it is still in production today as Jam Pac® Speeders. In 1967, Tootsietoy introduced the Playmate Series of preschool toys to compete with Fisher-Price. The company ventured away from realism in favor of the current style of toys being created for toddlers. This line was discontinued after 1971.

By 1973 vehicle production had reached an all-time high—nearly one hundred million toy cars and trucks were sold worldwide—and, according to an article in the *Chicago Tribune* on December 25, 1973, the company then employed over five hundred people.[17] The export business grew to a level that had not been achieved since 1957 and, for the first time since then, Strombecker exported more than it imported. Around 1970, the company bought the Rose O'Neill Kewpie doll line from Cameo Doll company, and used an outside organization to sell them until the line was sold to Playskool in the late 1970s. The Shure management obviously did not hesitate to gamble on toys that they felt satisfied the market for basic, inexpensive durable playthings. However, the toy business was plagued with problems relating to the rising costs of materials. A shortage of zinc occurred in the seventies when suppliers held on to what they controlled and waited for the price to go up, causing the price that manufacturers paid to shoot up from twenty cents to thirty-eight cents a pound.[18] A shortage of plastic only complicated these problems.

According to Joseph O'Brien, who began working for Dowst as a teenager in the forties, Strombecker also worked to become an industry leader in safety concerns, often working with government officials to develop better product standards. It was one of the first toy companies to use voluntarily only lead-free paints, as well as to incorporate age-grading and bilingual wording on the packaging of its products—policies developed by vice president Richard Shure.

In 1976, Strombecker celebrated the 100th anniversary of the Tootsietoy manufacturers. To mark the occasion, the company offered a limited number of plaques featuring a four-color illustration of the history of the company, a thermometer, and a barometer. The artwork was done by Richard Locher, an illustrator for the *Chicago Tribune* who drew the Buck Rogers and Dick Tracy cartoons and who designed many of the graphics for Strombecker's Gift Set boxes. The plaque sold as a limited edition piece for $29.95. Special T-shirts also designed by Locher for the centennial sold for $4.95 in children's sizes and $5.95 in adult sizes. Both items were advertised as exclusive in *Antique Toy World* that year. The T-shirt was also advertised by Strombecker on the back of some toy packages. No current values for these items are known.

In addition to the vehicle lines, the company acquired Esquire Novelty of Amsterdam, New York, in the early seventies and has become the leading producers of toy guns and rifles under the American West and Attack Force® brand names, as well as the exclusive distributor of Edison Giocattoli toy cap guns and caps made in Italy. They have created a very popular line of electronic sound and action guns, with trademarked names like the F/X Intimidator and the F/X Devastator, that have at least six different electronic weapon sounds and shoot strip or roll caps. In 1982, the Nichols Toy Gun line was purchased from Kusan, which is part of Bethlehem Steel. This purchase also included Marx gun molds.

In 1979 the company purchased ChemToy, and they now supply the market with popular bubble pipes, wands, and patented bubble mixes under the names of Mr. Bubbles® and Wonder® Bubbles. In addition, Strombecker assumed rights to a line of spring Disney character toys, which included bubble toys, jax, paddle balls, and jump ropes. In 1989, Strombecker purchased Sandberg Manufacturing Co., makers of wooden preschool products, many of which were already licensed under the Sesame Street name. The purchase allowed them to diversify and balance the line at a time when die-cast sales were dropping off. Strombecker is now the largest manufacturer of wooden preschool blocks, a line accounting for over 50 percent of its volume in wood. The company uses mainly U.S. wood for its colored and natural wood blocks, alphabet blocks, puzzles, pounding benches, shape sorters, magnetic alphabet boards, "Jumbo Kinder" log sets, and counting frames. Joy Toy, a company that had manufactured plastic action figures since 1973, was purchased in 1990. Included in this line with figurines are bags and buckets of plastic animals, dinosaurs, soldiers, and cowboys and Indians. Many Tootsietoy vehicles are now packaged and sold with complimentary figures from this line.

Myron Shure acknowledges that most of these new lines were also taken on when the former companies were having problems—following the same acquisition philosophy of the company since Dowst was acquired in 1926. The diversified line includes an assortment of novelty toys and seasonal products like Ruby's® Easter egg dyes, which are all sold under the Tootsietoy name, though some products are shipped in the former company's packaging while Strombecker uses up its inherited inventory of boxes from each acquisition. An addition to the line in 1990 was marbles, something the company had marketed thirty years before and a hobby that enjoys a resurgence at the present time. Strombecker felt that packaging them in attractive, durable plastic bags and jars as well as wrist packs would substantially increase their appeal and marketability to stores and customers alike.[19]

It is the bubbles, however, that have brought renewed attention to the company. In an article in May, 1992, the *Chicago Tribune* noted that not only was Strombecker the oldest toy company in America but it also made the "No. 1 selling toys in America: Tootsietoy's Mr. Bubbles and Wonder Bubbles, of which more than 50 million bottles are sold each year."[20] The formula is patented and kept under lock and key. The only ingredient openly discussed is the Lake Michigan water! According to the *Tribune,* the company even ships 55-gallon drums of solution to China for some of its more "labor-intensive" bubble toys. Their bubbles have been used on the Lawrence Welk Show, at the Ice Capades, and on the Mississippi riverboat *Delta Queen,* as well as by pipeline companies for use in leak diagnosis. The plant in Chicago alone produces over a quarter of a million bottles a day. The bubble wands come in all shapes, sizes, and characters—including patented trolls, swords, daggers, baseball bats, cross bows, and tennis rackets.

Today, the Strombecker Corporation is still based at the one-story plant on North Pulaski Road in Chicago, although there are five plants nationwide and one in Canada; it is still in the business of manufacturing economical vehicles of all types and sizes. According to the company's 1992 press kit, it produces over thirty million cars each year, and die-cast vehicles remain the mainstay of the entire product line. The list is extensive: Hard Body® (metal) cars and trucks, construction and farm equipment vehicles, Jam Pac® sets, motorcycles, airplanes, trailer trucks, the Hitch-Ups,® a full line of plastic vehicles and boats, and a wide assortment of boxed sets.

At the company's 1993 Toy Fair sales meeting, Myron Shure announced that 1992 was the greatest sales year in their corporate history. Despite the long recession, Strombecker was able to show a 15 percent increase in sales overall, and a 25 percent increase in the sales of die-cast vehicles. The die-cast vehicles are now manufactured in China while most of the plastic items are made at their Durant Plastics facility in Durant, Oklahoma, which was established in 1965 to make the slot-car racing tracks. The Durant facility operates around the clock, seven days a week, fulfilling company requirements for plastic items. They not only make all the plastic cars, trucks, planes, and boats sold in the line (proudly proclaiming "Made in U.S.A." on their packages); they also make many of the components used by other lines, like plastic blisters, the grips used on the Esquire guns, rifle components, and bubble toys and wands. True to policies that made the company solid in the past, Strombecker introduced new 7-inch and 10-inch vehicles at this year's Toy Fair, "a niche in plastics that," according to executive vice president John Schutz, "no other company has committed to."

Myron Shure, present Chairman of the Board of the Strombecker Corporation, enjoys sharing the history of Tootsietoys.

The company has indeed grown beyond its low-key image, with six facilities and over four hundred employees. But manufacturing has not ceased at the Chicago plants; on any given day, visitors can watch the assembly line produce metal cap guns, bottles of bubbles, and wooden preschool toys. Sales showrooms are located in Chicago, Dallas, Hong Kong, and New York; sales representatives are based in Illinois, Massachusetts, New York, Tennessee, Florida, Oregon, California, and Texas to cover the continental United States, as well as in Canada, Australia, France, Mexico, New Zealand, Puerto Rico, and England.

Tootsietoys have always been manufactured by a family-run company. After the war, leadership of the company passed to Nathan Shure's son, Joseph, whose own sons held different roles in the growth of the company at that time. Myron (known as "Mike" to his friends) was responsible for marketing, advertising, and promotions; Richard was in charge of administration and new product development; and Alan was in charge of production, though Richard took over the Tootsietoy product line production for part of the time. Myron became president after his father passed away; he passed the helm to Richard when he became Chairman of the Board. When Richard died in 1988, leadership passed to Myron's son, Daniel, who is currently president and Chief Executive Officer. This feeling of family, however, also extended beyond the front office and beyond the Shures; over the years, the company has employed brothers, fathers, sons, mothers, daughters, and cousins on the line and in the design and sales departments. Many have moved from the line to management and to vice presidencies. Each employee seems to have understood the significance of following the footsteps of his forebears. Daniel Shure, whose acquisition of Sandberg after becoming president brought the eyes of the toy trade on Strombecker again, was no exception. According to *Crain's Chicago Business*, the acquisition in 1989 of Sandberg and the Sesame Street license meant that Strombecker was "relieved of the necessity of developing a high-profile brand name—an expensive proposition considering the marketing muscle of such competitors as Playskool and Fisher-Price." When Daniel Shure became president, he considered making "Tootsietoy" the brand name for all Strombecker's toys again, a "strategy which would extend to appropriate products in other categories that the company might create or acquire."[21] That policy is in place at this time: the new red-and-white logo will be prominently featured on all of their products.

In retrospect, the story of Tootsietoys may be one of consistent success unparalleled for a toy company. Under the wise guidance and creativity of the Dowst brothers and the Shure family, the company survived many of the challenges that have confronted businesses over the last century. One hundred and seventeen years of production have passed since Dowst Brothers began with only a desire to publish the *National Laundry Journal*. Fifty years later, Nathan Shure provided the financial stability and direction to make sure the company continued to manufacture its popular toys. Although the Shure name never appeared on any of the products, the Shure family built the company to its present stature by seeking only to provide the best-quality basic toys for the least amount of money. That policy remains their spoken objective today: Daniel Shure announced to his staff at the Toy Fair meeting in 1993 that "We want to be the leading supplier of basic toys to the mass market."

Yet it is their sustained focus on the detail and durability of their toys and their willingness to take risks in new product lines that has made them a long-term success, and that will continue to make the collecting of Tootsietoys an ever-pleasing and popular pastime. While Myron Shure once told the *Chicago Sun-Times* that "We're jolly old toymakers now and we always have been,"[22] Daniel Shure will make sure that the Tootsietoy name remains recognized as every parent's "best bet for great basic toys" for years to come, "because if it's a Tootsietoy, it's 'Fun, Pure and Simple'."[23]

The Postwar Vehicle Lines

As one can see, the number of different Tootsietoy vehicles produced from World War II through 1969 was extensive. During this quarter century, eighteen lines were introduced, including a line of toys developed prior to the war. Though the most experienced collectors do not consider all of the postwar toys collectible, very few even know how many were produced. In addition, inexperienced or first-time collectors may find the variations very confusing. The following overview of production has been included to help a collector make informed decisions on the toys he or she may wish to assemble in a collection. It is the most current information available.

In 1945, the company began reissuing some of the car and truck models manufactured before the war. These pieces are easily distinguished from their prewar predecessors by their black rubber tires (prewar Tootsietoys mainly rode on white rubber tires). These items are discussed in Chapters 2 and 3. The practice of varying the color of the tires from prewar to postwar did not occur on airplanes or ships with metal wheels, however, which makes it very difficult (if not impossible) to distinguish prewar and postwar versions.

In 1947, the company greatly expanded the line of cars and trucks by adding new 3-inch, 4-inch, and 6-inch models. The number of new models offered each year varied. Some of the early postwar models remained on the production line for almost twenty years, with changes only in body color, the type of tires used, and the axle design, as well as the weight of the casting for some 3-inch series vehicles. In the fifties, changes significantly improved tire wear around the axle pin which had been caused by soft tire rubber and by an axle that did not turn with the tire. The first generation of patterned treaded tires on Tootsietoys were made from a better quality, harder rubber; they were replaced with plastic tires in the sixties.

Since many of the most knowledgeable collectors concentrate on acquiring metal Tootsietoy vehicles either individually or in gift sets, blister packs, and boxes, it is helpful to note that the primarily metal toys are found only in nine of the eighteen lines or series. For the purpose of general identification, we will classify these nine lines of metal toys as the **Postwar First Generation.** In the sixties, Strombecker developed a variety of toys that differed both in size and composition from the previous lines; the extensive use of plastic is the most obvious change. Many of these newer toys were designed for the preschool market, though there were also road racing sets and "electric battery-operated" train sets, new gift sets, blister packs, and a small quantity of toys quite similar to those of the first generation. For general identification, these remaining nine lines are classified as the **Postwar Second Generation**, a later series in metal and plastic. While many of them are not yet highly sought by collectors, there is growing interest in the Classic Antique and Pocket (HO) Series. A number of collectors have indicated that it is already difficult to find Midget and Collector Series sets. Tables 1 and 2 should help collectors define the lines carried in both generations.

The company coined the phrase "Jumbo" (as well as "Midget") during the prewar years; "Jumbo" signified new, larger sized toys. The term was used in many of their advertisements, on some sets, and on some blister packs. Many postwar collectors have associated "Jumbo" exclusively with all the 6-inch series of cars and trucks. However, in postwar years, the company used this phrase to identify many groupings of toys, such as three or four 3-inch cars on a blister card. There are several true 6-inch Jumbo "torpedo-styled" vehicles which were reissued prewar pieces; they are listed in Chapters 2 and 3.

The New Model Production chart (Table 3) details the number of models introduced each year for the most popular series covered in the remaining chapters. Note that 1945 and 1946 are not included in the chart, since all of the toys issued in those years were reissued prewar pieces. Some interesting observations become apparent from this type of chart. In 1951 and 1952 the development of new models seems low in comparison to other years through 1960. Although this period coincides with involvement in the Korean War, there is no evidence that involvement in the war affected production.

In 1957 the chart shows no new model production, since 1956 and 1957 were covered by a single catalogue according to company records; because of this, all new models are credited in 1956. 1959 saw the largest introduction of new models—thirty-six vehicles and airplanes, most of which were military items, and a new line of sports cars for the 6-inch series. After 1959 the development of new models for the more popular series greatly diminished, and the company redirected development toward other series, such as the Pocket, Midget, Classic, and Collector Series. One exception occurred in 1965 when the new 1959 Chevrolet Tractor Truck was introduced; however, it was short-lived.

Table 1: Postwar First Generation (Metal Toys)

	3" Series	4" Series	6" Series*	7" Series	Airplanes	Ships	Trailers	Trains	English Series
1945-1946	R	R	R	–	R	R	–	R	–
1947-1955	x	x	x	–	x	x	x	x	–
1956-1958	x	x	x	x	x	x	x	x	–
1959	x	x	x	–	x	x	x	x	–
1960-1961	x	x	x	–	x	x	x	x	x
1962-1969	x	x	x	–	x	x	x	x	–

* Includes the tractor trailer truck series containing units measuring 8" to 9" in length
R Reissued after the war
x Production years

Table 2: Postwar Second Generation (Later Series in Metal and Plastic)

	Classic Antique Series	Pocket (HO) Series	Midget Series	Collector Series	Super Series	Hitch-Ups Series	Racing Sets	Train Sets*	Playmate Series
1960-1961	x	x	–	–	–	–	–	–	–
1962-1963	1962	1962	–	–	–	–	x	x	–
1964-1965	–	–	–	–	x	–	x	x	–
1966-1967	–	–	x	x	x	–	x	x	x
1968	–	–	x	x	–	–	–	x	x
1969	–	–	x	x	–	x	–	x	x

* Electric and battery-operated

Table 3: New Model Production

	6" Cars	6" Trucks	Pull Trailers	Truck Trailers	Airplanes	Military Vehicles	4" Series	3" Series	Others
1947	2	2	–	–	1	1	3	1	–
1948	1	3	–	–	4	–	4	–	–
1949	2	4	–	4	–	2	1	9	–
1950	–	–	–	–	4	–	7	–	–
1951	1	–	–	–	2	–	–	2	2
1952	–	–	–	–	–	–	–	1	5
1953	3	2	–	1	1	–	3	1	–
1954	–	3	–	3	1	–	1	–	1
1955	4	1	–	1	–	1	4	7	4
1956	1	–	–	1	5	1	–	1	–
1957	–	–	–	–	–	–	–	–	2
1958	1	1	1	–	2	3	–	–	–
1959	7	3	1	2	2	12	1	4	–
1960	2	2	3	4	2	1	–	2	1
1961	–	–	1	1	–	1	3	2	1
1962	2	3	–	2	–	–	–	1	1
1963	–	–	1	1	–	–	–	1	–
1964	1	–	–	–	–	–	–	–	1
1965	–	–	–	5	–	1	–	–	–
1966	–	–	–	–	–	–	–	–	–
1967	–	–	–	2**	–	–	–	–	–
1968	–	–	–	1**	–	–	–	–	–
1969	–	–	6*	–	–	–	1*	–	–

* Denotes 1969/1970 production
** Variations to previously developed models

Table 4: Dealer Assortments

Year	Asst. No. (Size of Vehicles)	Remarks
1947	**2011 12 Oil Trucks** (6")	Four Types
1947-1948	**4730 12 Cars & Trucks** (6")	Four Types
1947-1949	**4615 12 Cars & Trucks** (4")	Six Types
1947-1948	**525 24 Cars & Trucks** (3")	Eight Types
1948	**1050 12 Fire Trucks** (4")	Three Types
1948-1955	**1200 12 Airplanes**	Four Types
1948-1949	**4829 12 Cars & Trucks** (6")	Four Types
1948	**4820 12 Trucks** (4")	Asst. Colors
1948-1956	**1152 12 Midget Racers** (4")	Asst. Colors
1949-1950	**2029 12 Oil Trucks** (6")	Four Types
1949	**4730 12 Cars & Trucks** (6")	Four Types
1949	**4615 12 Cars & Trucks** (4")	Six Types
1949-1954	**749 12 Cadillacs** (6")	Asst. Colors
1949-1954	**529 24 Cars & Trucks** (3")	Eight Types
1950-1952	**5025 12 Cars & Trucks** (6")	Six Types
1950-1954	**747 12 Greyhound Buses**	
1950-1956	**1180 12 Cars & Trucks** (4")	Six Types
1950-1956	**5030 12 Cars & Trucks** (6")	Six Types
1950-1956	**405 12 Badges**	Four Types
1953-1956	**285 12 Jeeps** (6")	Asst. Colors
1954-1956	**245 12 Tow Trucks** (6")	Asst. Colors
1954-1956	**249 12 Dump Trucks** (6")	Asst. Colors
1955-1956	**1210 24 Cars & Trucks** (3")	Eight Types
1956	**1319 12 Airplanes**	Five Types
1956	**7210 24 Cars & Trucks** (3")	Display Box
1959-1961	**1400 12 Dump Trucks** (6")	Asst. Colors
1959-1961	**1350 12 Jeeps** (6")	Asst. Colors
1959-1969	**1280 24 Sports Cars** (6")	Display Box
1959	**1250 12 Army Vehicles** (4")	Six Types
1959-1969	**1160 12 Airplanes**	Six Types
1959-1969	**1170 36 Cars & Trucks** (4")	Display Box
1959	**1100 72 Cars & Trucks** (3")	Display Box
1959-1964	**1010 72 Cars & Trucks** (3")	Four Types
1960-1964	**1011 36 Cars & Trucks** (3")	Assorted
1960	**1600 12 Farm Tractors**	
1962	**2300 12 Cars** (6")	Six Types
1962	**2350 12 Trucks** (6")	Four Types
1966-1969	**1010 72 Midget Vehicles**	Display Box
1966-1969	**1011 36 Midget Vehicles**	Display Box
1966-1969	**1015 72 Cars & Trucks** (3")	Display Box
1966	**1016 36 Cars & Trucks** (3")	Display Box

No values available.

It is interesting to note that, despite the many types of vehicles produced over the years, some of the ones most likely to be included in the product lines were not manufactured at all. For example, while the 4-inch series contains an ambulance and two fire chief cars, the 6-inch and 3-inch series apparently do not. There is no evidence to indicate the production of a police car in any series until the introduction of a 6-inch model in 1963. The 6-inch and 3-inch series each contain a bus, but the 4-inch series does not. These are only a few of the inconsistencies collectors have noted over the years.

The shift to plastics that started in the sixties actually had a positive effect on the design of the toys. It allowed for more detail to be incorporated in the vehicles, particularly in their interiors. It also allowed the company to hire more employees to run the injection molding machines.

According to Harry Brown, who retired as vice president of design in 1991, Strombecker continued to produce "premium" promotional items for various companies like U-Haul through the sixties and seventies. In U-Haul's case, they would specify exactly what Tootsietoy vehicle could be used to pull the U-Haul trailer. The item was sold exclusively to that company, and was not provided to the toy market through the Strombecker catalogue. Many were packaged on blister cards. How many different kinds of these promotional items were produced is not known.

Packaging

Tootsietoys, for the most part, were originally made to be sold to dealers and stocked in open counter bins at local "Five and Dime" stores. The earlier **Dealer Assortments** in plain cardboard boxes or plastic packages contained many unwrapped and unboxed individual vehicles to put in those bins. Consequently, nicks and scratches in the paint were probably fairly common as children rummaged through the bins to find the vehicle of their choice. Later assortments were marketed in well-designed boxes that could be placed on a countertop or that could stand alone on the floor. Other assortments included individually boxed items packed in a larger box. Because Dealer Assortments in complete form are rare and highly collectible, Table 4 lists all those advertised in the catalogues from 1947–1969.

These assortments usually included bulk quantities ranging from twelve dozen to twenty-four dozen products, depending on the size of the individual items. The 6-inch series were usually packaged as twelve dozen boxes or pieces per assortment, while the 3-inch and 4-inch series came in lots of twenty-four dozen or more. On occasion, these assortments have turned up at auctions and large toy shows. A No. 529 Dealers Assortment from 1949 is shown in Chapter 6.

Some of the 6-inch series toys, like the 1955 Greyhound Scenicruiser, were packaged in individual boxes to increase their marketability. For collectors, having a Tootsietoy in its original box can substantially increase its value, depending on the condition of the box. The **Individually Boxed Items** included tractor trailer and pull trailer units with 6-inch series vehicles, and are listed in Chapter 11. However, since individual 6-inch toys are most often found without their boxes, their descriptions are found in Chapters 2, 3, and 4. Each box was given a special identification number: the earlier series released in the fifties have a three-digit number; the later series from 1959 through 1960 were given four-digit numbers. Some boxes were promoted in the catalogues as **Viewer Packages** with cellophane windows in the front of the box to make the product visible and more enticing to children.

During the later years covered in this volume, the company began to provide a large number of units in **Cellophane Packaging, "Skin" Packaging,** and **Blister Packs.** Plastic packaging protected the product yet maintained its visibility. The earlier form of this packaging used a clear plastic bag sealed at the top to a piece of decorated cardboard which also

An assortment of the earlier and later boxed items. J. Gibson Collection.

served as a display hanger for the individual piece. This kept small accessories from being separated from the main vehicle or toy and provided some degree of protection to the paint finish. It also permitted the company to get their products into department and toy stores at a time when traditional "Five and Dime" stores were beginning to disappear. Metal tree racks were used to display the products, and these proved to be more visual, practical, and functional, increasing the sales of unmarred toys.

In 1956 the first **Display Rack**, No. 9000, was offered to retailers. This type of display may not have been very popular at first, since use of display racks did not appear to take hold in stores until 1962. By this time, the types of stores carrying Tootsietoy products included department stores and discount chains; the use of open counter bins diminished. Unlike the first display rack offered, newer racks were usually larger and capable of revolving, which meant they could be placed almost anywhere in a store. Some of the display racks designed to hold blister cards or packaged pieces are listed in Table 5.

Some of the most desired pieces of all, however, are the various **Boxed and Gift Sets** produced from the late forties through the sixties. The introduction of set boxes was truly a marketing marvel, for it provided a group of toys at a price usually lower than if the pieces were purchased separately, it allowed the company to use various pieces already in production, and it therefore increased production volume. Carrying

Table 5: Dealer Display Racks with Toys

Year	Assortment	Quantity
1956	**9000 Display Rack**	14 doz.
1962	**2495 Pocket Series**	8 doz.
1962	**3001 Classic Series**	6 doz.
1963	**2955 Toy Box**	6 doz.
1963	**2985 Bus Load of Toys**	6 doz.
1963	**2979 Jumbo Toy Box**	6 doz.
1963	**2992 Revolving Rack**	13 doz.
1963	**2997 Floor Merchandiser**	18 doz.
1963	**2999 Toy Dept. Rack**	33 doz.
1964	**3310 Toy Box**	10 doz.
1964	**3320 Jumbo Toy Box**	6 doz.
1964	**3325 Revolving Rack**	19 doz.
1964	**3335 Toy Dept.**	30 doz.
1965	**3315 Bus Load Toys**	6 doz.
1965	**3355 Revolving Rack**	21 doz.
1965	**3365 Total Toy Dept.**	30 doz.
1966	**1900 Bus Load Toys**	6 doz.
1966	**1905 Revolving Rack**	13 doz.
1966-1969	**1910 Toy Dept. Rack**	30 doz.

No values available for these items.

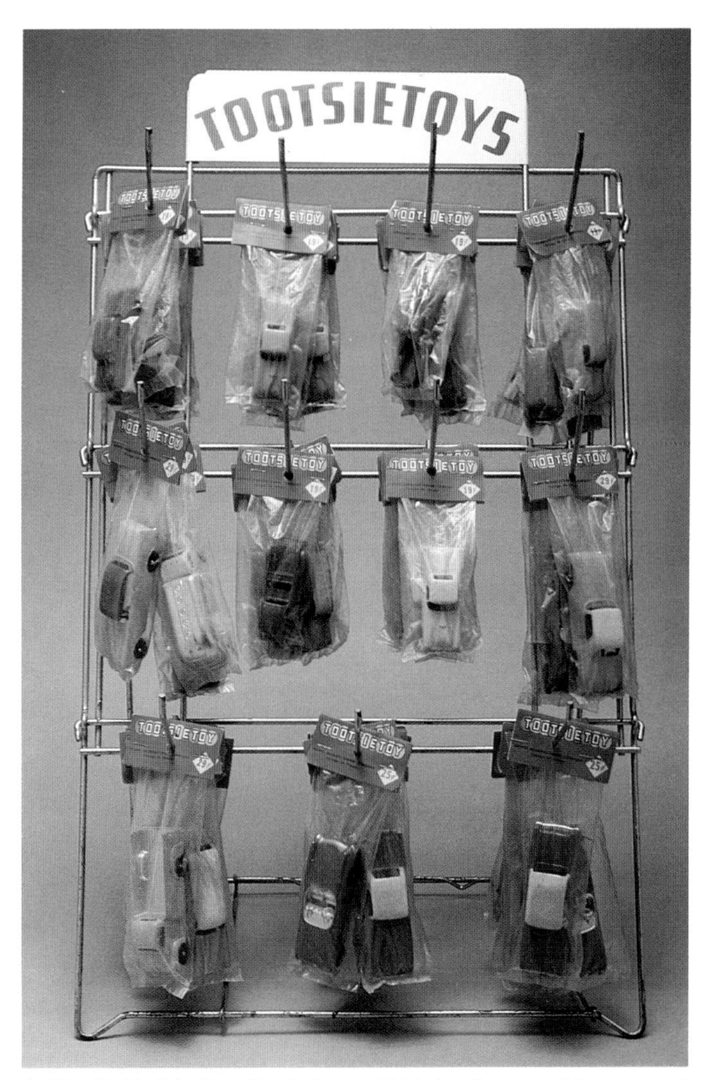

A No. 9000 Display Rack from 1956 is shown with assorted 3-inch and 4-inch vehicles in cellophane packaging. S. Butler Collection.

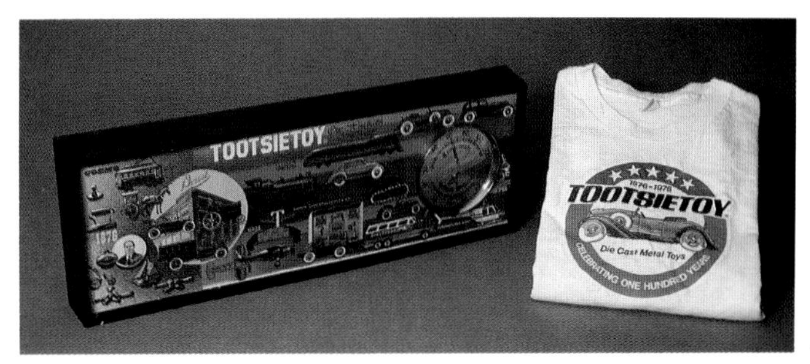

To celebrate the 100th anniversary of the manufacturers of Tootsietoys, Strombecker commissioned Richard Locher, an illustrator for the Chicago Tribune who also designed many of the gift set box graphics, to create the art for this Thermometer/Barometer plaque. D. Campbell Collection.

"Boxed Sets" or "Gift Sets" in the line was not a new practice after the war, since this form of packaging was used as far back as 1925 for dollhouse furniture. In 1930 Dowst introduced a unique form of packaging for five different gift sets: a heavy cardboard can with a tin top and bottom, which Louis Hertz identified as "Akana (a can of)" packaging in *The Complete Book of Building and Collecting Model Automobiles.* This packaging lasted a very short time and was replaced by the more conventional Tootsietoy boxed set packages we know today.

Some of the earliest boxes were illustrated with graphics that remained on those sets for nearly a quarter of a century, even when the contents of the box changed. A good example of this is the prewar Tootsietoy Playtime Toys box featuring a variety of fairy tale characters in front of a castle's large wooden door; it was offered from before the War through 1955. Detailed designs like this were used on both large and small gift sets; the company took great pride in the artistic graphics used on the box tops. Many of the designs involved bold geometric shapes and colors that seem quite striking and ahead of the times. In 1939 the company received the national Toy Packaging Award; a blue ribbon was added to the cover of a set of war ships commemoratingthisachievement.

With the reintroduction of gift sets after the war, the company continued to use excellent color graphics on box tops to promote set contents. These graphics usually featured good renditions of the vehicles inside which were depicted in an action scene, and fair representations of buildings and scenery.

A number of gift sets were illustrated only with colorful graphic designs of the Tootsietoy name and set identification information. From a marketing aspect, they were not as appealing because they did not identify the contents of the box for the buyer. Most of the boxes had yellow interiors; however, some boxes—such as those for convoy sets with an ocean background—featured graphic designs that were carried from the cover into the interior. Over time, as the amount of metal used in the vehicles decreased (and as more plastic was used), so too did the quality of the graphics. Box tops gave way to "viewer windows" so that the contents could easily be seen and touched. A game board was added to the back of many of the sets for additional play value. This kind of packaging clearly identified the contents of the set; it also unfortunately marked the end of an era for the art form associated with the earlier gift sets.

The late-sixties Postwar Second Generation gift sets were substantially different from earlier ones. Promoted as value sets, they contained up to eighteen individual pieces as well as a game on the back of the packaging. The company also introduced a **Platform Display Box** package which featured a new line of Midget vehicles and an associated building for added play value. In 1968 and 1969, these Platform Display items included a Farm Set, a Fire Station, and a Super Service Station. They can be found in Chapter 12; they are all in little demand by collectors at the present time.

Information on all individually boxed items, boxed sets, and blister packs, as well as some of the accessory items to be used with them, will be found in Chapters 11 and 12.

Without a doubt, the entire line of Tootsietoys, especially those covered in this volume, is testament to the company's long-standing tradition of offering the best, basic toys for the best price. That these toys are becoming collectible is most fitting; few companies exist that can boast such a record of success, or that can proclaim the same commitment—to

A countertop ring display featuring the 1950 Chevy from the 3-inch series in various colors. S. Butler Collection.

quality and affordability while maintaining its commitment to manufacture its own products—that existed when the company began. That commitment, according to Joseph O'Brien, has been "the catalyst for its growth, the reason for its profitability, its strength, and its character, and the sustaining element all these years."

Notes

[1]The available literature disagrees on which Dowst brother saw the Linotype machine at the World's Columbian Exposition. Charles O. Dowst: Steven Sommers, "A Century of Chicago Toys," *Chicago History,* 1982: Fall & Winter. Samuel: Daniel Shure, Strombecker's roots were buttons, but its future is toys," *The Toy Book,* January 1990; Joan Fleming, "Tootsietoys Now Popular Collectibles," *Collectors News,* 1980: Vol. XX, No. 12.

[2]Louis H. Hertz, *The Complete Book of Building and Collecting Model Automobiles* (New York: Crown Publishers, 1970), 117.

[3]Strombecker Corporation, *1976 Catalogue,* Anniversary insert (1976). Fleming, "Tootsietoys Now Popular Collectibles."

[4]Hertz, *Building and Collecting Model Automobiles,* 251.

[5]Ibid., 199.

[6]Dorothy Kahn Jaffe, "Chicago Toy Firm Outproduces Detroit's," *The Christian Science Monitor*, 15 August 1958, Business-Research page.

[7]Hertz, *Building and Collecting Model Automobiles,* 116.

[8]Jaffe, "Firm Outproduces Detroit's."

[9]Ibid.

[10]Ibid.

[11]Barnard K. Leiter, "Talk About Small Cars...They Make Millions Here," *Chicago Daily News*, 27 September 1958.

[12]Ibid.

[13]Jim Arpy, "Where wood still reigns as king," *Quad City Times* (1981). Edwin Darby, "Strombecker; Are The First 90 Years The Hardest?", *Chicago Sun-Times,* 2 September 1966, Business News.

[14]Arpy, "Where Wood Still Reigns."

[15]Darby, "First 90 Years."

[16]Alvin Nagelberg, "The Merry Toymaker," *The Chicago Tribune,* 25 December 1973, section 3.

[17]Ibid.

[18]Ibid.

[19]Dorothy J. Gaiter, "Makers of Marbles Get Kids to Shoot Clearies Again," *The Wall Street Journal,* 14 August 1992, Marketplace.

[20]Barbara Mahany, "Bubble vision; The more you know, the clearer things become," *The Chicago Tribune,* 28 May 1992, Tempo magazine.

[21]Joanne Cleaver. "Toy firm's growth plan built on blocks," *Crain's Chicago Business*, 1 May 1989.

[22]Darby, "First 90 Years."

[23]Shure, "Strombecker's roots were buttons."

CHAPTER 2

Six-Inch Sedans, Station Wagons, Convertibles, Sports Cars, and Jeeps

This is the first of several chapters covering the various 6-inch Tootsietoy vehicles. It presents the sedans, station wagons, convertibles, roadsters, sports cars, and civilian jeeps produced from 1947 through 1969, as well as a special series of reissued prewar cars known as the Jumbo Series. Reissued prewar pieces can be distinguished from actual prewar pieces by the color of their tires: most prewar pieces have white rubber tires, although a few have white-painted wooden wheels; the postwar reissued vehicles have black rubber tires. The axle spacers remained the same. These reissued toys are given a variable date of production as 1942/1946 to denote the uncertain date of manufacture.

Throughout all the chapters, you may find that some of the later vehicles have a higher dollar value than similar earlier ones. This may be caused by actual collector demand for the item, its "looks," or the apparent difficulty in locating the item at toy shows, train shows, specialty stores, flea markets, or antique stores and auctions. Low production runs also play a major part in availability and value.

Clearly in this series the most difficult car to find is the 1955 Chrysler Regent. Although this vehicle has been identified by some collectors as a Chrysler 300, it was designated as a Chrysler Regent in the 1955 catalogue. The 1951 Buick Experimental Sportster Convertible with unpainted side panels and the 1950 Chrysler Windsor Convertible follow the 1955 Chrysler Regent as difficult to find. The Chrysler Windsor Convertible is especially difficult to locate in any color but gray. The 1947 Buick Estate Wagon has a reputation of being difficult to find, and since it was only available in 1948, it usually commands an inflated price. The 6-inch series also includes a number of vehicles, such as the Packard Patrician, produced with a special lithographed chassis, they are all considered rare pieces. When collecting toys from this series, look for vehicles that contain separate cast parts which could have been easily broken or lost, followed by those having a tin chassis, a two-tone paint scheme, and any items which contain a trailer hitch, since in this series castings of the same vehicle were made with and without this feature.

In the introduction, mention is made that a number of what could be considered *popular* vehicles were not offered in every series. A good example is an ambulance, which was produced in the 4-inch series, but not in the 6-inch or 3-inch series. At first it is difficult to understand why there is no ambulance in the 6-inch series. One possible explanation may be that the company tried to produce vehicles to a similar scale for each of their popular gift box sets. This is most evident in the contents of the Fire Department Set, which utilized vehicles from both the 6-inch and 4-inch series that are relatively to scale. Adding a 6-inch ambulance that would be as large as the fire trucks in this set would not have maintained the realistic scale appearance. Therefore, it is possible that the designers saw no real need or advantage in producing either a 6-inch ambulance or fire chief car; these toys would not have been available for set use, an overlapping of markets that seemed to dominate the production line.

Yet another puzzling observation is the absence of a police car in this series until 1964. A police car certainly would seem to have been an ideal item to include in the boxed sets of various 6-inch cars and trucks. Perhaps the difficulty in making a sedan look like a police car was one reason for this absence. By studying all of the vehicles made at that time, it appears that while there were a number of different sedans made, none were well-suited for a police vehicle. For example, a toy company based in Chicago, Illinois, would logically produce one similar to the local Chicago police department vehicle. But at that time, Cook County mainly used Fords, and none of the vehicles in production were Fords. In addition, the company in the early fifties was not noted for using decals or stickers to identify a vehicle, let alone to improve its looks, which could have easily created a generic-looking police car.

(Above) A 1955 Packard with a tin chassis and the original box. J. Gibson Collection.

(Opposite page top) Several Jumbo vehicles reissued after the war with the telltale black rubber tires. **Top:** *Jumbo Pickup Truck and Jumbo Coupe (the prewar version with wooden tires), S. Butler Collection.* **Middle:** *Jumbo Convertible and Jumbo Bus.* **Bottom:** *Jumbo Tow Truck and Jumbo Sedan. The Pickup Truck (restored), Bus, and Tow Truck are described in Chapter 3.*

(Opposite page bottom) **Top:** *Civilian Willys-style Jeeps, without painted features, on their original boxes. S. Butler Collection.* **Middle:** *Civilian Jeeps with painted features. S. Butler Collection.* **Bottom:** *1947 Buick Estate Wagon, 1947 Kaiser, and 1942 Rocket Roadster, S. Butler Collection.*

Most of the vehicles in this chapter were manufactured with silver-painted features including front and rear bumpers, headlights, grilles, and rear taillights; some also have silver-painted emblems and door handles. Toys with extensive painted features are usually more valuable. You will find some toys both with and without painted features from the same year. Some pieces were first produced with painted features and, in later years, without.

Some of these models underwent a change in wheel and axle design and tire type over time. Unlike some of the other series, the types of tires and axles in 6-inch series are not a major concern, nor do they substantially affect their value. Generally, the type of tire and axle design incorporated can distinguish the period of production (late forties, fifties, or sixties). Throughout the postwar, prewar reissued, and tractor trailer truck series, the following variations in tire design were produced. Exact dates that each of these types of tires were used on specific vehicles are not known.

Wherever a listing refers to "Tootsietoy tires," it means that "TOOTSIETOY" appears on both the inside and outside of the sidewalls of the tires.

The first cars listed in this chapter—the Jumbo reissued cars—can be distinguished by their generic torpedo style. The expression "torpedo" is widely used by collectors to denote a body styling wherein all side surfaces, including the fenders, are flush. At the present time, these pieces are not seen as highly desirable since they do not model a prototype of their era (one of the appealing features of most Tootsietoys). Additional Jumbo reissued vehicles are listed in Chapter 3 with the 6-inch trucks, vans, and buses.

Beginning in 1954 a small number of 6-inch cars were manufactured with a lithographed tin chassis. This chassis was mounted to the underside of the car by using cast pins located at each end of the car body. The lithograph provided a bottom view of the car motor, transmission, rear axle, gas tank, and spare tire but did not provide any support for the car axles and wheels that were mounted the same way as previous models. Collectors may come across units where the tin chassis has been removed. This will be apparent by the existence of the two broken pins which are part of the body casting. The 6-inch cars with lithographed chassis are very rare and will cost substantially more to acquire. The following vehicles are known to exist with this feature: 1954 Cadillac; 1954/1955 Experimental Coupe; 1954 Buick Wagon; 1955 Packard; and the 1956 Dodge Panel Truck.

By 1969, the company only offered five different 6-inch cars: the 1954 Volkswagen; 1956 Mercedes 190SL; 1932 Hot Rod; 1956 Jaguar; and the 1956 Porsche. Only the Hot Rod came with painted features. More information pertaining to these vehicles can be found in Chapter 4 on the trailer sets. In addition to the toys presented in the first three chapters, vehicles from the 6-inch series may be referenced in Chapters 8, 9, 10, and 11.

Based on historical data, catalogue advertisements, and data obtained from Strombecker, the best known information on production years for each piece is included with the listings. **Note:** The *last* detail in each listing will be any information cast into the underside of the vehicle. Most vehicles included

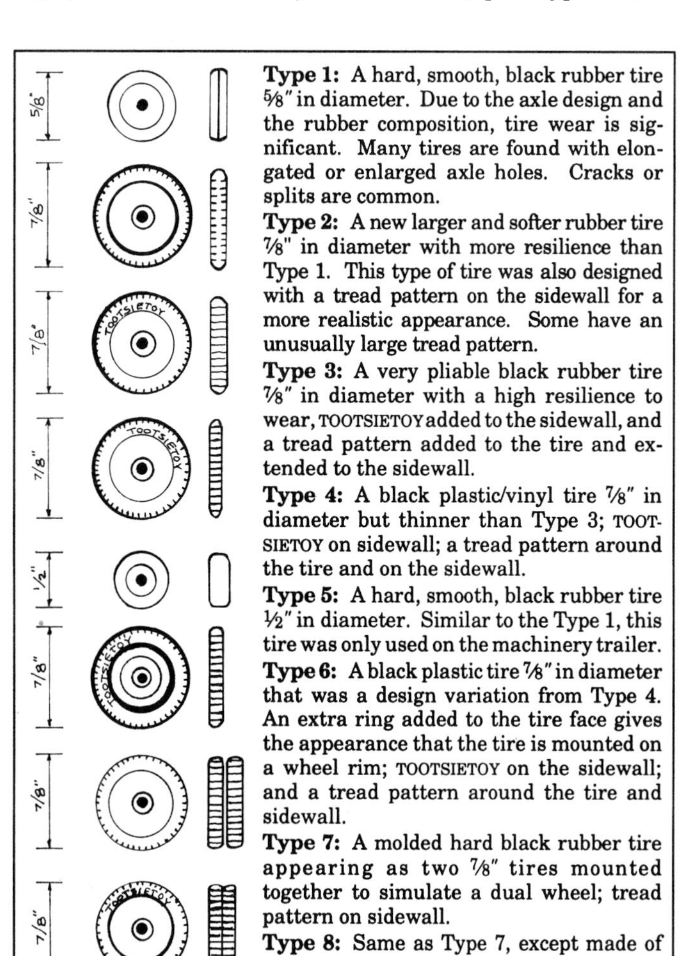

Type 1: A hard, smooth, black rubber tire ⅝" in diameter. Due to the axle design and the rubber composition, tire wear is significant. Many tires are found with elongated or enlarged axle holes. Cracks or splits are common.

Type 2: A new larger and softer rubber tire ⅞" in diameter with more resilience than Type 1. This type of tire was also designed with a tread pattern on the sidewall for a more realistic appearance. Some have an unusually large tread pattern.

Type 3: A very pliable black rubber tire ⅞" in diameter with a high resilience to wear, TOOTSIETOY added to the sidewall, and a tread pattern added to the tire and extended to the sidewall.

Type 4: A black plastic/vinyl tire ⅞" in diameter but thinner than Type 3; TOOTSIETOY on sidewall; a tread pattern around the tire and on the sidewall.

Type 5: A hard, smooth, black rubber tire ½" in diameter. Similar to the Type 1, this tire was only used on the machinery trailer.

Type 6: A black plastic tire ⅞" in diameter that was a design variation from Type 4. An extra ring added to the tire face gives the appearance that the tire is mounted on a wheel rim; TOOTSIETOY on the sidewall; and a tread pattern around the tire and sidewall.

Type 7: A molded hard black rubber tire appearing as two ⅞" tires mounted together to simulate a dual wheel; tread pattern on sidewall.

Type 8: Same as Type 7, except made of plastic with TOOTSIETOY on sidewall.

ARMY JEEP
ARMY JEEP

G E LN

some information underneath the toy; it is included here in small capitals letters—without reference to the underside location in an effort to reduce the number of repetitious phrases in the listings. With few exceptions, the information appears on the toy in capital letters.

JUMBO CONVERTIBLE: (1942/1946) Open-styled car resembling a 1935 Auburn Roadster. Body painted red, yellow, orange, green, blue, or silver. Long sleek body has elongated hood with slanted front grille; large front and rear fenders with open wheel wells; headlights on top of fender; a small windshield; and a single "roll and pleated" seat without any other additional interior details. Smooth black rubber tires with axle spacers. TOOTSIETOY MADE IN UNITED STATES OF AMERICA.

(A) Body and features same color. **15 40 45**

(B) Same as (A) with silver-painted features, bumpers, and front grille. **20 45 50**

(C) Same as (B) with two-tone seat area. **25 50 55**

JUMBO COUPE: (1942/1946) Torpedo-styled two-door coupe resembling a Pierce Arrow or Packard; body painted red, yellow, orange, blue, green, or silver. Two-piece windshield; elongated hood; sloping front grille; headlights on top of fender next to hood; large stone guards on rear fenders. Body extends through wheel wells; axles extend through sides of car body; smooth black rubber tires with axle spacers. TOOTSIETOY MADE IN UNITED STATES OF AMERICA.

(A) Body and features same color. **15 40 45**

(B) Same as (A) with silver-painted features, bumpers, grille, and headlights and two-tone paint. **20 45 50**

JUMBO SEDAN: (1942/1946) Torpedo-styled four-door sedan somewhat resembling a Hupmobile or Packard; body painted red, yellow, orange, blue, green, or silver. Body extends over wheel wells, front fenders extend the length of the car; vertical and horizontal air vents behind the front wheel wells; a long hood with a protruding panel along top of hood; oversized headlights; a one-piece windshield; door hinges and door handles; small rear trunk. Axles extend through sides of car; smooth black rubber tires with axle spacers. TOOTSIETOY MADE IN U.S.A.

(A) Body and features same color. **15 30 35**

(B) Same as (A) with two-tone paint and silver-painted bumpers, front grille, and headlights. **20 45 50**

CIVILIAN JEEP: (1949-1955) World War II Willys Jeep in civilian colors; available in dealer packs, as a boxed piece, and in sets. Body and features painted red, yellow, silver, orange, or blue; cast windshield and steering wheel in natural metal finish. Casting contains molded star in a circle on the hood, W-2017590 in front of the star; headlights on front fenders; U-shaped trailer hitch molded on rear body panel. Smooth rubber tires with axle spacers. TOOTSIETOY MADE IN U.S.A. 4.

(A) Slender three-spoke steering wheel. **15 22 25**

(B) Same as (A) but cast steering wheel has three thick spokes and large center hub painted silver; patterned rubber tires with axle spacers; no casting identification on underside of body. **15 22 25**

(C) Body, windshield, and steering wheel same color. S. Butler Collection. **20 30 35**

G E LN

1932 HOT ROD: (1959-1969) Two-door topless roadster; body painted red, yellow, orange, green, or blue; silver-painted motor, seat and dash area, front grille, and rear bumper. Body casting includes detailed interior, exposed motor compartment, and large rear bumper; no headlights, taillights, or front fenders. Patterned rubber Tootsietoy tires, no axle spacers. TOOTSIETOY CHICAGO 24 U.S.A.

(A) As described above. **10 25 30**

(B) Patterned plastic Tootsietoy tires, no axle spacers, rear trailer hitch. **15 30 35**

1940 FORD CONVERTIBLE: (1962-1966) Body painted red, orange, green, blue, or dark red; silver-painted features front and rear bumpers, front grille, and interior. On some vehicles the interior is painted gold. Body casting includes open detailed seats, dash, and steering wheel; no front windshield; large rounded front fenders with headlights; open wheel wells; V-shaped hood; and running boards between front and rear fender. Patterned rubber Tootsietoy tires, no axle spacers. TOOTSIETOY CHICAGO 24 U.S.A. 01043.

(A) As described above. **18 40 45**

(B) Patterned plastic Tootsietoy tires, no axle spacers. **15 35 40**

(C) Same as (B) with detailed interior painted same as body color. **15 35 40**

(D) Same as (B); body and features painted same color. **10 35 40**

1942 ROCKET ROADSTER: (1947-1949) Convertible, sometimes called a Chrysler Thunderbolt. Body painted red, orange, yellow, blue, or green; silver-painted features include front and rear bumpers, air flow vents on both front fenders, rear fender mud guards, hood emblem, grille, headlights, and taillights. Raised fin extends through trunk to rear bumper, smaller fin extends from each taillight to back of seat panel; body sides extend over front and rear wheel wells. Axle assembly is mounted through body sides; smooth rubber tires with axle spacers. TOOTSIETOY MADE IN UNITED STATES OF AMERICA 745.

(A) Painted features. **15 30 40**

(B) Same as (A) with silver-painted seat and dash. **15 30 40**

(C) Same as (A) except air flow vents same color as body. **15 30 40**

(D) Same as (A) with red-painted seat and dash; body painted yellow. **20 40 50**

1947 BUICK ESTATE WAGON: (1948) Four-door station wagon with simulated wood treatment on all doors and back side panels; body painted maroon; two-tone models came in maroon or green with cream doors, rear side panels, and rear door. Silver-painted features include front and rear bumpers, front grille, and headlights. Front fenders extend to rear fenders; body sides extend through front and rear wheel wells. Axle assemblies mounted through body sides; smooth rubber tires with axle spacers. TOOTSIETOY MADE IN U.S.A..

(A) Painted features. **20 60 70**

(B) Two-tone paint, painted features. **30 55 65**

(C) Same as (B) with silver trim on fenders. J. T. Riley Collection. **30 55 65**

	G	E	LN

1947 KAISER: (1947-1949) Four-door touring sedan; body painted red, medium green, yellow, orange, blue, gray, or maroon; two-tone models came in either red, blue, or maroon with cream roof. Silver-painted features include front and rear bumpers, door handles, trunk handle, front hood emblem, and headlights. Two-piece front windshield. Body sides extend through front and rear wheel wells; axle assemblies mounted through body sides; smooth rubber tires with axle spacers. TOOTSIETOY MADE IN UNITED STATES OF AMERICA 746.

	G	E	LN
(A) Painted features.	20	40	45
(B) Two-tone paint, painted features.	20	45	55

1948 CADILLAC: (1949-1954) Four-door sedan; body painted red, yellow, gray, blue, or green; two-tone models came in red, blue, turquoise, or maroon with cream or white roof. Silver-painted features include front and rear bumpers, front grille, and headlights. Two-piece windshield, three-piece rear window, swept rear fenders; body sides extend through front and rear wheel wells. Axle assembly mounted through body sides; smooth rubber tires with axle spacers. TOOTSIETOY MADE IN UNITED STATES OF AMERICA.

	G	E	LN
(A) Painted features.	12	30	35
(B) Two-tone paint, painted features.	15	35	40

1949 BUICK ROADMASTER: (1949-1950) Four-door sedan; body painted green, red, yellow, or blue; two-tone models came with white or cream roof. Silver-painted features include front and rear bumpers, front grille, headlights, and taillights. Body sides extend through front and rear wheel wells; two-piece front windshield; sloping roof and trunk; four simulated portholes on each front fender. Axle assemblies mounted through body sides; smooth rubber tires with axle spacers. TOOTSIETOY MADE IN UNITED STATES OF AMERICA.

	G	E	LN
(A) Painted features.	20	35	45
(B) Two-tone paint, painted features.	20	40	50

1950 CHRYSLER WINDSOR CONVERTIBLE: (1951-1955) Body painted gray but may be found in yellow, red, green, or blue. Silver-painted features include front and rear bumpers, grille, headlights, cast windshield, and dashboard. Body features a one-piece cast windshield, steering wheel, dashboard unit, and convertible tour cover; CHRYSLER clearly identified on the rear trunk; body sides extend through front and rear wheel wells. Axle assemblies mounted through body sides; patterned rubber tires with axle spacers. TOOTSIETOY MADE IN U.S.A.

	G	E	LN
(A) Body painted gray.	35	80	100
(B) Any other color. Rare.	45	125	150

1951 BUICK EXPERIMENTAL XP300 SPORTSTER CONVERTIBLE: (1953-1959) A model of a futuristic automobile. Body painted red, yellow, orange, medium green, or blue. Silver-painted features include front and rear bumpers, front grille, windshield, dashboard, and steering wheel assembly, rear taillights, center rear assembly above bumper, and headlights. Body features a one-piece cast windshield, dashboard, and steering wheel; two distinct rear fender fins extend from the simulated bucket seats to the rear bumper; a center fin extends the full length of the back portion of the car; no hood or trunk lines are provided in the body casting. Body sides extend over rear wheels; open front wheel wells; rear axle assembly extends through car body sides; patterned rubber tires with axle spacers. TOOTSIETOY CHICAGO 24 U.S.A.

	G	E	LN
(A) Painted features.	20	45	55
(B) Same as (A) except TOOTSIETOY U.S.A.	20	45	55
(C) Same as (A) with unpainted side panel. Rare. S. Butler Collection.	40	70	75

1952 LINCOLN CAPRI: (1953-1958) Two-door hardtop; body painted red, gray, blue, or medium green; two-tone models in red, blue, or medium green with cream, white, or tan roof. Silver-painted features include front and rear bumpers, front grille, and headlights. Body features include open front wheel wells, three-piece rear window, and oval-shaped rear taillights; body sides extend through rear wheel wells to simulate fender skirts; large bumper guards on front bumper. Axle assembly for rear wheels extend through body sides; patterned rubber tires with axle spacers. TOOTSIETOY MADE IN U.S.A.

	G	E	LN
(A) Painted features.	15	35	45
(B) Two-tone paint, painted features.	20	40	50
(C) Same as (A) or (B); no casting identification.	15	35	45

1953 CHRYSLER NEW YORKER: (1953-1954) Four-door sedan; body painted green, red, blue, gray, or yellow; two-tone models came in red, blue, or green with white or cream roof. Silver-painted features include front and rear bumpers, front grille, and headlights. Body contains four-piece side windows, three-piece rear windows; open front wheel well; V on front and rear of car; CHRYSLER on rear trunk. Body sides extend over rear wheels to simulate fender skirts; rear axle assembly extends through body sides; patterned rubber tires with axle spacers. TOOTSIETOY MADE IN U.S.A.

	G	E	LN
(A) Painted features.	15	40	50
(B) Two-tone paint, painted features.	20	45	55

1954 BUICK CENTURY WAGON: (1955-1959) Four-door station wagon; body painted green, red, or blue; two-tone models in red, blue, or green with white or cream roof. Silver-painted features include bumpers, front grille, taillights, and headlights. Body sides extend through rear wheels; open front wheel wells; three simulated oval portholes on sides of front fenders. Rear axle extends through body sides; patterned rubber Tootsietoy tires with axle spacers. BUICK CENTURY TOOTSIETOY CHICAGO U.S.A.

	G	E	LN
(A) Painted features.	20	35	45
(B) Two-tone paint, painted features.	25	40	50
(C) Same as (A) with trailer hitch.	25	40	50
(D) Same as (B) with trailer hitch.	30	45	55
(E) Same as (B) with tin chassis. Rare.	45	65	90

1954 CADILLAC 62 SEDAN: (1955-1959) Four-door sedan; body painted red, blue, medium green, or gray. Two-tone models in red, green, orange or blue with cream roof; gray with red or blue roof; or red, green, and blue with white roof. Silver-painted features include front and rear bumpers, headlights, taillights, and front grille. Body contains four-piece side windows and swept-up rear taillights; body sides extend over rear wheels to simulate fender skirts with open front wheel well; Cadillac emblem on the front and rear; large

Top: *1952 Lincoln Capri.* **Middle:** *1951 Buick Experimental XP300 Sportster and 1948 Cadillac.* **Bottom:** *1949 Buick Roadmaster and 1950 Chrysler Windsor Convertible.*

Top: *1954 Cadillac 62 Sedan with original box; 1955 Packard Patrician with original box. S. Butler Collection.* **Middle:** *1954 Buick Century Wagon.* **Bottom:** *1954/1955 Experimental Coupe and 1953 Chrysler New Yorker.*

Top: *1956 Jaguar XK 140 and 1956 Mercedes 190SL.* **Middle:** *1956 Porsche Spyder and 1954 MG Classic, S. Butler Collection.* **Bottom:** *1956 Austin-Healy.*

Top: *1962 Ford Station Wagon and 1956 CJ5 Jeep with Snowplow in color variations. C. Jones and S. Butler Collections.* **Bottom:** *1932 Hot Rod and 1940 Ford Convertible. S. Butler Collection.*

G E LN

bumper guards on front bumper. Patterned rubber tires with axle spacers. TOOTSIETOY MADE IN U.S.A. CADILLAC 62.

	G	E	LN
(A) Painted features.	20	35	45
(B) Two-tone paint, painted features.	25	40	50
(C) Patterned rubber Tootsietoy tires, no axle spacers, trailer hitch, CADILLAC on rear trunk, two-tone paint. CADILLAC TOOTSIETOY CHICAGO 24 U.S.A.	25	45	55
(D) Same as (C) with painted features.	20	40	45
(E) Same as (B) with tin chassis. Rare.	40	65	75

1954/1955 EXPERIMENTAL COUPE: (1958-1964, 1967) Two-door coupe resembling either a 1954 Buick Experimental Coupe or a 1955 Chrysler "Falcon" Experimental; may have intended it to look like a convertible with the top up. Body painted light blue, blue, medium green, red, or orange. Silver-painted features include front and rear bumpers, front grille, headlights, taillights, and lower body strip extending the length of the car. Body has finned rear fenders with large slanted taillights; SPECIAL in front bumper between two large bumper guards; simulated center panel lines extending length of hood and trunk. TOOTSIETOY CHICAGO 24 U.S.A.

	G	E	LN
(A) Patterned rubber tires, no axle spacers.	15	40	45
(B) Same as (A) with patterned plastic Tootsietoy tires, no axle spacers.	15	40	45
(C) Same as (A) with tin chassis. Rare.	35	65	75

1954 MG CLASSIC: (1959-1967) Two-seat sports car convertible; body painted blue, green, red, yellow, or orange. Silver-painted features include bumpers, headlights, and front grille. Body casting includes detailed dash and steering wheel; no windshield; spare tire mounted over rear trunk; large flat tonneau area behind car seat; engine vents on both sides of hood; directional lights on the top of front fenders. Patterned rubber Tootsietoy tires, no axle spacers. TOOTSIETOY CHICAGO 24 U.S.A. CLASSIC MG.

	G	E	LN
(A) Painted features.	10	20	25
(B) Patterned plastic Tootsietoy tires, body and features painted single color.	8	20	25
(C) Same as (B) with trailer hitch.	15	30	35

1954 VOLKSWAGEN: (1959-1960, 1962-1964, 1968-1969) Two-door sedan; body painted red, yellow, green, blue, gold, or orange. Silver-painted features on some models include front and rear bumpers, headlights, and taillights. Body, often described as a "VW Bug," contains large headlights, air vent under rear window, open wheel wells, and distinctive hood and rear body panels. Patterned rubber Tootsietoy tires, no axle spacers. TOOTSIETOY CHICAGO 24 USA VOLKSWAGEN.

	G	E	LN
(A) Painted features.	10	25	28
(B) Body and features painted same color.	8	20	25
(C) Same as (B) with patterned plastic Tootsietoy tires, no axle spacers.	8	20	25

1955 CHRYSLER REGENT: (1955) A rare two-door hardtop painted in a two-tone finish; lower body in red, blue, green, or gray; roof in gray, red, green, or cream. Silver-painted features include front and rear bumpers, taillights, headlights, and front two-piece grille. Body casting features a one-piece windshield, large side windows with side vent windows, and open wheel wells on front and rear. Patterned rubber Tootsietoy tires, no axle spacers. Casting identification unknown. This car was featured in No. 7000 Playtime Set and in assortment No. 5030. **NRS**

1955 PACKARD PATRICIAN: (1955-1959) Four-door sedan; body found in green, blue, gray, red, or cream; two-tone colors came in red, cream, green, or blue with a green or cream roof, or gray with a red or blue roof. Silver-painted features include front and rear bumpers, headlights, taillights, and front grille. Body features include rear wheel fender skirts and PACKARD on rear trunk; small circle with a V through it on front grille; open front wheel wells; trailer hitch. Rear axle does not protrude through car body sides; patterned rubber Tootsietoy tires, no axle spacers. PACKARD TOOTSIETOY CHICAGO 24 U.S.A.

	G	E	LN
(A) Painted features.	15	35	45
(B) Two-tone paint, painted features.	25	40	50
(C) Two-tone paint, painted features; patterned rubber tires with axle spacers, rear axle extends through side of car body, no trailer hitch. PACKARD PATRICIAN TOOTSIETOY CHICAGO U.S.A.	25	40	50
(D) Same as (C) without two-tone paint.	20	35	45
(E) Same as (B) with tin chassis. Rare.	40	65	90
(F) Body and features same color.	12	25	35

1956 AUSTIN-HEALY: (1959-1961) Four-seat sports car convertible; body painted green, blue, gold, red, or orange. Body and features painted single color. Body casting includes detailed dash and steering wheel, oval front grille, hood scoop, and small rear trunk. Patterned rubber Tootsietoy tires, no axle spacers. TOOTSIETOY CHICAGO 24 U.S.A. AUSTIN.

	G	E	LN
(A) As described above.	10	30	35
(B) Patterned plastic Tootsietoy tires.	10	30	35

1956 JAGUAR XK 140: (1959-1964, 1968-1969) Two-door sports car with hardtop; body painted blue, light blue, medium green, red, or yellow. Silver-painted features include front and rear bumpers, front grille, and headlights. Body casting features oval side windows; two-piece windshield; oval upright front grille; headlights between grille and front fenders; rear oval window; taillights located between rear fender and trunk. Patterned rubber Tootsietoy tires, no axle spacers. TOOTSIETOY CHICAGO 24 USA JAGUAR XK 140.

	G	E	LN
(A) Painted features.	10	20	25
(B) Body and features same color.	8	20	25
(C) Same as (B) with patterned plastic Tootsietoy tires, no axle spacers.	8	20	25

1956 JEEP CJ5: (1956-1962) Body and features painted red, orange, yellow, blue, or silver; cast windshield and steering wheel painted silver. Body features a detailed interior; open wheel wells; U-shaped trailer hitch; USA 20965148 on left and right sides of front hood in small cast print; and headlights and front grille on flat panel between front fenders. Patterned rubber Tootsietoy tires, no axle spacers. TOOTSIETOY CHICAGO U.S.A. ¼ TON M-38 JEEP- 1.

	G	E	LN
(A) As described above.	18	30	35
(B) Patterned plastic Tootsietoy tires.	15	25	30

1956 JEEP CJ5 WITH SNOWPLOW: (1958-1961, 1963) Body painted red or blue; snowplow painted yellow; cast windshield and steering wheel painted silver; all other features painted the same as the body color. Body features a

G E LN

detailed interior; open wheel wells; U-shaped trailer hitch; USA 20965148 on left and right of front hood in small cast print; headlights and front grille on flat panel between front fenders. Snowplow is held to body behind front wheels by a cast pin on plow inserted through a hole on each side of body. Patterned plastic Tootsietoy tires, no axle spacers. TOOTSIETOY CHICAGO U.S.A. ¼ TON M-38 JEEP-2. **25 40 50**

1956 JEEP CJ5: (1962-1966) Body painted blue, red, silver, yellow, or orange. Silver-painted features include front bumper, front grille, headlights, and rear trailer hitch. Body cast with windshield in down position. Detailed interior with molded steering wheel, open wheel wells, and trailer hitch. USA 20965148 on left and right sides of front hood. Patterned rubber Tootsietoy tires, no axle spacers; painted features. TOOTSIETOY CHICAGO 24 U.S.A. 3.

(A) As described above. **10 20 25**

(B) Patterned plastic Tootsietoy tires; body and features same color. **8 18 23**

1956 MERCEDES 190SL: (1959-1964, 1968-1969) Two-door coupe; body and features painted gray, light blue, or blue. Body casting includes Mercedes emblem on trunk and front grille; 190SL on trunk below emblem; open wheel wells front and rear; one-piece windshield; small oval rear window. Patterned rubber Tootsietoy tires, no axle spacers. TOOTSIETOY CHICAGO 24 USA MERCEDES 190SL.

(A) As described above. **10 20 25**

(B) Patterned plastic Tootsietoy tires. **8 20 25**

1956 PORSCHE SPYDER: (1959-1964, 1968-1969) Single-seat sports car roadster; body painted red, gold, yellow, blue, green, or orange. Body and features painted single color. Body casting includes steering wheel, rear engine grille, PORSCHE on front and rear, SPYDER on left front fender only. Patterned rubber Tootsietoy tires, no axle spacers. TOOTSIETOY CHICAGO 24 U.S.A. PORSCHE.

(A) As described above. **10 20 25**

(B) Patterned plastic Tootsietoy tires. **8 20 25**

1959 FORD COUNTRY SEDAN: (1959-1967) Four-door station wagon; body painted light blue with gray top, green or red with cream top. Silver-painted features include front and rear bumpers, front grille, headlights, and taillights. Body casting contains dual headlights; large circular taillights; open front wheel wells; trailer hitch. Body casting extends over rear wheels; rear wheel axle mounted inside body casting. Patterned rubber Tootsietoy tires, no axle spacers. TOOTSIETOY CHICAGO 24 U.S.A. FORD COUNTRY SEDAN P-10296. Shown in Chapter 4.

(A) As described above. **12 25 28**

(B) Patterned plastic Tootsietoy tires. **12 25 28**

1959 OLDSMOBILE CONVERTIBLE: (1960-1968) Body painted red, green, yellow, blue, orange, or turquoise. Silver-painted features include front and rear bumpers, front grille and lights, seats, and front windshield. Body casting contains dual headlights; undersized windshield; trailer hitch; seats; steering wheel; large flat hood and trunk. Patterned rubber Tootsietoy tires, no axle spacers. OLDSMOBILE TOOTSIETOY CHICAGO 24 U.S.A. P-10310. Shown in Chapter 4.

(A) As described above. **14 27 35**

(B) Patterned plastic Tootsietoy tires. **12 25 30**

(C) Same as (B) with windshield and seats painted same color as body. **10 25 30**

(D) Same as (B) with seats painted same color as body. **10 25 30**

(E) Same as (D) with windshield and tour cover painted gold or silver. **12 25 35**

1962 FORD STATION WAGON: (1964-1968) Four-door wagon; body painted red, blue, orange, or green; two-tone models came in red, blue, or green with white roof. Silver-painted features are front and rear bumpers, front grille, headlights, and taillights. Body extends over rear wheels to simulate fender skirts; large wide hood; grille with dual headlights; six roof strips for luggage rack; large rear taillights; and a trailer hitch. Patterned rubber Tootsietoy tires, no axle spacers. TOOTSIETOY CHICAGO 24 U.S.A. 01049-2.

(A) Painted features. **10 18 20**

(B) Two-tone paint with painted features. **12 20 25**

(C) Body and features same color. **8 15 20**

(D) Same as (C) with patterned plastic Tootsietoy tires, no axle spacers. **8 15 20**

(E) Same as (B) with police sticker on hood which reads SHERIFF. **20 45 50**

CHAPTER 3

Six-Inch Trucks, Vans, and Buses

The 6-inch trucks, vans, and buses, including those that were produced before the war but reissued after the war, those produced from 1947 through 1969, and the Jumbo Series, are covered in this chapter. The major differences between the original prewar vehicles and those reissued postwar were, again, a change in the type and color of tire and in some cases the body colors used. Prewar vehicles had white rubber tires; postwar used black rubber tires. The first trucks included in this chapter belong to the Jumbo Series reissued immediately following the war and, for the most part, are not yet in high demand. They appear to be generic productions rather that direct copies of any specific vehicles. The best-looking vehicle of this Jumbo Series is the Pickup Truck, which can be found in the two-tone paint scheme; while most of the Jumbo vehicles were not produced in two-tone paint, those included in special gift sets were. These toys are more readily found without any painted features. The most difficult vehicle to find in the entire series is the Jumbo Bus with postwar black tires in a two-tone paint scheme. See Chapter 2 for a picture of these reissued units. The reissued 1937 Reo

1937 Reo Tanker Trucks in Standard, Sinclair, Texaco, and Shell oil company versions. Note unusual yellow color on the Sinclair. S. Butler Collection.

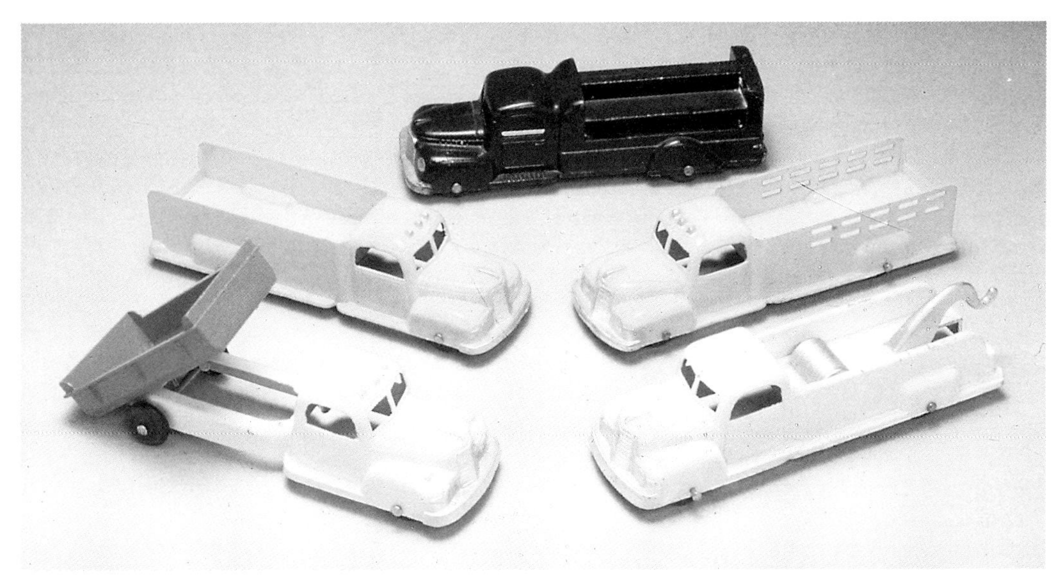

Top: *1948 Diamond T Bottle Truck.* **Middle**: *1947 Diamond T Truck and 1947 Diamond T Stakeside Truck, S. Butler Collection.* **Bottom**: *1947 Diamond T Dump Truck and 1947 Diamond T Tow Truck.*

Top: *1947 Mack Fire Truck with original box; S. Butler Collection.* **Middle:** *1947 Mack Dump Trucks in color variations.* **Bottom:** *1946 International Standard Oil Truck and 1946 International Sinclair Oil Truck.*

Tanker Truck was produced in four oil company versions, a two-tone paint scheme, and painted features. Each version can be somewhat difficult to find today.

The postwar 6-inch series contains the 1959 International Metro Van, the most difficult to find; the 1947 Mack and 1956 Ford Stakeside Trucks, both with the TOOTSIETOY tin top, two 1946 International Oil Trucks with different oil company names, and the 1949 Ford Tanker Trucks, some of which are difficult to locate; there are twenty-seven different models that are relatively easy to find. The 1947 Diamond T trucks are excellent productions. Properly identifying the correct model year for these trucks has been difficult. Many collectors and prior publications identify them as 1940 International trucks; however, research of company records, other publications, and catalogues has led to the conclusion that the basic truck was not an International. It seems to have been modeled after the Diamond T truck produced by the C. A. Tilt Company of Chicago, since they were produced beginning in 1947; they are listed here, then, as 1947 and 1948 trucks. The Tootsietoy model contains a low-profile cab, roof lines, and roof running lights that are very similar to 1947 and 1948 Diamond T trucks. The 1940 International cab does not have these features. The Diamond T series contains five different models; all utilize the same cab except for the bottle truck, which was only offered in 1948. For this model, the headlights were positioned more to the outside face of the fender. Because the bottle truck was only produced for one year, it is a desirable piece to have. The dump truck produced from 1948 to 1952 is also very collectible, thanks to the quality of the casting. The solid stakeside truck offered only in 1953 can be somewhat difficult to find. Collectors should examine the tires on all of these units before purchasing them for signs of cracking, splitting, and elongation.

Three units were produced with removable parts: the 1947 Mack Stakeside Truck, the 1956 Ford Stakeside Truck with a tin TOOTSIETOY bed cover, and the 1960 El Camino with a camper top and boat. The removable pieces are easily lost, which makes it difficult to find these items intact today. This has substantially affected the value of the 1947 and 1956 Stakeside Trucks found with the bed covers, but has had little effect on the price of the El Camino, perhaps because the quality of the camper top is somewhat average. It should be noted that the 1960 El Camino was made with and without a hole in the truck bed floor for mounting the camper top. Some collectors believe that this El Camino was also made into a tow truck. However, research has not turned up any evidence to support that claim. It is more likely that someone used a tow hoist assembly from a 1947 Mack Tow Truck and installed it in an El Camino unit with a hole in the truck bed. The existing hole would have to have been slightly enlarged to do this, but the tow assembly could then be mounted to the truck bed by flaring the mounting pin (a delicate but not impossible procedure) from the underside of the bed.

The F-700 Ford Truck was made with and without a Ford hood emblem, which has little effect on the value. There is, however, a discrepancy in how this unit is identified by collectors. While the casting includes the designation "F-700," some collectors believe the truck actually resembles an F-600; the F-700 was a heavier truck.

The 1955 Greyhound Bus, a model of a Scenicruiser, was produced in two different paint schemes. The earlier version is painted in three colors: blue and silver with a cream roof. The later version is painted only in blue and silver, which reflected changes in the prototype Scenicruiser. Both variations were available boxed as well as in the later blister packs. See Chapter 11 for additional 6-inch units which were sold as boxed units.

By the end of 1968, only the 1955 Mack Cement Truck, the 1955 Scenicruiser Bus, and the 1962 Ford Econoline Pickup Truck were still in production. The body and features of the pickup truck were painted in the same color. A two-tone paint scheme was still provided for the cement truck and bus.

The method for mounting the tires using axle spacers with pins is featured on all of the reissued toys. (For additional information and drawings of the tires used on these vehicles, refer to Chapter 2.)

Based on historical data, catalogue advertisements and data obtained from Strombecker, the best known information on production years for each piece is included with the listings. **Note:** The *last* detail in each listing will be information cast into the underside of the vehicle. Most vehicles included some information underneath the toy; it is included here in small capitals letters without reference to the underside location in an effort to reduce the number of repetitious phrases in the listings. With few exceptions, the information appears on the toy in capital letters.

	G	E	LN

JUMBO BUS: (1942/1946) Prewar reissued torpedo-styled Greyhound bus; body painted blue, silver, orange, green, red, or yellow. Silver-painted features include front bumper, grille, and headlights; some units also contain a silver roof which extends to the back of the bus and rear bumper. Body features a short front hood with painted hood trim; headlights connected to motor hood; split front windshield; front fenders; covered wheel wells; seven windows on each side; front and rear bumpers; GREYHOUND on each side of roof; raised panel in center of roof extending almost the entire roof length. Axles extend through body sides; smooth black rubber tires with axle spacers. TOOTSIETOY MADE IN UNITED STATES OF AMERICA.

	G	E	LN
(A) Painted features with silver roof.	35	65	70
(B) Same as (A), roof painted same color as bus body.	35	60	65
(C) Body and features same color.	30	45	50

JUMBO PICKUP TRUCK: (1942/1946) Prewar reissued pickup truck resembling an International; body painted red, yellow, orange, green, blue, or silver. Cab has a two-piece windshield; no rear window; protruding fenders with running board extending to truck bed; headlights in fenders; two small running lights in front of windshield; a large front grille with radiator cap; solid body mold between front bumper and truck front. Truck bed contains hump to allow for rear axle clearance and large wheel well covers. Smooth black rubber tires with axle spacers. TOOTSIETOY MADE IN UNITED STATES OF AMERICA.

	G	E	LN
(A) Body and features same color.	18	30	35
(B) Same as (A) with silver-painted front bumper, grille, and headlights.	20	35	40
(C) Same as (B) with silver-painted interior truck bed.	20	35	40
(D) Same as (C) with white-painted truck roof and window area.	25	40	50
(E) Same as (B) without solid body mold between front bumper and truck front.	25	40	50
(F) Same as (E) with interior of truck bed painted silver and white roof and window area.	30	50	60

JUMBO TOW TRUCK: (1942/1946) Prewar reissued tow truck resembling a Chevy truck; painted silver, yellow, red, blue, green, or orange; two-tone versions painted red and silver, yellow and brown, and green and cream. Truck cab features a two-piece windshield; no rear window; large light on rear of cab roof; headlights on top of fender extending to truck hood; protruding front and rear fenders; open wheel wells in

G E LN

front and rear; and a running board extending from the front fenders to the rear of the truck. Casting also includes four motor vents and one cab vent on each side of truck hood, and a tow bar and hook molded in one piece. Smooth black rubber tires with axle spacers. TOOTSIETOY MADE IN U.S.A.

(A) Body and features same color. 20 35 40

(B) Same as (A) with two-tone paint; silver-painted front bumper, grille, and headlights. 25 45 50

(C) Same as (A) with patterned rubber tires. 20 35 45

(D) Same as (A) or (B) without solid body mold between front bumper and body. 20 35 45

1937 REO TANKER TRUCK: (1947) Prewar reissued oil tanker truck produced in four different company names. Silver-painted features include grille, bumpers, headlights, and tank. Truck body features cab-over-motor design, split windshield, large front grille, V-shaped front bumper, and closed wheel wells in the front and rear; the tanker body has a rear bumper, a simulated rear door, four bands across the upper portion of tank, and a large round hatch cover in the center of the tank. Oil company names in large black lettering occur on a flat panel on each side of body tank. Axles extend through the body sides; smooth black rubber tires with axle spacers.

(A) STANDARD oil truck; cab and lower body painted red. 30 45 50

(B) SINCLAIR oil truck; cab and lower body painted green. 30 45 50

(C) TEXACO oil truck; cab and lower body painted red. 30 45 50

(D) SHELL oil truck; cab and lower body painted yellow. 30 45 50

(E) Same as (B), except cab and lower body painted yellow. S. Butler Collection. 40 65 100

1946 INTERNATIONAL OIL TRUCK: (1949-1955) Tanker truck; body casting features three protruding running lights on roof of cab and three simulated running lights on top rear of truck; four filler caps on top; three simulated doors on each side of tanker body; two rear doors with taillights on each side. Hood contains long air vents on each side; a large front grille and protruding front fenders; and headlights in fender next to grille. Oil company names cast into tanker body on both sides. Truck body extends over wheel wells in front and rear. Axle extends through body sides front and rear; smooth rubber tires with axle spacers. TOOTSIETOY MADE IN U.S.A. **Note:** Some collectors believe this truck also came in Texaco and Shell versions; however, there is no evidence that they were ever produced.

(A) STANDARD oil truck painted red; front bumper, grille, headlights, and oil company name painted silver. 20 45 55

(B) SINCLAIR oil truck painted medium green; front bumper, grille, headlights, and oil company name painted silver. 20 45 55

1947 DIAMOND T TRUCK: (1953) Solid-side truck; body painted red, yellow, orange, green, or blue. Silver-painted features include front bumper, roof lights, headlights, and front grille. Body casting features three running lights on cab roof; rounded front hood and closed wheel well fenders; headlights in fender next to horizontal-style front grille; air vents on each side of hood; a two-piece windshield; large side windows and rear cab window; and covered rear fenders protruding from truck's side. Back of truck body is open with taillights located outside of truck sides. A narrow running board extends from back of front fender to truck rear. Axles extend through body sides; smooth rubber tires with axle spacers. TOOTSIETOY MADE IN UNITED STATES OF AMERICA. 20 35 40

1947 DIAMOND T DUMP TRUCK: (1948-1953) Truck body and frame painted red, blue, green, yellow, or orange; dump bed painted red, blue, green, yellow, orange, or silver. Silver-painted features include front bumper, grille, and headlights. Truck contains a dump bed which tilts to up position and which is connected to truck body at rear axle. Cab has three running lights on top of cab and one on top of front fender; a rounded front hood; covered front wheel wells; headlights in the fenders next to a horizontal-style front grille; air vents on each side of hood; a two-piece windshield; large side windows; and rear wheels outside of truck frame under dump bed. Front axle extends through closed wheel wells; smooth rubber tires with axle spacers. TOOTSIETOY MADE IN UNITED STATES OF AMERICA can be found on underside of dump bed; no markings on truck body. 25 40 45

1947 DIAMOND T TOW TRUCK: (1948-1952) Body painted red, yellow, blue, green, or orange. Silver-painted features include front bumper, grille, and headlights. All models include a cable reel in the truck bed with a one-piece tow bar and hook assembly. Truck body contains a two-piece windshield; large side windows and rear cab window; a single light on cab roof facing rear of truck; a rounded front hood; covered front fender wheel wells; a headlight in front face of fender next to a horizontal-style front grille; air vents on each side of truck hood; running board extending from the front fender to the back of truck. Rear truck body contains a half cable spool protruding from body floor and a large open slot in the center extending from the rear of the truck to the back of the tow bar assembly. Truck sides extend over wheel wells to form square rear fenders. Axles extend through body sides; smooth rubber tires with axle spacers. TOOTSIETOY MADE IN UNITED STATES IN AMERICA.

(A) Painted features include tow bar and cable reel. 25 40 45

(B) Painted features include tow bar; cable reel same as body color. 20 35 40

(C) Painted features include cable reel; tow bar same as body color. 20 35 40

(D) Painted features; tow bar and cable reel same as body color. 15 35 40

1947 DIAMOND T STAKESIDE TRUCK: (1947-1953) Stakeside truck; body painted in red, yellow, green, orange, or blue. Silver-painted features include front bumper, roof lights, headlights, and front grille. Truck cab has three running lights on roof; rounded front hood and front fenders; closed front wheel wells; headlights in front face of fender next to a horizontal-style front grille; air vents on each side of truck hood; and a running board extending from the front fender to rear of truck. Truck cab has a two-piece windshield, large side windows, and rear cab window. Truck body sides contain five

Clockwise from left: *1947 Mack Truck with variable sides; 1947 GMC Bus; 1947 Mack Tow Trucks in various colors, S. Butler Collection; 1955 Mack Cement Truck; and 1947 Mack Truck with even sides and* TOOTSIETOY *tin top.*

	G	E	LN

rows of open slots to simulate stakes; an open rear tailgate; taillights on the outside. Truck body extends over rear wheel well to form a square rear fender. Axles extend through body sides; smooth rubber tires with axle spacers. TOOTSIETOY MADE IN UNITED STATES OF AMERICA 748. **15 30 35**

1948 DIAMOND T BOTTLE TRUCK: (1948) Truck cab resembles a 1947 Diamond T Truck except that the headlights are located on the outside face of the front fender. Body painted orange, blue, yellow, red, or green. Silver-painted features include front and rear bumper and grille. Casting includes two-piece windshield; rounded front hood; closed wheel wells on front fenders; horizontal-style front grille; air vents on each side of hood; hood ornament; running boards beneath each door; large side windows; no rear cab window. Rear truck body contains two open storage compartments extending the length of the truck body on each side; rear wheel housing in teardrop design, unlike square type on the 1947 model. Axles extend through body sides; smooth rubber tires with axle spacers. TOOTSIETOY MADE IN U.S.A. 754. **25 40 55**

1947 GMC BUS: (1947-1955) Silver-side Greyhound Lines bus; silver roof, blue-painted side window panel and bus front. Silver-painted features include sides below window areas, front bumper, and rear of bus. Simulated corrugated siding has GREYHOUND LINES and Greyhound dog cast in. Sides of body extend over wheel wells; axles extend through body sides. Smooth rubber tires with axle spacers. TOOTSIETOY MADE IN 2 U.S.A.

	G	E	LN
(A) Blue and silver.	**20**	**40**	**45**
(B) Same as (A) but painted red and silver. C. Jones Collection.	**25**	**50**	**60**
(C) All-blue with silver front bumper.	**20**	**35**	**40**

1947 MACK DUMP TRUCK: (1954-1966) Truck body painted red, yellow, blue, green, or dark red; dump body painted silver, yellow, green, red, blue, or dark blue. Silver-painted features include front bumper and front grille. Cab casting includes protruding front fenders; headlight and directional and/or running light on fender; running boards on both sides of body. Dump bed is held to truck body by rear axle assembly; dump bed has a revolving rear dump door; straight subframe under dump bed. Rear dual wheels consist of four separate tires. Patterned rubber tires with axle spacers. Cast-in under cab: TOOTSIETOY MADE IN U.S.A.; under dump bed: 1.

	G	E	LN
(A) Painted features.	**20**	**30**	**35**
(B) Rear dump door missing.	**10**	**18**	**20**

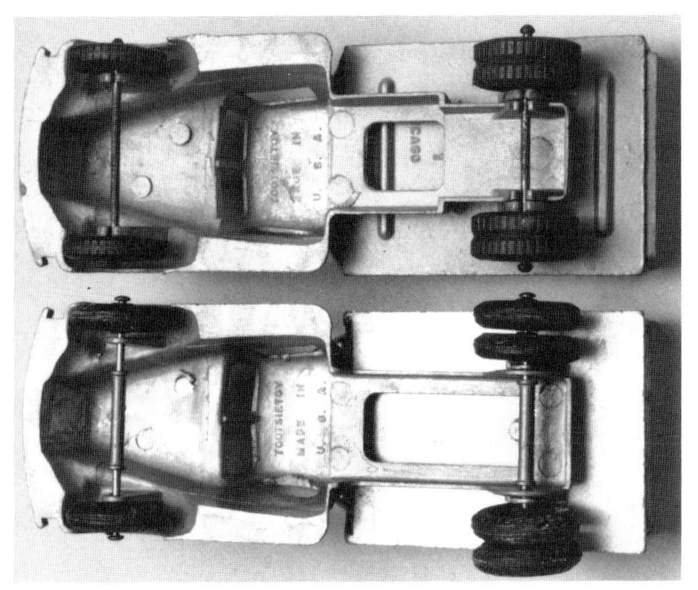

Frame and wheel variations for the 1947 Mack Dump Truck.

G E LN

(C) Patterned rubber Tootsietoy tires with axle spacers; TOOTSIETOY 2 CHICAGO 24 U.S.A. cast under dump bed. Molded dual rear tires. 18 22 25

(D) Patterned plastic Tootsietoy tires, no axle spacers, molded dual rear tires; step in subframe under dump bed; under dump bed TOOTSIETOY 1 CHICAGO 24 U.S.A. 18 22 25

(E) Same as (C) or (D) but rear dump door missing. 10 15 18

1947 MACK FIRE TRUCK: (1953-1958) Body painted red with silver-painted front bumper and large front grille. Crew cab has three windows on each side; a divided front windshield; protruding fenders with running boards extending between front and rear fenders; open wheel wells on front and rear; MACK cast on rear step; fire hose on reel protruding from rear of truck; emergency light on roof; and two fire extinguishers in body casting, one on each side. Open rear truck bed has two hooks outside driver's side to hold ladder, and two hooks on opposite side for two black fire hoses. Patterned rubber tires with axle spacers. TOOTSIETOY MADE IN THE U.S.A.

(A) With cast ladder and two black fire hoses. 25 55 70

(B) With cast ladder, hoses missing. 20 35 45

(C) Ladder and hoses missing. 15 25 30

(D) Same as (A) with silver-painted running boards. Rare. S. Butler Collection. 30 65 85

1947 MACK TOW TRUCK: (1954-1966) Body painted white, yellow, red, or green. Silver-painted features include front bumper, grille, and tow assembly on those truck bodies painted red, yellow, or green. White body has red-painted features including the front grille, roof warning light, and zebra-striped front and rear bumpers; silver-painted tow assembly. Red truck also found with white trim. Tow hook resembles a Christmas tree ornament hook. The short rear body has a toolbox behind cab. Truck cab features protruding front fenders with headlights and directional/running light and running board on both sides. Molded dual rear tires. TOOTSIETOY MADE IN U.S.A. 2.

G E LN

(A) Patterned rubber Tootsietoy tires, axle spacers. 15 35 40

(B) Patterned plastic Tootsietoy tires, no axle spacers. 15 35 40

(C) Same as (B) with ESSO on roof and red star on each door; yellow truck body with silver features. (Observed at a toy show.) NRS

1947 MACK TRUCK: (1954-1957) Solid, step-up stakeside truck; body painted red, yellow, blue, or green. Two-tone versions painted red, yellow, blue, or green with a silver-painted truck bed and bed sides. Silver-painted features include front bumper and large grille. Body features open rear truck body with rounded corners behind truck cab; open rear tailgate; protruding front fenders with headlight and directional/running lights; and open wheel wells front and rear. Patterned rubber Tootsietoy tires with axle spacers. TOOTSIETOY MADE IN U.S.A.

(A) Painted features with two-tone paint. 20 40 45

(B) Painted features. 15 35 40

(C) Painted features; patterned plastic Tootsietoy tires. 15 35 40

1947 MACK TRUCK: (1958-1959) Solid, even stakeside truck; body painted red, yellow, blue, orange, or green. Silver-painted features include front bumper and large front grille. Body features open rear truck body with open rear tail gate; two running lights on roof; protruding front fenders with headlights and directional/running lights; and open wheel wells front and rear. Patterned rubber Tootsietoy tires with axle spacers. TOOTSIETOY CHICAGO 24 U.S.A.

(A) Painted features. 20 35 40

(B) With tin TOOTSIETOY bed cover; silver with black lettering. Rare. 45 75 100

(C) Painted features; patterned plastic Tootsietoy tires with axle spacers. 20 35 40

(D) Same as (C), body and features painted same color. 15 35 40

(E) Same as (B) with all-silver tin bed cover, or bed cover painted the same as truck. Rare. 45 70 90

1949 FORD TANKER: (1949-1952, 1963) Gas truck; body casting contains three protruding running lights on cab roof, short front hood, protruding fenders, oval-style grille with headlights, and five filler caps on top of fuel tank; gas company names and emblems featured on both sides of tanker body. Body sides extend over front and rear wheel wells; axles extend through body sides; smooth rubber tires with axle spacers. TOOTSIETOY MADE IN U.S.A. **Note:** Some collectors believe this truck was also produced in a Standard or a Sinclair version; however, there is no evidence that these exist.

(A) SHELL truck painted yellow or orange; front bumper, grille, headlights, and gas company name painted silver. 20 40 45

(B) TEXACO truck painted red; front bumper, grille, headlights, and gas company name painted silver. 20 40 45

(C) Painted orange or blue; body and features painted same color in any gas company name. 20 40 45

Top: *1956 Ford Stakeside Truck with* TOOTSIETOY *tin top.* **Middle:** *1949 Ford "Shell" Tanker, S. Butler Collection; 1956 Dodge Panel.* **Bottom:** *1949 Ford "Shell" Tanker and 1949 Ford "Texaco" Tanker.*

	G	E	LN

1955 GREYHOUND SCENICRUISER BUS: (1955-1969) Raised upper deck with windows over storage compartment. Lower body painted silver including dog and GREYHOUND. Middle section and lower roof painted blue; upper roof top and window area painted cream. Body features include simulated corrugated sides; GREYHOUND; Greyhound dog; and SCENICRUISER. Small patterned tires, single tandem rear tires; no axle spacers. No cast-in identification on underside.

	G	E	LN
(A) As described above with cream, blue, and silver paint scheme.	30	50	60
(B) Same as (A) except lower body and roof top painted silver; middle section, lower roof section, and upper window area painted blue.	25	45	50

1955 MACK CEMENT TRUCK: (1959-1969) Body painted red or orange; cement drum painted yellow, orange, red, or cream. Silver-painted features include front bumper, grille, and headlights. Body casting features a two-piece revolving cement drum; three running lights on cab roof; protruding fenders with headlights in center of fender; large vertical front grille; and rear dump shoot. Cement drum rotates on a worm gear axle that meets a round gear set in truck body (the drum contains spaced teeth extending around cement drum which rides on round gear). Drum rotates as wheel assembly is turned. Patterned rubber Tootsietoy tires, no axle spacers; dual tandem molded rear tires. TOOTSIETOY CHICAGO 24 U.S.A. P-10240.

	G	E	LN
(A) As described above.	20	40	45
(B) Patterned plastic Tootsietoy tires.	20	40	45
(C) Same as (B) without painted features.	15	35	40
(D) Same as (C) without axle gear (non-revolving cement drum). C. Jones Collection.	15	35	40

1956 DODGE PANEL TRUCK: (1959-1966) Two-tone model with top, window area, and side panels painted cream or light yellow. Lower truck body and hood in green, blue, or red. Silver-painted features include front and rear bumpers, grille, and headlights. Body casting includes wraparound windshield; open front wheel wells; side vent windows and double rear window; raised panel down center of hood with V-8 emblem; headlights in fenders; and directional lights under headlights. Truck body extends over rear wheels; rear axle mounted inside of truck body. Patterned rubber Tootsietoy tires, no axle spacers. TOOTSIETOY CHICAGO 24 U.S.A.

	G	E	LN
(A) As described above.	25	40	45
(B) Patterned plastic Tootsietoy tires.	25	40	45
(C) Same as (B) without painted silver features.	20	35	40

Top: *1959 Metro Van (restored; side decals are missing); 1955 Greyhound Scenicruiser Bus with original box, S. Butler Collection.* **Middle:** *1962 Ford Fuel Truck and 1960 Chevrolet El Camino with camper top and boat.* **Bottom:** *1962 Ford Econoline Pickup Truck and 1960 Chevrolet El Camino.*

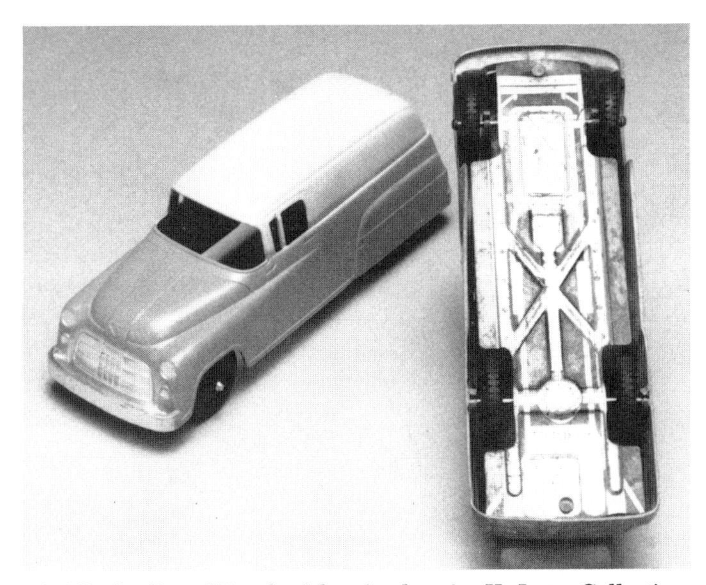

1956 Dodge Panel Truck with a tin chassis. K. Jestes Collection.

	G	E	LN
(D) Same as (B) with painted features; body painted solid red, blue, or medium green.	**18**	**35**	**40**
(E) Same as (A) with tin chassis. Rare.	**30**	**65**	**75**

1956 FORD STAKESIDE TRUCK: (1960-1964) F-700 stakeside truck resembling an F-600; body painted red, green, or light blue. Silver-painted features include front bumper and front grille assembly. Body casting features wraparound windshield; large front grille with headlights and V-8 emblem located in center; protruding front fenders with open wheel well; running board under side doors; truck bed extending over dual rear wheels; simulated stakeside truck body. Ford emblem on front of truck hood. Patterned rubber Tootsietoy tires, molded dual rear tires, no axle spacers. TOOTSIETOY CHICAGO 24 U.S.A. FORD F-700.

	G	E	LN
(A) Painted features.	**25**	**40**	**45**
(B) With silver TOOTSIETOY tin top; black lettering. Rare.	**40**	**80**	**100**
(C) Patterned plastic Tootsietoy tires; no Ford emblem on truck hood; painted features. TOOTSIETOY CHICAGO 24 U.S.A.	**25**	**40**	**45**

	G	E	LN
(D) Same as (C) except body and features same color.	20	35	40

1959 METRO VAN: (1959) International delivery truck in a two-piece casting: truck body containing detailed interior, and an exterior shell. Van interior painted yellow; body painted light blue. No other painted features. Body contains open wheel wells front and rear; open side door; driver's compartment over front wheels; clear sticker PARCEL SERVICE on side panel. TOOTSIETOY CHICAGO 24 USA METRO TRUCK NO. SM130. **Note:** The letter N is cast backwards.

	G	E	LN
(A) Rubber tires; PARCEL SERVICE.	50	125	150
(B) Same as above, but sticker missing.	35	65	75
(C) Patterned plastic Tootsietoy tires, no axle spacers, and PARCEL SERVICE.	50	125	150
(D) Same as (C) but sticker missing.	35	65	75

1960 CHEVROLET EL CAMINO: (1960-1967) Two-door sedan with an open pickup-type rear truck bed. Body painted red, blue, green, or maroon. Silver-painted features include front and rear bumpers, large front grille, and headlights. Casting contains large window area for car cab; dual headlights; twin taillights; trailer hitch; and open wheel wells front and rear. Patterned plastic Tootsietoy tires, no axle spacers. CHEVROLET EL CAMINO TOOTSIETOY CHICAGO 24 U.S.A.

	G	E	LN
(A) Painted features.	15	22	25
(B) Body and features same color.	12	18	20

1960 CHEVROLET EL CAMINO WITH CAMPER TOP AND BOAT: (1962-1964) Vehicle is painted blue; truck camper is molded red plastic; small plastic boat is a two-piece unit with a brown bottom and a white top. Silver-painted features on El Camino include front and rear bumpers, front grille, and headlights. El Camino body has open wheel wells, dual headlights, twin taillights, and trailer hitch. Truck bed is cast with a hole in the middle to accept a molded pin in the bottom of the camper body. Top of camper contains two pins that match holes in boat top (boat is mounted upside-down). Patterned plastic Tootsietoy tires, no axle spacers. CHEVROLET EL CAMINO TOOTSIETOY CHICAGO 24 U.S.A.

	G	E	LN
(A) Painted features.	25	40	45
(B) Vehicle body and features same color.	20	40	45
(C) Same as (A) except boat has a white hull with a brown top.	25	40	45

1962 FORD ECONOLINE PICKUP TRUCK: (1962-1969) Pickup truck; body painted red, yellow, orange, or blue. Silver-painted features include front and rear bumpers, headlights, grille, and taillights. A cab-over-motor design with a large front windshield and a three-piece rear cab window; body extending over wheel wells; large headlights with directional lights; and a trailer hitch. Front and rear axles mounted inside of body casting. Patterned plastic Tootsietoy tires, no axle spacers. TOOTSIETOY CHICAGO 24 U.S.A.

	G	E	LN
(A) Painted features.	15	30	35
(B) Body and features same color.	10	25	30
(C) Same as (A) with silver truck bed. J. T. Riley Collection.	15	30	35

1962 FORD FUEL TRUCK: (1962-1966) Tanker truck painted red, orange, or blue. Silver-painted features include front bumper, large front grille, dual headlights, rear bumper, four rear fuel ports, and tanker top catwalk. A cab-over-motor truck design with open wheel wells; a large front windshield; a small door window; a two-piece rear cab window; and three simulated doors on each side along bottom of body. Patterned plastic Tootsietoy tires, no axle spacers. TOOTSIETOY CHICAGO 24 U.S.A. 01046.

	G	E	LN
(A) Painted features.	15	30	35
(B) Body and features same color.	10	25	30

CHAPTER 4

Six-Inch Car and Truck Pull Trailer Sets and Separate Trailers

The popular Tootsietoy car and trailer sets produced after the war were, for the most part, offered in blister packages, although some earlier units were offered in boxes. They are presented here because they are most often encountered out of any packaging. In Chapter 11, you will find them listed as blister packs or boxed pieces with a value assigned for packaging that is present and intact.

It is interesting to note that while many 6-inch vehicles were manufactured with a trailer hitch after 1958, not all were offered in a trailer set. The following vehicles were capable of pulling a trailer and, except for the World War II Jeep, were marketed with one: 1932 Hot Rod; 1959 Oldsmobile Convertible; 1956 Jeep; 1954 Cadillac; 1954 MG; 1955 Packard; 1959 Ford Station Wagon; 1960 El Camino; 1962 Ford Station Wagon; 1962 Ford Econoline Pickup Truck; and the Army Jeep.

By 1968 the production of trailer sets was limited to the 1962 Ford Wagon with a U-Haul trailer, the 1962 Ford Wagon with a trailer and race car, and the 1959 Oldsmobile Convertible with Chris-Craft boat and trailer. In 1968 the company planned to produce a Rambler Station Wagon pulling a U-Haul trailer. The 1962 Ford Wagon was used instead, and the Rambler was never made. No car and trailer sets were offered in 1969.

The values assigned to toys in this chapter do not reflect original items found in blister packs or boxes. It can be expected that the values for such units, considered to be in mint condition because they have not been removed from the box or blister pack, will be substantially higher than the values given here for items in Like New (LN) condition.

For information on the type of tires provided on the pull vehicles, see Chapter 2; for trailer tire information, see the box at the left. Cast-in information on the underside of each vehicle appears last in each listing.

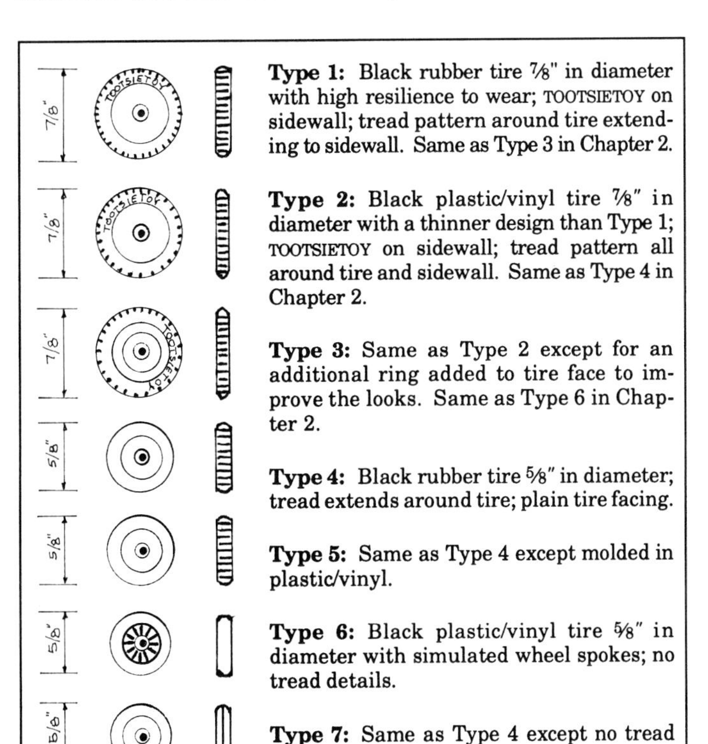

Type 1: Black rubber tire 7/8" in diameter with high resilience to wear; TOOTSIETOY on sidewall; tread pattern around tire extending to sidewall. Same as Type 3 in Chapter 2.

Type 2: Black plastic/vinyl tire 7/8" in diameter with a thinner design than Type 1; TOOTSIETOY on sidewall; tread pattern all around tire and sidewall. Same as Type 4 in Chapter 2.

Type 3: Same as Type 2 except for an additional ring added to tire face to improve the looks. Same as Type 6 in Chapter 2.

Type 4: Black rubber tire 5/8" in diameter; tread extends around tire; plain tire facing.

Type 5: Same as Type 4 except molded in plastic/vinyl.

Type 6: Black plastic/vinyl tire 5/8" in diameter with simulated wheel spokes; no tread details.

Type 7: Same as Type 4 except no tread pattern.

	G	E	LN

1932 FORD HOT ROD, TRAILER, AND RACE CAR: (1964, 1966-1967) Three-piece unit. Ford hot rod; body painted red with silver features, patterned plastic tires, no axle spacers, and TOOTSIETOY CHICAGO 24 U.S.A. Trailer is painted yellow with patterned plastic tires, no axle spacer, and TOOTSIETOY CHICAGO 24 U.S.A. P-10336. Midget race car is blue, red, or orange, approximately 4" in length, with patterned plastic tires, no axle spacers, and TOOTSIETOY CHICAGO 24 U.S.A. P-10334.

	G	E	LN
(A) As described above.	40	60	65
(B) With plastic driver ("Terrible Tommy"). Part of the 1966 "Go-Group" Series.	40	60	70

1954 MG WITH CHRIS-CRAFT BOAT: (1964, 1966-1967) A three-piece unit. MG Classic sports car convertible; body

Top: *1954 Cadillac and Trailer with a Chris-Craft Boat, Trailer, original box.* **Middle:** *1959 Ford Wagon and Trailer with a Chris-Craft Boat.* **Bottom:** *1959 Oldsmobile Convertible with Chris-Craft Boat and Trailer, S. Butler Collection.*

Blister packages. **Left:** *1959 Oldsmobile Convertible, Horse Trailer, and horse; S. Butler Collection.* **Right:** *1962 Ford Station Wagon, a U-Haul Trailer and a load of tires.*

G E LN

painted red, blue, or green; patterned plastic tires; no axle spacers; and TOOTSIETOY CHICAGO 24 U.S.A. CLASSIC MG. Yellow boat trailer has a TEE-NEE sticker; smooth rubber tires; no axle spacer. TOOTSIETOY CHICAGO 24 U.S.A. TEE-NEE OB-70. Chris-Craft boat is brown and white plastic; TOOTSIETOY CHICAGO 24 U.S.A. CHRIS-CRAFT CAPRI.

(A) As described above. **45 70 75**

(B) With plastic driver ("Pony-Tailed Terry"). Part of the 1966 "Go-Group" Series. **45 70 75**

1954 MG WITH U-HAUL TRAILER: (1966-1967) Two-piece item. MG Classic sports car convertible; body painted red, blue, or green; patterned plastic tires; no axle spacers; TOOTSIETOY CHICAGO 24 U.S.A. CLASSIC MG. Orange U-Haul trailer carries a load of black tires; patterned plastic tires; no axle spacer; TOOTSIETOY U.S.A.

(A) As described above. **40 60 65**

(B) With plastic driver ("Tubby Teddy"). Part of the 1966 "Go-Group" Series. **40 60 70**

1954 CADILLAC AND TRAILER WITH BOAT: (1959) Three-piece item. Four-door sedan; blue body with a white roof. Silver-painted features include front and rear bumpers, front grille, headlights, and taillights. Patterned rubber Toot-

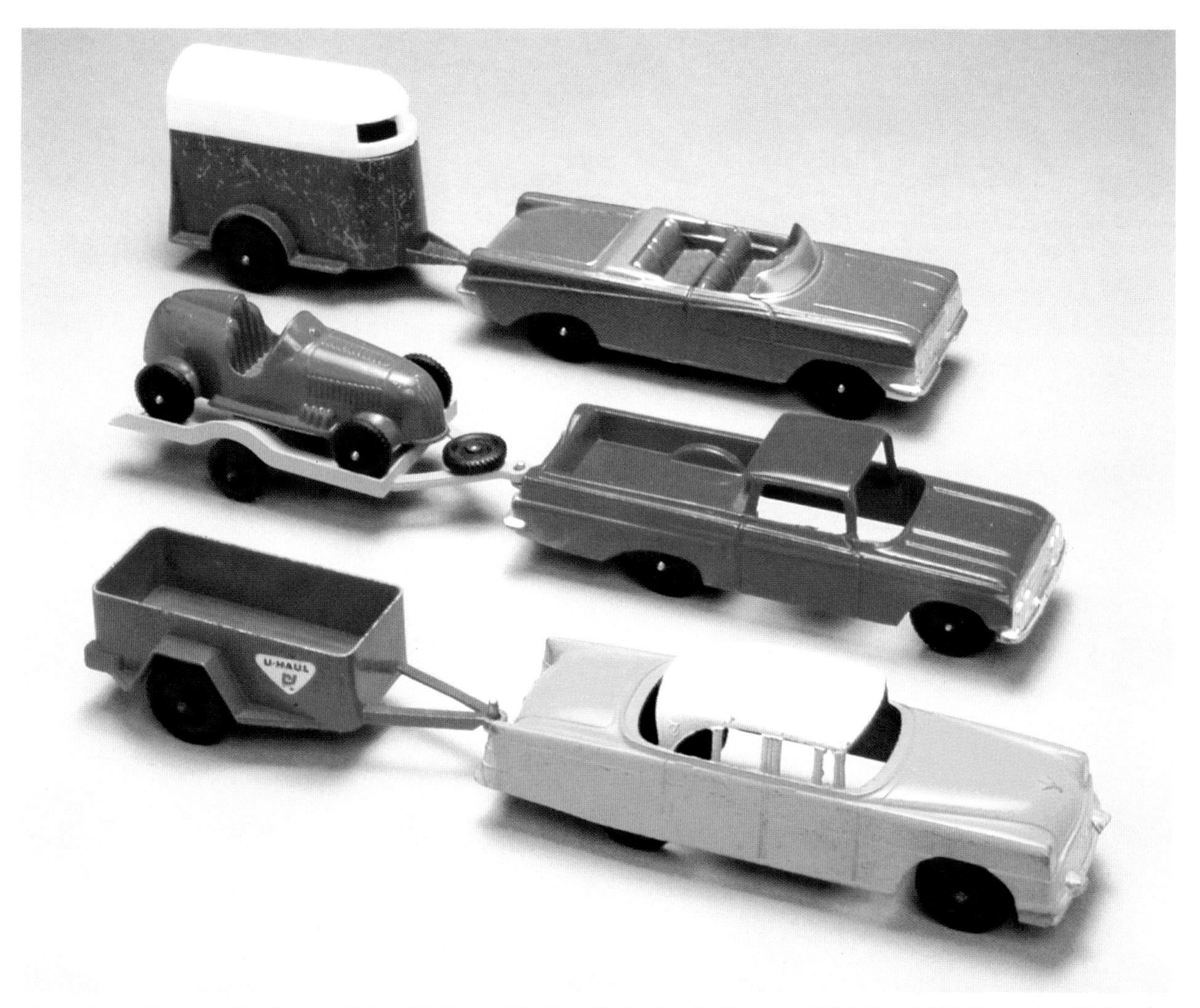

Top: *1959 Oldsmobile Convertible with Horse Trailer, S. Butler Collection.* **Middle:** *1960 Chevrolet El Camino with Trailer and Race Car.* **Bottom:** *1955 Packard with U-Haul Trailer.*

G E LN

sietoy tires, no axle spacers; CADILLAC TOOTSIETOY CHICAGO 24 U.S.A. Boat trailer is painted yellow with TEE-NEE sticker on right side of panel behind front hitch; trailer fenders covering the wheels to the axle; rubber tires, no axle spacer; TOOTSIETOY CHICAGO 24 U.S.A. TEE-NEE OB-70. Chris-Craft boat has a one-piece brown plastic hull with a white molded plastic top featuring two seats, windshield, and steering wheel; TOOTSIETOY CHICAGO 24 U.S.A. CHRIS-CRAFT CAPRI. H. Van Curler Collection.
40 60 70

1954 CADILLAC AND U-HAUL TRAILER: (1959) Two-piece unit. Four-door sedan has a blue body with a white roof. Silver-painted features include front and rear bumpers, front grille, headlights, and taillights. Patterned rubber Tootsietoy tires, no axle spacers; CADILLAC TOOTSIETOY CHICAGO 24 U.S.A. Orange U-Haul trailer has same tires as sedan; U-Haul stickers on each side of trailer and along back. TOOTSIETOY U.S.A.
40 55 65

1955 PACKARD WITH BOAT AND TRAILER: (1959) Three-piece unit. Four-door sedan with a light blue body and white roof. Silver-painted features include front and rear bumpers, headlights, taillights, and front grille. Patterned rubber Tootsietoy tires, no axle spacers; rear axle does not extend through car body sides; open front wheel wells; PACKARD TOOTSIETOY CHICAGO 24 U.S.A. Boat trailer is yellow with a TEE-NEE sticker on right side of panel behind front hitch. Molded two-piece plastic Chris-Craft boat with brown hull and white top; hull has two seats; windshield; and steering wheel; TOOTSIETOY CHICAGO 24 U.S.A. CHRIS-CRAFT CAPRI. J. Gibson Collection.
40 60 70

1955 PACKARD WITH U-HAUL TRAILER: (1959) Four-door sedan; body painted green with a cream roof. Silver-painted features include front and rear bumpers, headlights, taillights, and front grille. Patterned rubber Tootsietoy tires, no axle spacers; rear axle does not extend through car body sides; open front wheel wells; PACKARD TOOTSIETOY CHICAGO 24 U.S.A. Orange U-Haul trailer has a U-Haul paper sticker on each side and across the rear. Trailer tires are the same size and type as the Packard. TOOTSIETOY U.S.A.
40 60 65

1956 JEEP WITH HORSE TRAILER: (1964-1965) Jeep painted red or blue; body and features painted same color. Jeep windshield molded into casting; patterned plastic Toot-

Top: *1959 Ford Wagon with Camper Trailer, S. Butler Collection.* **Upper middle:** *1960 Chevrolet El Camino with Refreshment Stand, C. Jones Collection.* **Lower middle:** *1962 Ford Station Wagon with U-Haul Trailer.* **Bottom:** *1962 Ford Econoline Pickup Truck with Solid-Side Trailer, S. Butler Collection.*

G E LN

sietoy tires; no axle spacers; TOOTSIETOY CHICAGO U.S.A.-3. Horse trailer painted orange; does not have a plastic trailer cover; patterned plastic Tootsietoy tires; no axle spacers. TOOTSIETOY CHICAGO 24 U.S.A. P-10300. **25 40 45**

1959 FORD WAGON WITH CAMPER TRAILER: (1960-1961, 1963-1967) Country Sedan station wagon; body painted blue with a light blue roof. Silver-painted features include front and rear bumpers, front grille, headlights, and taillights. Patterned rubber Tootsietoy tires, no axle spacers; TOOTSIETOY CHICAGO 24 U.S.A. FORD COUNTRY SEDAN P-10296. Two-piece camper trailer: trailer body is metal, trailer sides and roof are molded red plastic. Trailer tires are the same size and design as the Ford wagon. TOOTSIETOY CHICAGO 24 U.S.A. P-10306. **35 55 60**

1959 FORD WAGON WITH RACE CAR AND TRAILER: (1960, 1964) Country Sedan station wagon; body painted blue with a light blue roof. Silver-painted features include front and rear bumpers, grille, headlights, and taillights. Patterned rubber Tootsietoy tires, no axle spacers; TOOTSIETOY CHICAGO 24 U.S.A. FORD COUNTRY SEDAN P-10296. Yellow race car trailer carries a blue or red 4" race car. TOOTSIETOY MADE IN U.S.A. P-10334. **45 60 65**

1959 FORD WAGON AND TRAILER WITH BOAT: (1959-1961, 1963-1967) Three-piece item. Country Sedan station wagon; body painted blue with a light blue roof. Silver-painted features include front and rear bumpers, front grille, headlights, and taillights; patterned rubber Tootsietoy tires, no axle spacers; TOOTSIETOY CHICAGO 24 U.S.A. FORD COUNTRY SEDAN P-10296. Boat trailer is painted yellow with TEE-NEE sticker on right front panel behind trailer hitch, trailer fenders extending to axle, smooth rubber tires, no axle spacer; TOOTSIETOY CHICAGO 24 U.S.A. TEE-NEE OB-70. Chris-Craft boat is made of plastic with a brown bottom and white top; TOOTSIETOY CHICAGO 24 U.S.A. CHRIS-CRAFT CAPRI.

G E LN

(A) As described above. **30 50 55**

(B) Same as (A) except boat trailer has patterned rubber tires, no axle spacers, and two small pins that match corresponding holes in boat bottom to secure boat to trailer; Chris-Craft Capri boat has a white bottom with a dark brown top. **30 50 55**

(C) Country Sedan wagon has patterned plastic Tootsietoy tires, no axle spacers; boat trailer has patterned plastic tires, no axle spacer; Chris-Craft Capri boat has a blue bottom with a white top. Boat trailer and boat connection same as (B) above. **30 45 50**

1959 OLDSMOBILE WITH U-HAUL TRAILER: (1960-1961, 1963, 1966) Two-piece item. Oldsmobile convertible; body painted green with silver-painted features, patterned tires, no axle spacers, and OLDSMOBILE TOOTSIETOY CHICAGO 24 U.S.A. Orange U-Haul trailer has patterned tires, no axle spacer; TOOTSIETOY U.S.A. There is no trailer load. **35 45 50**

G E LN

1959 OLDSMOBILE CONVERTIBLE WITH HORSE TRAILER: (1960-1961, 1963) Three-piece item. Convertible's body is green or yellow with silver-painted features including front and rear bumpers, front grille, headlights, windshield, and tour cover behind rear seat. Casting includes dual headlights, steering wheel, and seats. Patterned rubber Tootsietoy tires, no axle spacers; OLDSMOBILE TOOTSIETOY CHICAGO 24 U.S.A. P-10310. Horse trailer painted red, dark maroon, or orange. Cast body has high sides and an open rear; top of trailer is white plastic. Patterned rubber Tootsietoy tires, no axle spacer; TOOTSIETOY CHICAGO 24 U.S.A. P-10300.

(A) As described above. **35 55 60**

(B) Same as (A) except convertible and horse trailer have patterned plastic Tootsietoy tires, no axle spacers; horse trailer has a short trailer connection and does not include a plastic top. Pins for holding top have been eliminated from side casting. **20 45 50**

1959 OLDSMOBILE CONVERTIBLE WITH BOAT AND TRAILER: (1964) Three-piece unit. Oldsmobile convertible painted yellow or green with silver-painted features including bumpers, front grille, and, on some units, windshield and tour cover. Boat trailer is yellow with a TEE-NEE sticker on right side of panel behind front hitch. Molded two-piece plastic Chris-Craft boat has white or blue hull with dark brown or white top; two seats, windshield, and steering wheel molded into hull; TOOTSIETOY CHICAGO 24 U.S.A. CHRIS-CRAFT CAPRI.

(A) Oldsmobile convertible in green with silver features including windshield and tour cover; blue and white boat with patterned plastic Tootsietoy tires, no axle spacers. **40 55 60**

(B) Oldsmobile convertible in yellow with painted features; boat in dark brown and white, patterned rubber Tootsietoy tires, no axle spacers. **40 55 60**

1960 CHEVROLET EL CAMINO WITH BOAT AND TRAILER: (1966) A Chevrolet El Camino pickup truck; body and features painted red. Patterned plastic Tootsietoy tires, no axle spacer. Boat trailer painted yellow; no Tee-Nee sticker on right front panel behind trailer hitch; trailer fenders extend to axle; patterned plastic tires, no axle spacers; TOOTSIETOY CHICAGO 24 U.S.A. TEE-NEE OB-70. Two-piece molded plastic Chris-Craft boat has white bottom with blue top; TOOTSIETOY CHICAGO 24 U.S.A. CHRIS-CRAFT CAPRI. **35 55 65**

1960 CHEVROLET EL CAMINO WITH TRAILER AND RACE CAR: (1961, 1963, 1966) A Chevrolet El Camino pickup truck; body painted red or dark red. Some may have silver-painted features including front and rear bumpers, front grille, and headlights. Patterned rubber Tootsietoy tires, no axle spacers. Trailer is painted dark yellow or yellow including a spare tire mounted on the trailer tongue. Trailer wheels are located under trailer frame; no fenders; patterned rubber tires, no axle spacer; TOOTSIETOY CHICAGO 24 U.S.A. P-10336. Blue Midget Racer approximately 4" in length; casting includes open seat area with steering wheel and the numeral 3 near back of racer on both sides. Wheels are outside of race car body; patterned rubber tires, no axle spacers. Race car and trailer have the same-sized tires. TOOTSIETOY MADE IN U.S.A. P-10334.

(A) As described above. **45 60 65**

G E LN

(B) Same as above except all wheels on El Camino, trailer, and race car are patterned plastic tires, no axle spacers. Trailer is painted a light yellow. **40 55 60**

1960 CHEVROLET EL CAMINO WITH REFRESHMENT STAND: (1960-1961, 1963) Rare two-piece set. El Camino pickup truck body painted red or blue. Silver-painted features include front and rear bumpers, grille, and headlights. Patterned rubber Tootsietoy tires, no axle spacers. Refreshment trailer is yellow plastic on a die-cast metal frame; red, blue, and white paper stickers extending from left side, down full length, and across back. Trailer tongue has two propane tanks. Large Tootsietoy tires, no axle spacer. TOOTSIETOY CHICAGO 24 USA P-10312. **50 70 85**

1962 FORD WAGON AND TRAILER WITH RACE CAR: (1964-1968) Three-piece item with four-door station wagon; body painted red or orange; patterned plastic Tootsietoy tires, no axle spacers. Trailer painted light yellow; spare tire mounted on the trailer tongue; trailer wheels located under trailer frame, no fenders. Patterned plastic tires, no axle spacer; TOOTSIETOY CHICAGO 24 U.S.A. P-10336. Blue Midget Racer approximately 4" in length; casting includes detailed open seat area with racing number behind seat; wheels outside of car body; patterned plastic tires, no axle spacers; TOOTSIETOY MADE IN U.S.A. P-10334. **35 55 60**

1962 FORD WAGON AND TRAILER WITH BOAT: (1966, 1968) Three-piece item with four-door station wagon; body painted red with white top. Silver-painted features include front grille and bumper, rear panel, taillights, and trailer hitch. Patterned tires, no axle spacers; TOOTSIETOY CHICAGO 24 U.S.A. 01049-2. Boat trailer painted light yellow with TEE-NEE sticker on right front panel behind trailer hitch; trailer fenders extend to axle; patterned rubber tires, no axle spacers; TOOTSIETOY CHICAGO 24 U.S.A. TEE-NEE OB-70. Two-piece molded plastic Chris-Craft boat has white bottom with dark brown top; TOOTSIETOY CHICAGO 24 U.S.A. CHRIS-CRAFT CAPRI. **30 55 60**

1962 FORD STATION WAGON WITH U-HAUL TRAILER: (1964-1968) Two-piece unit. Four-door station wagon painted red or orange with no painted features; or red with silver-painted features including the front bumper, grille, headlights, rear bumper, taillights, and trailer hitch; or red with a white roof and painted features as described above. Patterned tires, no axle spacers; TOOTSIETOY CHICAGO 24 U.S.A. 01049-2. Orange U-Haul trailer has a U-Haul paper sticker on each side and across the rear. Trailer tires are the same size and type as the station wagon. TOOTSIETOY U.S.A.

(A) As described above, with load on trailer consisting of nine sets of dual molded tires. **25 40 45**

(B) Same as (A) with load of four plastic barrels. **25 40 45**

(C) Same as (A) with load of appliances. **35 45 50**

(D) Wagon painted orange with no painted features; patterned plastic Tootsietoy tires, no axle spacers. U-Haul trailer with patterned plastic Tootsietoy tires, no axle spacer; no trailer load. **25 30 35**

(E) Wagon painted red with white top; tires and trailer same as (A) above; no load in trailer. **30 40 45**

G E LN

1962 FORD ECONOLINE PICKUP TRUCK WITH TRAILER: (1963) Four-piece unit; red pickup truck with silver-painted features; yellow stake trailer with a die-cast body and plastic side stakes; a plastic bull; and a cowboy. Was advertised as a ranch set in 1963.

(A) As described above. Rare. 30 55 65

(B) With solid-side (horse) trailer; no pins for trailer top. 25 40 50

Six-Inch and Four-Inch Pull Trailers

Trailers that were sold as individual items without a vehicle to pull them are described below. Many of these trailers were used in the pull trailer sets listed previously. However, they were also sold by themselves so that a child could attach them to different vehicles they might already have, which means they will be encountered individually by the collector.

In the 6-inch series, there are a number of trailers which are difficult to find, especially the Tandem Trailer with Cabin Cruiser and the Stakeside Trailer introduced in 1963, the Refreshment Trailer, and then the Camping Trailer. Since many of the trailers contain plastic parts or components, it is advisable to examine these units carefully for cracks, chips, or broken parts before purchasing them.

The company found it necessary to make improvements in their boat trailer so that the boat would stay on the trailer during play. This was accomplished by adding two pins to the trailer base and two corresponding holes to the bottom of the plastic boat. Therefore there are two types of Trailers with Chris-Craft Boat.

The following trailers have been divided into two separate categories: the first eight are from the Postwar First Generation series and the later ones from the Postwar Second Generation. The second generation of trailers had smaller, plastic-spoked tires. However, a wide variety of tires was used by the company over the years due to trailer size and improvements in tire design and composition.

The second generation of trailers were primarily intended for the 4-inch series and Hitch-Ups. However, many of these units could also be used with the 6-inch series.

Based on historical data, catalogue advertisements and data obtained from Strombecker, the best known information on production years for each piece is included with the listings. Cast-in information on the underside of each vehicle appears last in each listing.

Postwar First Generation Trailers

CAMPING TRAILER: (1960-1967) 6" long; also known as a house trailer. Two piece unit: metal frame with four tabs, and plastic body with walls and roof. Tabs in frame snap into corresponding slots in body. Trailer available in white, light blue, or red; large front window, small window in rear; right side has door with small window, two small windows, and one large window; left side has two small and two large windows; one air vent on roof; short trailer tongue with propane tanks; large patterned plastic Tootsietoy tires, no axle spacer. TOOTSIETOY CHICAGO 24 U.S.A. P-10306. 20 28 30

Top: *Camping Trailer, H. Van Curler Collection.* **Upper middle left:** *Trailer with Chris-Craft Boat.* **Upper middle right:** *Refreshment Stand Trailer, C. Jones Collection.* **Middle:** *Boat Trailer for Chris-Craft Boat and Solid-Side Horse Trailer with no pins for trailer top.* **Lower middle left:** *Midget Racer with Trailer.* **Lower middle right:** *Horse Trailer.* **Bottom:** *Trailer for Midget Racer and U-Haul Trailer.*

G E LN

HORSE TRAILER: (1961, 1963-1965) Two-piece trailer: body and sides are a metal casting with a rounded front, open wheel well, narrow fenders; plastic top is molded in white. Body painted red, dark maroon, or orange.

(A) 3¾" long; three cast pins in the top of the trailer sides and front to hold the plastic top; simulated doors on each side; open rear of trailer; large patterned rubber tires, no axle spacer. Plastic top has two small front windows; three vents on each side; simulated extension of doors from trailer bottom. TOOTSIETOY CHICAGO 24 U.S.A. P-10300. 8 15 20

(B) 3½" long; no cast pins or simulated doors on each side; open rear of trailer; large patterned plastic tires, no axle spacer. Trailer body is the same size as (A) with a shorter trailer tongue. TOOTSIETOY CHICAGO 24 U.S.A. P-10300. 8 13 15

(C) Same as (A) but missing trailer top. 5 7 8

(D) Same as (A) with patterned plastic tires. 8 15 20

(E) Same as (A) with white plastic horse. 10 18 22

REFRESHMENT STAND TRAILER: (1960-1961, 1963) 4⅜" long. Two-piece trailer has metal frame with four tabs, and plastic wall-and-roof body. Tabs in frame snap into corresponding slots in body. Trailer is light yellow plastic with a red, blue, and white paper sticker beginning on left side, extending the full length of trailer and across back. Trailer contains open service windows with counter and awnings along front, left side, and rear of trailer. Right side of trailer has one large window and door with small window. Top of trailer has two round vents. Very short trailer tongue with two propane tanks; large patterned plastic Tootsietoy tires, no

Top: *Horse Trailer with long frame, trailer hitch, and pins for trailer top.* **Bottom:** *Horse Trailer with short frame, trailer hitch, and pins eliminated for the trailer top.*

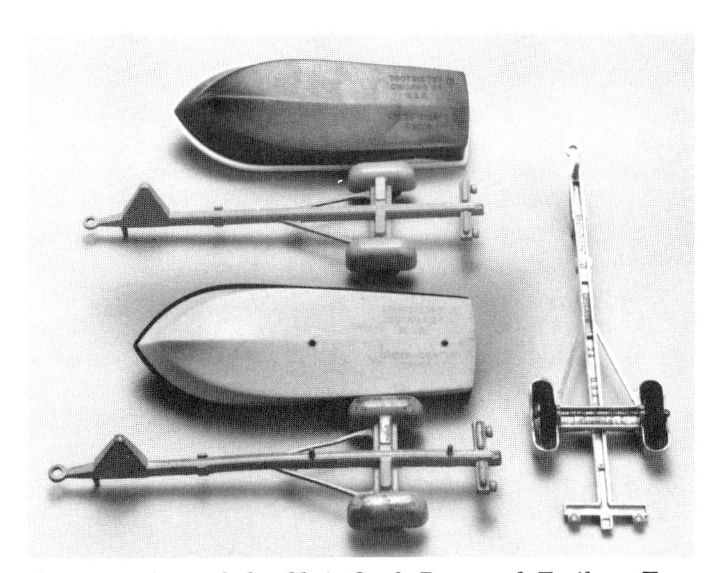

Two variations of the Chris-Craft Boat and Trailer. **Top:** *Without mounting pins.* **Bottom:** *With mounting pins in trailer and corresponding holes in boat's bottom.*

	G	E	LN

axle spacer. TOOTSIETOY CHICAGO 24 U.S.A. P-10312. Information from the C. Jones Collection.

	G	E	LN
(A) As described above.	25	45	55
(B) With refreshment sign on roof.	25	55	65

STAKE TRAILER: (1963) 4½" long. Yellow trailer introduced in 1963 for the 6-inch series of vehicles. Trailer body is die-cast metal with upper side stakes made of plastic. Unit was first introduced in No. 2912 Ranch Set with the Jumbo Series Ford Econoline Pickup Truck. Patterned plastic tires, no axle spacer. Casting identification not verified. **20 30 35**

G	E	LN

TANDEM-WHEEL TRAILER WITH CABIN CRUISER: (Date unknown) Approximately 6" long. Trailer has tandem single wheels; fenders extend over wheels. Cabin cruiser is made of two plastic molded parts which snap together: boat hull and cabin top. Further information requested. **NRS**

TRAILER WITH CHRIS-CRAFT BOAT: (1959, 1961, 1963-1968) 6" long. Yellow boat trailer with TEE-NEE sticker on a triangle panel at front of trailer; fenders extending over wheels to axle; two rear taillights in casting; smooth rubber tires, no axle spacer; single axle. TOOTSIETOY CHICAGO 24 U.S.A. TEE-NEE OB-70. Capri-style speedboat is made of two pieces of molded plastic, a brown boat hull with a white top; two seats, steering wheel, and windshield all molded in top piece. TOOTSIETOY CHICAGO 24 U.S.A. CHRIS-CRAFT CAPRI.

(A) As described above. **13 18 25**

(B) Same as (A) except boat has a white hull with a dark brown top; trailer has patterned rubber tires, no axle spacer; two cast pins match two corresponding holes in boat bottom. **12 18 25**

(C) Boat has a blue or white bottom with a white or blue top; trailer is light yellow, with patterned plastic tires, no axle spacer; two cast pins match two corresponding holes in boat bottom. **10 18 25**

TRAILER WITH RACE CAR: (1960-1961, 1963-1968) 4½" long. Yellow car trailer with single axle assembly mounted under trailer; no fenders; patterned rubber tires, no axle spacer; TOOTSIETOY CHICAGO 24 U.S.A. P-10336. Blue Midget Racer approximately 4" in length; casting includes open single seat, steering wheel, external exhaust pipe, and racing number on each side of body behind seat; patterned rubber tires, no axle spacers. Race car color and number may vary. TOOTSIETOY MADE IN U.S.A. P-10334.

(A) As described above. **15 25 30**

(B) Same as above except that the trailer is light yellow; tires on trailer and race car are patterned plastic tires, no axle spacers. **15 25 30**

U-HAUL TRAILER: (1958-1959, 1961, 1963-1968) 4" long. Orange trailer with U-HAUL on each side and on rear; sides of trailer are even all around; large patterned rubber tires, no axle spacer; TOOTSIETOY U.S.A. **6 9 10**

Postwar Second Generation Trailers

ATV TRAILER: (1969-1970) 4" long. Wide, flat trailer for the Hitch-Ups; painted blue. Casting has depressed floor sections for ATV rear and front wheels. Small plastic spoked tires, no axle spacer. TOOTSIETOY CHICAGO U.S.A. H/U ATV 60755. **2 3 4**

BOAT TRAILER: (1969-1970) 4" long. Yellow trailer (also called a "float on") for the Hitch-Ups. Casting includes highly detailed cross supports; fenders over wheels; two protruding pins near front of trailer to hold boat. Small plastic spoked tires, no axle spacer. TOOTSIETOY CHICAGO U.S.A. 60722. **2 3 4**

CYCLE TRAILER: (1969-1970) 4" long. Narrow trailer for the Hitch-Ups; painted blue. Casting includes two slots on

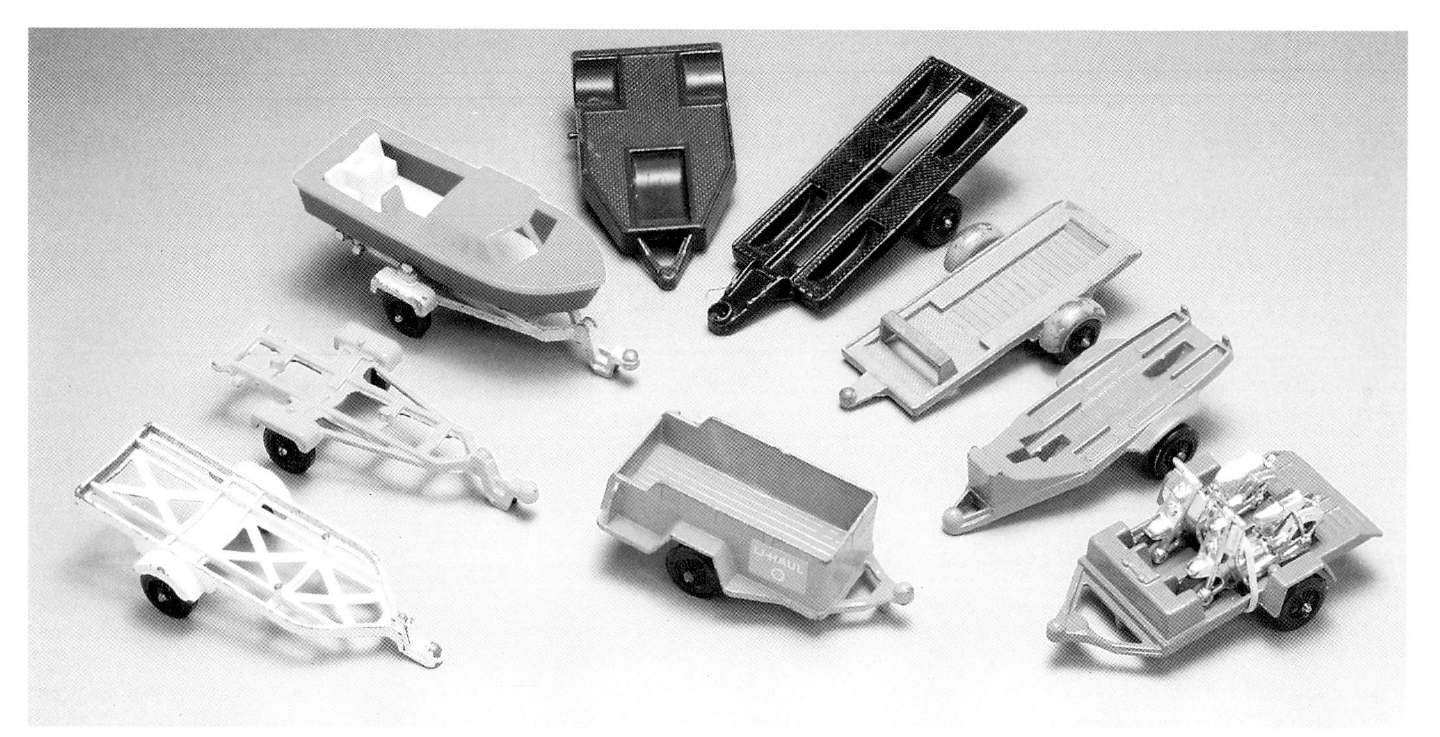

Clockwise from left: *Float-on Boat Trailer; Boat Trailer for Cabin Cruiser; Cabin Cruiser with Trailer; ATV Trailer; Twin Cycle Trailer; Snowmobile Trailer; Motorcycle Trailer; Twin Scooter Trailer.* **Center:** *U-Haul Trailer.*

G E LN

each side of trailer to hold the cycle tires; open slots in trailer center; no fenders. Small plastic spoked tires, no axle spacer. **3 4 5**

GENERATOR TRAILER: (1969-1970) 2¾" long. Trailer for the Hitch-Ups; painted green. Casting includes floor compartment, raised front section with power feed connections and compartment. Small plastic spoked tires, no axle spacer. TOOTSIETOY MADE IN U.S.A. **3 4 5**

MOTORCYCLE TRAILER: (1969-1970) 4" long. Narrow orange trailer for the Hitch-Ups. Casting includes two slots in center of trailer to hold motorcycle tires; walkway on each side of trailer with narrow fenders. Small plastic spoked tires, no axle spacer. TOOTSIETOY CHICAGO U.S.A. 2. **2 3 4**

SMALL TRAILER WITH CABIN CRUISER: (1969) 4" long. Small cast yellow or orange trailer intended for Hitch-Ups. Casting contains two pins in the bottom frame which correspond to two holes in the bottom of the boat; small plastic spoked tires; no axle spacer; trailer fender over wheel; TOOTSIETOY CHICAGO U.S.A. The plastic cabin cruiser is made up of three parts glued together: blue boat hull; red top of boat and cabin with one seat; white boat floor, rear seats, and cabin wall. TOOTSIETOY HONG KONG. **6 10 12**

G E LN

SMALL U-HAUL TRAILER: (1969) 3" long. Orange trailer for 4-inch series and Hitch-Ups with paper U-HAUL stickers on each side and on rear of compartment. Casting includes narrow fenders over open wheel wells; rear outside wall support on both sides; sides of trailer with step down at back and across rear of trailer. Small plastic spoked tires, no axle spacer. TOOTSIETOY CHICAGO U.S.A.

(A) As described above. **4 5 6**

(B) Same as above except for large U-HAUL sticker; no rear sticker. Small plastic spoked tires; large lettering on trailer bottom: TOOTSIETOY CHICAGO U.S.A. **3 4 5**

(C) Same as (A) with load of plastic appliances. **5 8 10**

SNOWMOBILE TRAILER: (1969-1970) 4" long. Narrow trailer painted light blue for Hitch-Ups; casting includes rounded fenders; raised crossbar at front of trailer; open under crossbar; raised section next to fenders; depressed center section. Small plastic spoked tires, no axle spacer. TOOTSIETOY CHICAGO U.S.A. 1970. **3 4 5**

TWIN SCOOTER TRAILER: (1969) 3" long. Wide-body trailer for the Hitch-Ups; painted red. Casting has two sets of slots to hold two small plastic motor scooters; full fender over wheels. Small plastic spoked tires, no axle spacer. Scooters have a chrome finish, rubber tires. TOOTSIETOY CHICAGO U.S.A. 1969. **5 8 10**

CHAPTER 5

Four-Inch Cars, Jeeps, and Trucks

The 4-inch series of cars and trucks may be the most popular series for collectors. Despite their smaller size, the detail cast into these vehicles is unusually good, and, in general, much better than that of the 3-inch or 6-inch series. While there were thirty-five different vehicles developed for this series (not including military pieces), most can be found if variations and color are not an issue. There are, however, a number of pieces which are very difficult to find. All of the 1937 Mack fire trucks, both the prewar reissued and the postwar units, clearly fall into this category. There are five different types and/or variations listed, and there may be as many as ten different variations of the 1937 Mack fire truck. In addition, the 1938 Federal Truck (postwar production), 1941 International Panel Truck, 1947 Pull Wagon, 1950 Pontiac Fire Chief Chieftain, 1960 Rambler Wagon, and the 1969 Ford LTD (in any color except blue) are all difficult to find.

In the 4-inch series, at least thirteen different vehicles were made with a two-tone paint finish, which makes these units more collectible. These particular toys were among the first to be manufactured for gift sets, and are therefore usually the oldest variation of that toy to have been made. Some of these vehicles were made for more than twenty years, but in later years were painted in a single body color and with wheel and axle design changes. The vehicles seen with two-tone paint finishes include the 1937 International Wagon (postwar); 1949 Ford Tanker Truck; 1949 Chevy Panel Truck; 1949 Ford Stakeside Truck; 1950 Dodge Pickup Truck; 1950 Pontiac Chieftain; 1952 Mercury Four-Door Sedan; 1954 Ford Ranch Wagon; 1954 Oldsmobile Two-Door Hardtop; 1955 Thunderbird; 1956 Chevrolet Cameo Pickup Truck; 1949 Oldsmobile Convertible; and 1969 Ford LTD Hardtop.

The company seemed to limit its special cars and trucks to those that could be cast in the 4-inch size and still remain somewhat in scale to the others. Therefore, the series only contains fire trucks, pickup trucks, small delivery type vans, and the 1949 Ford Tanker and Stakeside Trucks. It is unclear, however, why certain vehicles which could have been manufactured in this series (such as a tow truck, a bus, a dump truck, or a farm tractor) were not!

Unlike the 6-inch series, the 4-inch series *does* include an ambulance, a fire chief car, and a police car. The police car is a blue 1954 Ford Wagon that has no markings or special casting identification; it is only identifiable as a police car by its color and because it comes in a blister package with a police badge. Once it is removed from the package, it is no longer "obviously" a police car! The 1950 Pontiac Fire Chief Car could have been classified as a police car if it had been made in blue; however it has only been found in red to date, and therefore is classified as a fire chief car.

In the 4-inch series, only three vehicles were produced to pull a trailer or some other unit: the Jeep, the Army Half-Track discussed in Chapter 8, and the 1969 LTD Ford. The total line of vehicles produced in the late sixties (see Chapter 12) was designed to make more extensive use of trailer pulling capabilities. The 1969 LTD was the only vehicle capable of pulling the newer line of trailers; but it was actually not offered until 1970, and was the last all-metal vehicle offered in the 4-inch series. The other two vehicles mentioned above were designed with a different trailer hitch that could only be attached to military units.

By 1969, the company had reduced the number of different 4-inch vehicles it featured to only seven. They were the Jeep, a 1953 Corvette, two 1949 Ford trucks, a 1959 Pontiac Star Chief, a 1956 Chevrolet Pickup Truck, and the 1960 Chrysler Convertible.

The various types of tires made for this series are shown below.

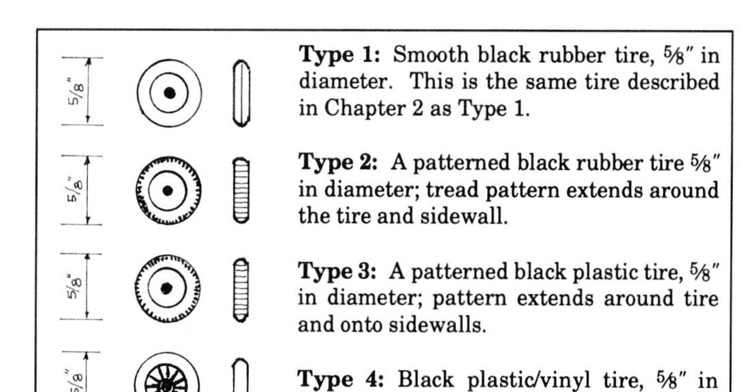

Type 1: Smooth black rubber tire, 5/8" in diameter. This is the same tire described in Chapter 2 as Type 1.

Type 2: A patterned black rubber tire 5/8" in diameter; tread pattern extends around the tire and sidewall.

Type 3: A patterned black plastic tire, 5/8" in diameter; pattern extends around tire and onto sidewalls.

Type 4: Black plastic/vinyl tire, 5/8" in diameter with simulated wheel spokes; no tread pattern.

There have been and will continue to be disagreements among collectors about the proper identification of some of the early vehicles in this series. Even when consulting all of the reference books available today, it is still difficult to correctly identify the model year for certain pieces! Some vehicles seem to be generic productions or combinations of vehicles. The company's effort to produce low-cost toys probably played a significant part in their design and production. Small changes to simplify a casting may have resulted in various deviations, such as a toy with the correct type of windows but incorrect headlight placement. Changes such as these could make a vehicle look like one or two other models, especially in the early years when so many of the prototypes were similar in style and design. The automotive industry, in many instances, made few changes from year to year before introducing a totally new body design. The casting on many of the Tootsietoy pieces is not detailed enough to allow one to distinguish these small changes from year to year. It is certain that the debates identifying these toys will continue, but that is, to some, the exciting part of our hobby.

From 1946 through 1954, the Midget Racer (often referred to as an Offenhauser) was sold to the A. C. Gilbert Company for use on its American Flyer S Gauge operating flatcars Nos. 715 and 915. Because of the demand by train collectors to acquire these units intact, it may be a little more difficult to find this race car by itself.

In general, the vehicles in this chapter are listed numerically by model year and grouped by type. Cars are listed first, followed by the trucks. See Chapters 8 and 11 for other 4-inch vehicles and additional information. Based on historical data, catalogue advertisements, and data obtained from the Strombecker Company, the best known information on production years for each piece is included in the listings. Cast-in information on the underside of each vehicle appears last in each listing.

Cars

CIVILIAN JEEP: (1947-1969) World War II Willys-style Jeep painted red, silver, orange, light blue, blue, yellow, or green. Body and features painted the same color. Casting contains front and rear seats; steering wheel; windshield in down position; five-point star in circle on hood; large front grille; headlights on fender; open wheel wells; eyelet trailer hitch; front bumper; no rear bumper. Seats do not extend above body. Smooth rubber tires with axle spacers.

A 1969 Ford LTD Hardtop with a U-Haul Trailer and a load of furniture can go for $25 to $35. K. Jestes Collection.

	G	E	LN
(A) As described above; star on hood points toward front. TOOTSIETOY MADE IN U.S.A.	14	20	22
(B) Patterned rubber tires, no axle spacers; star on hood points toward windshield. TOOTSIETOY MADE IN U.S.A. JEEP.	12	18	20
(C) Same as (A) but no axle spacers; star on hood points toward windshield. TOOTSIETOY MADE IN U.S.A. JEEP.	12	17	20
(D) Patterned plastic tires, no axle spacers; star on hood points toward windshield. TOOTSIETOY MADE IN U.S.A. JEEP.	10	15	18

MIDGET RACER: (1948-1968) Race car often called an Offenhauser; painted red, yellow, orange, green, silver, blue, or gray; body and features painted same color. Body casting contains a racing number in each side of car body behind driver's seat: 3, 5, 7, and 8 have been observed. Casting includes a detailed interior with a steering wheel and two gauges on the dash to the right of the steering wheel; some versions contain a single gauge to the right of the steering wheel. Other details include exhaust pipes on each side of the body; air vents on both sides and top of front hood; and a vertical front grille. Smooth rubber tires, no axle spacers. TOOTSIETOY MADE IN U.S.A. P-10334.

	G	E	LN
(A) As described above.	15	22	25

Midget Racers in various colors and with different racing numbers; S. Butler and K. Jestes Collections.

Top: *1941 Chrysler Convertible, S. Butler Collection; 1937 International Wagon.* **Middle:** *1938 Buick Experimental Convertible and 1941 Buick Special, S. Butler Collection.* **Bottom:** *Pull Wagon (restored), S. Butler Collection; 1949 Oldsmobile Convertible.*

	G	E	LN
(B) Patterned rubber tires.	12	18	20
(C) Patterned plastic tires.	12	18	20

PULL WAGON: (1947) Rare and unusually modern-looking toy wagon first shown in the 1947 catalogue. Body painted red with a silver front panel and wagon floor. Wagon has a bent, shaped wire handle. Body sides cover front and rear wheels; axles extend through sides of wagon; smooth black rubber tires with axle spacers. TOOTSIETOY MADE IN U.S.A. **25 50 60**

1937 INTERNATIONAL WAGON: (1947-1949) Four-door "Woody" wagon sometimes referred to as a Ford; body painted red, tan, orange, or yellow. Two-tone colors: fenders and roof red, tan, maroon, green, or blue; hood and sides light yellow or cream. Silver-painted features include front and rear bumpers, grille, and headlights. Body casting includes simulated wood panels on side doors and rear sides; a wraparound front grille; large front bubble fenders; headlights in fender extending to front grille; two-piece front windshield and rear window; running board between front and rear fenders. Body casting extends over wheel wells; axles extend through body sides; smooth rubber tires with axle spacers. TOOTSIETOY MADE IN UNITED STATES OF AMERICA NO. 1046.

	G	E	LN
(A) Painted features.	20	35	40
(B) Two-tone paint with painted features.	20	40	45

1938 BUICK EXPERIMENTAL CONVERTIBLE: (1947-1949) Single-seat roadster also known as the "Y" Job; body painted green, yellow, red, or blue. Silver-painted features include front and rear bumpers, grille, and headlights. Body casting contains small solid windshield with three front supports; a long hood; large front fenders extending into side doors; small running light on top of the front fenders; headlights in the fender face; V-shaped rear body with elongated rear fenders; two rear taillights; license plate in center of the rear just above rear bumper. Body casting extends over front and rear wheel wells. Car interior contains only seat and flooring details. Smooth rubber tires with axle spacers. TOOTSIETOY MADE IN U.S.A. **15 30 35**

1941/1942 BUICK SPECIAL: (1947-1949) A two-door fastback sedan; body painted red, blue, green, orange, or yellow. Silver-painted features include front bumper, grille, and rear bumper. Body casting contains two-piece front windshield; single rear window; long hood; front fenders which extend back to side door; vertical front grille; headlights in front fender beyond grille; rear trunk outline; license plate. Rear fenders follow roof and trunk slope. Body casting ex-

	G	E	LN

tends over wheel wells; axles extending through body sides; smooth rubber tires with axle spacers.

	G	E	LN
(A) As described above.	15	30	35
(B) TOOTSIETOY MADE IN U.S.A. underneath.	15	30	35

1941 CHRYSLER CONVERTIBLE: (1947-1949) A twin-seat convertible in red, blue, green, orange, or yellow. Silver-painted features include front bumper, grille, and rear bumper. Body casting contains small solid windshield with three front supports; front horizontal grille extending through front fenders and including headlights; tour cover around rear seat; rear trunk outline; license plate; simulated trim on front fender and top of hood. Interior details limited to front and rear seats and flooring. Body casting extends over wheel wells; axles extend through body sides; smooth rubber tires with axle spacers. TOOTSIETOY MADE IN U.S.A. **15 30 35**

1949 MERCURY FIRE CHIEF CAR: (1953-1960) Four-door sedan; body painted red. Silver-painted features include front bumper and grille, rear bumper, and headlights. Body casting includes warning light on roof with FIRE CHIEF molded into roof casting; two-piece windshield; single rear window; narrow vertical front grille; two large bumper guards on front and rear bumpers; smooth side body lines; front fenders match hood line; rear fenders match sloping trunk line. Body sides extend over wheel wells; axles extend through body sides. Smooth rubber tires with axle spacers. TOOTSIETOY MADE IN U.S.A.

	G	E	LN
(A) As described above.	20	35	40
(B) Same as (A) with no axle spacers.	20	35	40

1949 MERCURY SEDAN: (1950-1952) Four-door sedan; body painted red or blue. Silver-painted features include front and rear bumpers, grille, and headlights. Body casting contains a two-piece windshield; single rear window; narrow vertical front grille; two large bumper guards on front and rear bumpers; and a large hood ornament; smooth side body lines; front fenders match hood line; rear fenders match sloping trunk line. Body sides extend over wheel wells; axles extend through body sides; smooth rubber tires with axle spacers. TOOTSIETOY MADE IN U.S.A.

	G	E	LN
(A) As described above.	15	30	35
(B) Same as (A), no axle spacers.	15	30	35

1949 OLDSMOBILE CONVERTIBLE: (1950-1954) Body painted yellow, red, blue, or maroon. Silver-painted features include front bumper and grille, headlights, and rear bumper. Body casting includes solid windshield; tour cover behind rear seat; front and rear seats; flooring; narrow front grille extending length of front bumper; headlights in fenders; directional light directly under each headlight; front fender line extending to rear fender; rear trunk matching rear fender line at back of car; three-piece hood ornament above globe-and-ring emblem on front of hood. Body sides extend over wheel wells; axles extend through body sides; smooth rubber tires, axle spacers. TOOTSIETOY MADE IN U.S.A.

	G	E	LN
(A) As described above.	18	30	35
(B) Same as (A), no axle spacers.	18	30	35
(C) Same as (B) but body and features same color.	15	25	30
(D) Same as (A) with maroon body, yellow interior, and windshield. Rare. J. Gibson Collection.	20	40	50

1950 PONTIAC CHIEFTAIN: (1950-1954) Two-door sedan; body painted blue, red, gray, cream, or green. Silver-painted features include front and rear bumpers, front grille, and headlights. Body casting includes two-piece windshield; single rear window; small rear side windows; a five-strip panel in center of hood and rear trunk; bumper guards on front and rear bumpers; narrow grille extending width of car. Body sides extend over wheel wells; axles extend through body sides; smooth rubber tires with axle spacers. TOOTSIETOY MADE IN U.S.A.

	G	E	LN
(A) As described above.	15	30	35
(B) Same as (A), no axle spacers.	15	30	35
(C) Same as (A) in two-tone colors.	20	40	45

1950 PONTIAC FIRE CHIEF CHIEFTAIN: (1950-1954) Two-door fire chief car; body painted red. Silver-painted features include front and rear bumpers, front grille, and headlights. Body casting includes two-piece windshield; single rear window; small rear side windows; a warning light on roof; five-strip panel in center of hood and rear trunk; bumper guards on front and rear bumpers; narrow grille extending width of car. Body sides extend over wheel wells; axles extend through body sides; smooth rubber tires with axle spacers. TOOTSIETOY MADE IN U.S.A.

	G	E	LN
(A) As described above.	15	35	40
(B) Same as (A), no axle spacers.	15	35	40

1952 MERCURY SEDAN: (1953-1954, 1958) Four-door sedan; body painted blue, red, yellow, or orange; two-tone colors in green or red body with cream roof. Silver-painted features include front and rear bumpers, grille, headlights, and taillights. Body casting contains one-piece windshield; large front and rear bumpers; narrow grille between front fenders; air scoop on hood; slanted rear fenders with large taillights extending from top of fender to rear bumper; circle emblem on trunk. Top of fender line extends length of car. Body sides extend over wheel wells; axles extend through body sides; smooth rubber tires with axle spacers. TOOTSIETOY MADE IN U.S.A.

	G	E	LN
(A) As described above; painted features.	10	20	25
(B) Same as (A) with two-tone colors.	10	25	30
(C) Same as (A) but no axle spacers.	10	20	25
(D) Same as (C) with two-tone colors.	10	25	30
(E) Painted features; patterned rubber tires, no axle spacers.	10	20	25

1953 CHEVROLET CORVETTE: (1955-1969) Single-seat sports car; body painted red, blue, gold, dark blue, green, or cream. Silver-painted features include taillights, emblem, grille, headlights, rear lower panel, and interior including dash. Body casting includes open wheel wells; open interior; no windshield; bucket seats; detailed dashboard with steering wheel; narrow grille with vertical bars; twin-flag emblem on front hood; license plate on rear trunk numbered 3030; rounded front fenders with guarded headlights; rear fenders extending straight back with small round taillights. TOOTSIETOY MADE IN U.S.A. CHEVROLET CORVETTE.

	G	E	LN
(A) Painted features; smooth rubber tires, no axle spacers.	15	30	35
(B) Body and features same color; patterned rubber tires, no axle spacers.	10	18	20
(C) Same as (B) but patterned plastic tires.	10	18	20

G E LN

1954 FORD RANCH WAGON: (1955-1960) Four-door station wagon; body painted green, blue, or red; two-tone colors of blue, red, or green with cream or light blue, roof painted in gray. Silver-painted features include front and rear bumpers, headlights, taillights, and front grille. Body casting contains one-piece windshield; three side windows on each side; single rear window; Ford emblem on front and rear hoods; open front wheel wells; simulated rear fender skirts; front grille extends width of body; front hood ornament. Body sides extend over rear wheels; top of fender line extends length of car body; rear wheels mounted inside body; smooth rubber tires, no axle spacers. TOOTSIETOY CHICAGO U.S.A. FORD RANCH WAGON.

(A) As described above; two-tone color with painted features. 17 30 35

(B) Same as (A) except solid color. 15 25 30

(C) Same as (A) except patterned rubber tires. 17 30 35

(D) Same as (C) in solid color. 15 25 30

(E) Body and features same color; patterned rubber tires. 10 20 25

1954 OLDSMOBILE 98 HOLIDAY: (1955-1960) Two-door hardtop; body painted red, blue, gray, or green; two-tone colors of gray, orange, blue, red, or green body with a cream, gray, or blue roof. Silver-painted features include front and rear bumper, grille, headlights, and taillights. Body casting includes one-piece windshield; a vent window with single window on each side. Box-design type of body with style line on each side extending from front fender to beyond side door; small round taillights; front grille covering width of hood and extending under front headlights; rocket ornament on front hood. Car was made in two styles with variations in the width of the front and rear bumpers, and in open or covered wheel wells. Axles extend through body sides; smooth rubber tires with axle spacers.

(A) Two-tone paint with painted features; body casting extends over wheel wells; thick front and rear bumpers; TOOTSIETOY MADE IN U.S.A. OLDS 98 HOLIDAY. 20 35 40

(B) Same as (A) in solid colors; painted features. 20 30 35

(C) Two-tone paint with painted features; body casting contains open wheel wells, thin front and rear bumpers; no axle spacers. TOOTSIETOY CHICAGO U.S.A. HOLIDAY OLDS 98. 25 35 40

(D) Same as (C) in solid colors; painted features. 20 30 35

1955 FORD THUNDERBIRD: (1955-1967) Two-door coupe; body painted red, yellow, orange, green, gray, cream, blue, or light blue; two-tone colors of red, yellow, blue, gray, or green body with cream, red, green, blue, or yellow roof. Silver-painted features include front and rear bumpers, grille, and headlights. Casting includes open wheel wells; long hood with cone-shaped vent; one-piece windshield; single side windows; large rear window; small slanted air vents on side of front fenders; top of fender line extending length of car body; Ford emblem on front and rear hoods; small fin-style rear fenders with round taillights; headlights in fenders; oval-shaped front grille; front bumper guards.

(A) Two-tone colors with painted features; smooth rubber tires with axle spacers. TOOTSIETOY MADE IN U.S.A. FORD THUNDERBIRD. 15 30 40

(B) Same as (A) without two-tone paint. 12 25 35

G E LN

(C) Painted features; smooth rubber tires, no axle spacers. TOOTSIETOY MADE IN U.S.A. FORD THUNDERBIRD. 12 30 35

(D) Painted features; patterned rubber tires, no axle spacers. TOOTSIETOY CHICAGO U.S.A. FORD THUNDERBIRD. 12 25 30

(E) Body and features same color; patterned plastic tires, no axle spacers. TOOTSIETOY CHICAGO U.S.A. FORD THUNDERBIRD. 10 20 25

1959 PONTIAC STAR CHIEF: (1961-1969) Four-door sedan in red, turquoise, blue, or green. Silver-painted features include front and rear bumpers, headlights, and grille. Body casting contains large one-piece windshield; three windows on each side; and a large rear window; wide, flat hood and front fenders; twin headlights in the small grille area, separated by narrow body panel; open front wheel wells; fender skirt over rear wheel well; long, wide rear trunk with twin fins extending the length of the trunk; oval-shaped taillight under each fin. Rear axle mounted inside of car body. TOOTSIETOY CHICAGO 24 U.S.A. PONTIAC STAR CHIEF 10299.

(A) Painted features; patterned rubber tires, no axle spacers. 12 25 30

(B) Same as (A) but body and features same color. 10 20 25

(C) Body and features same color; patterned plastic tires, no axle spacers. 10 20 25

1960 CHRYSLER CONVERTIBLE: (1961, 1963-1964, 1968-1969) Full-size, two-door convertible; body painted red, turquoise, green, blue, or light blue. Silver-painted features include front and rear bumpers, dual headlights, and front grille. Body casting contains detailed interior with front and rear seats, steering wheel, molded windshield, and tour cover behind rear seat; dual front headlights; horizontal grille between dual headlights; raised narrow panel in center of hood; open wheel wells; two style lines on body side extending length of car; long, thin fins on top of rear fenders; raised style line down middle of trunk; rear bumper with license plate in center. Patterned plastic tires, no axle spacers. CHRYSLER TOOTSIETOY CHICAGO 24 U.S.A.

(A) As described above with painted features. 12 20 25

(B) Same as (A) but body and features same color; no axle spacers. 10 15 20

(C) Same as (A); patterned rubber tires. 15 25 30

1960 RAMBLER WAGON: (1961, 1963) Four-door station wagon; body painted blue or green. Silver-painted features include front and rear bumpers, front grille, and dual headlights. Body casting contains one-piece windshield; luggage rack on rear of roof; rear wheel support struts visible through rear side windows; wide, square front grille; small dual headlights above grille; wide, flat front fenders with sloping hood; side door windows with long rear side window; front and rear bumpers indented for license plate; large cone-shaped taillights; open wheel wells. Patterned rubber tires, no axle spacers. RAMBLER TOOTSIETOY CHICAGO 24 U.S.A.

(A) As described above; with painted features. 15 25 30

(B) Same as (A); patterned plastic tires. 15 25 30

(C) Same as (A); body and features same color. 12 22 50

1969 FORD LTD HARDTOP: (1970) Two-door hardtop; body and features painted blue. A large item for this series; casting includes concealed headlights; a wide panel in center

(Above) **Top:** *Civilian Jeep and 1950 Pontiac Fire Chief Chieftain.* **Middle, from left:** *1952 Mercury Sedan; Civilian Jeep with star on hood variation; 1949 Mercury Sedan; and 1950 Pontiac Chieftain.* **Bottom:** *1953 Chevrolet Corvette, S. Butler Collection, and 1949 Mercury Fire Chief Car.*

(Below) **Top:** *1954 Oldsmobile 98 Holiday, S. Butler Collection.* **Middle:** *1960 Chrysler Convertible; 1960 Rambler Wagon, S. Butler Collection; and 1954 Ford Ranch Wagon.* **Bottom:** *1954 Oldsmobile 98 Holiday with two-tone paint and painted features, 1959 Pontiac Star Chief, and 1955 Ford Thunderbird, S. Butler Collection.*

Top: *1938 Federal Truck, S. Butler Collection; 1969 Ford LTD Hardtop.* **Bottom:** *1937 Mack Hook and Ladder Fire Truck; 1941 International Panel Truck, S. Butler Collection; and 1941 International Ambulance, C. Jones Collection.*

	G	E	LN

of hood extending to center section of grille between headlights; a one-piece windshield; large single side windows; front fenders extending beyond headlights; lower trim line between open wheel wells; square taillights on front and rear bumper; trailer hitch; and large wide trunk. 1969 LTD FORD TOOTSIETOY MADE IN U.S.A.

	G	E	LN
(A) Body and features painted blue; plastic tires with simulated wire wheels, no axle spacers.	10	18	20
(B) Two-tone colors reported with silver-painted features; patterned plastic tires, no axle spacers.			NRS
(C) Silver-painted features; patterned plastic tires, no axle spacers.			NRS

Trucks

1937 MACK HOOK AND LADDER FIRE TRUCK: (1942/1946, 1948) Rare fire truck painted red with three silver-painted removable ladders that can be connected to form one long ladder. Silver metal fireman as driver cast with a pin to insert in a hole in the truck seat. Body casting contains large front fenders with headlights; running board extending from front fender to rear fender on each side; open front seat; dashboard extending above top of front hood; front bumper, but no rear bumper; and large vertical grille as the radiator. Rear portion of fire truck has two large openings along sides. Rear top of truck has two half-circle openings to hold a ladder in an upright position. Each side has two small cast hooks to hold one ladder. The third ladder is mounted to the top of the truck body. Body casting extends over wheel wells; axles extend through body sides. Smooth rubber tires with axle spacers. TOOTSIETOY MADE IN UNITED STATES OF AMERICA.

	G	E	LN
(A) As described above.	40	75	85
(B) Same as (A) except no fireman; no hole in seat; three ladders.	35	70	75
(C) (1942/1946) Open wheel wells, smooth rubber tires with axle spacers; red truck body; silver features including front bumper, headlights, and front grille; fireman; and three ladders.	40	65	75
(D) Same as (A) with silver-painted features including headlights, front bumper, and grille.	40	60	70
(E) Same as (A), (B), or (D), ladders missing.	25	45	50
(F) Same as (C), ladders missing.	25	50	55

1937 MACK HOSE TRUCK: (1948) Rare fire truck; body painted red. Body casting includes a fire hose cannon at the rear of the truck body which rotates on a cast pin running from the bottom of the cannon through truck body; silver fireman as driver with a cast pin to hold him to the seat; large front fenders with headlights; running board extending from front fenders to rear fender on each side; open front seat with dashboard extending above top of front hood; simulated hose reel behind the front seat; large vertical grille as the radiator. Body extends over wheel wells; axles extend through body sides; smooth rubber tires with axle spacers. TOOTSIETOY MADE IN UNITED STATES OF AMERICA.

	G	E	LN
(A) As described above.	35	75	85
(B) Same as (A) but no fireman or hole in seat.	30	65	75
(C) Open wheel wells, smooth rubber tires with axle spacers; red truck body; silver-painted features including front bumper, headlights, grille, front pumper, rear fire hose cannon, hose reel, and fireman.	40	70	80

G E LN

(D) Same as (A) with silver hose cannon, bumper, grille, and headlights. 40 75 85

(E) (1942/1946) Maybe prewar reissue. Open wheel wells, black smooth rubber tires, axle spacers; red truck body; silver front bumper and pumper, front grille, headlights, hose reel, and hose cannon. Silver fireman on front seat and rear step. NRS

(F) Same as (E) except firemen painted blue. NRS

(G) Same as (F) without fireman on rear step; no hole in rear step. NRS

1937 MACK PUMPER TRUCK: (1948) Rare fire truck; body painted red with one removable silver ladder, and a silver fireman with cast pin to hold him to the seat. Body casting includes large front fenders with headlights; running boards extending from front fenders to rear fender on each side; front bumper; open front seat with dashboard extending above top of front hood; fire hoses in side casting; hose reel behind seat; protruding rear step; large vertical grille as the radiator. Body extends over wheel wells; axles extend through body sides; smooth rubber tires with axle spacers. TOOTSIETOY MADE IN UNITED STATES OF AMERICA.

(A) As described above. 35 70 80

(B) Same as (A) but no fireman or hole in seat. 30 70 75

(C) (1942/1946) Open wheel wells; smooth rubber tires with axle spacer, red truck body; silver front bumper, headlights, grille, hose reel. Silver fireman and ladder. 35 70 75

(D) Same as (A) with silver front bumper, headlights, grille, and hose reel. 35 70 75

1938 FEDERAL TRUCK: (1948) Open high-sided truck; body painted green, blue, red, silver, or white. Silver-painted features include front bumper, grille, and headlights. Body casting contains a two-piece windshield; single-window doors; no rear window; protruding fenders on front and rear; hood and front grille protruding from front windshield; headlights behind front grille between hood and front fenders; high truck sides; front of truck bed extending to top of truck cab. Body extends over wheel wells; axles extend through body sides; smooth rubber tires with axle spacers. TOOTSIETOY MADE IN UNITED STATES OF AMERICA NO. 1010.

(A) Painted features. 20 40 45

(B) Body and features same color. 20 35 40

1941 INTERNATIONAL AMBULANCE: (1948-1949) Panel truck painted as an ambulance; body painted red, tan, or white with a red cross on the roof. Body casting includes two-piece windshield; door window on each side; two small rear windows; warning light on roof and hood above front grille; large front fenders with headlights between narrow horizontal front grille; front bumper; no rear bumper; double rear doors. Body sides extend over wheel wells; axles extend through body sides; smooth rubber tires with axle spacers. TOOTSIETOY MADE IN U.S.A.

(A) As described above with open rear windows and an opening between front bumper and truck body. 20 40 45

(B) Same as (A) with silver-painted features including front bumpers, grille, and headlights; open rear windows. 20 40 45

(C) Same as (A) with molded rear windows and front bumper. 20 40 45

G E LN

(D) Same as (B) with molded rear windows and front bumper. 20 40 45

1941 INTERNATIONAL PANEL TRUCK: (1948-1949) Panel truck; body painted orange, blue, red, or green. Body and features painted same color. Body casting includes two-piece windshield; door window on each side; two small rear windows; large front fenders with headlights between narrow horizontal front grille; front bumper; no rear bumper; double rear doors. Body sides extend over wheel wells; axles extend through body sides; smooth rubber tires with axle spacers. TOOTSIETOY MADE IN U.S.A.

(A) As described above with open rear windows and an opening between front bumper and truck body. 15 35 40

(B) Same as (A) except silver-painted features including front bumper, grille, and headlights. 20 40 45

(C) Same as (A) with molded rear windows and front bumper. 15 35 40

(D) Same as (B) with molded rear windows and front bumper. 20 40 45

1947 PICKUP TRUCK: (1947-1949) Futuristic-looking pickup truck sometimes called a Hudson; body painted orange, red, dark red, dark orange, blue, green, or yellow. Silver-painted features include front bumper, grille, and headlights. Body looks very much like the 4" Pull Wagon, with the addition of a truck cab. Body casting has a front bumper; no rear bumper or taillights; two-piece windshield; side door windows; no rear window; rounded cab roof extending up from a wide V-shaped front grille; rectangular headlights. Body extends over wheels; axles extend through body sides; smooth rubber tires, axle spacers. TOOTSIETOY MADE IN U.S.A.

(A) Painted features. 15 35 40

(B) Body and features same color. NRS

1949 CHEVROLET AMBULANCE: (1953-1960) Panel truck painted as an ambulance; body painted yellow or white with a red cross and warning light on roof, or red with a white cross. Silver-painted features include front bumper, grille, and headlights. Body casting contains a two-piece windshield; side door windows and two open or molded rear windows; protruding front fenders; wide hood and horizontal front grille; headlights in fender; front and rear bumpers. Body sides extend over wheel wells; axles extend through body sides; smooth rubber tires with axle spacers. TOOTSIETOY MADE IN U.S.A.

(A) Painted features; open rear windows. 25 40 45

(B) Same as (A); body and features same color except for cross and warning light. 15 35 40

(C) Same as (B) except patterned rubber tires, no axle spacers; molded rear windows. 15 30 35

(D) All-blue including warning light and cross. E. Cruts Collection. 15 30 35

1949 CHEVROLET PANEL TRUCK: (1950-1953) Body painted green, yellow, blue, red, orange, or black. Silver-painted features include front bumper, grille, and headlights. Body casting contains two-piece windshield; side door windows; two open or molded rear windows; protruding front fenders; wide hood and horizontal front grille; headlights in fender; front and rear bumpers. Body sides extend over wheel

Top: *1950 Dodge Pickup Trucks with and without painted features, S. Butler Collection.* **Bottom:** *1956 Chevrolet Cameo Carriers with and without painted features and two-tone paint, S. Butler Collection; 1949 Chevrolet Ambulance; and 1949 Chevrolet Panel Truck.*

G E LN

wells; axles extend through body sides; smooth rubber tires with axle spacers. TOOTSIETOY MADE IN U.S.A.

(A) Painted features; open rear windows. **15 30 35**

(B) Same as (A) but body and features painted same color. **12 25 30**

(C) Same as (A) but no axle spacers. **15 30 35**

(D) Same as (B) but no axle spacers. **12 25 30**

(E) Same as (D) with molded rear windows. **10 20 25**

(F) Same as (A) or (B) in two-tone colors. **15 40 45**

1949 FORD STAKESIDE TRUCK: (1950-1969) Solid-side, open-body truck; body painted red, yellow, blue, green, orange, dark red, or light blue; two-tone colors include red, green, orange, yellow, or blue body with silver truck bed and inside walls. Silver-painted features include the front bumper, grille, and headlights. Body casting contains a short front hood; protruding front fenders; oval-style front grille with headlights; one-piece windshield; side-door windows; open or molded rear window. The rear bed of truck is open. Smooth rubber tires with axle spacers.

(A) Two-tone paint with painted features; body sides extend over front and rear wheel wells; axles extend through body sides, open rear cab window; large wheel housing in truck bed. TOOTSIETOY MADE IN U.S.A. **15 30 35**

(B) Same as (A) without two-tone paint scheme. **10 25 30**

G E LN

(C) Two-tone paint scheme with painted features; open wheel wells front and rear; smooth rubber tires, no axle spacers; open rear cab window; small wheel housing in truck bed. TOOTSIETOY CHICAGO USA. **15 25 30**

(D) Same as (C) in solid colors; painted features. **10 20 25**

(E) Painted features; open wheel wells front and rear; patterned rubber tires, no axle spacers; open rear cab window; small housing in truck bed. TOOTSIETOY CHICAGO U.S.A. **10 20 25**

(F) Same as (E) except body and features same color. **8 15 20**

(G) Body and features same color; open wheel wells front and rear; patterned plastic tires, no axle spacers; molded rear cab window; small wheel housing in truck bed. TOOTSIETOY CHICAGO U.S.A. **8 12 15**

1949 FORD TANKER TRUCK: (1950-1969) Body painted red, yellow, blue, orange, or green; also two-tone colors of red, blue, green, or yellow truck cab and lower body with silver tank. Silver-painted features include front bumper, grille, and headlights. Body casting contains three protruding running lights on cab roof; short front hood; protruding front fenders; oval-style grille with headlights; and five filler caps on top of fuel tank. Cab has one-piece windshield; side door window but no rear window. Rear tank body has simulated equipment doors on both sides and

Top: *1949 Ford Tanker Truck, S. Butler Collection, and 1949 Ford Stakeside Truck in two color variations.* **Bottom:** *1949 Ford Tanker Truck in two-tone paint with painted features; 1947 futuristic-looking Pickup Truck, S. Butler Collection.*

	G	E	LN

at rear of tank; two protruding rear lights over rear doors. Body sides extend over front and rear wheel wells. Smooth rubber tires with axle spacers.

	G	E	LN
(A) Two-tone paint with painted features; axles extend through body sides. TOOTSIETOY MADE IN U.S.A.	16	25	30
(B) Painted features; axles extend through body sides. TOOTSIETOY MADE IN U.S.A.	15	23	25
(C) Painted features; axles extend through body sides, patterned rubber tires with axle spacers. TOOTSIETOY MADE IN U.S.A.	15	23	25
(D) Same as (C) but body and features same color.	10	16	20
(E) Painted features; axles mounted inside of truck body; patterned rubber tires, no axle spacers. TOOTSIETOY CHICAGO U.S.A.	15	18	20
(F) Same as (E) but body and features same color.	10	15	18
(G) Same as (A) except axles mounted inside truck body.	15	25	30
(H) Body and features same color; axles mounted inside of truck body; patterned plastic tires, no axle spacers. TOOTSIETOY CHICAGO U.S.A.	10	15	18

1950 DODGE PICKUP TRUCK: (1950-1960) Body painted red, blue, green, orange, or yellow. Silver-painted features include front bumper, grille, and headlights. Body casting contains a two-piece front windshield; side door windows; three rear windows: a center window with a small corner window on each side; protruding front fenders extending into the door; headlights in front fenders with a three-bar horizontal front grille; and bumpers in front and rear. Tailgate is molded in a closed position. Body casting extends over wheel wells; axles extend through body sides; smooth rubber tires with axle spacers. TOOTSIETOY MADE IN U.S.A.

	G	E	LN
(A) As described above.	15	25	30
(B) Same as (A) but no axle spacers.	15	25	30
(C) Same as (A) with silver-painted truck bed.	15	30	35

1956 CHEVROLET CAMEO CARRIER: (1959-1969) Pickup truck; body painted orange, red, dark turquoise, green, yellow, blue, or cream; two-tone colors of red, blue, green, or orange body with silver truck bed and interior bed side walls. Silver-painted features include front and rear bumpers; front grille; headlights and taillights. Body casting includes large single front windshield; headlights in the protruding front fenders; rounded hood with Chevy emblem above front grille; large rear cab window; door windows with vent windows; rear tailgate molded in closed position; oval-shaped taillights; license plate in rear bumper; two bumper guards; no fender wells in truck bed; open wheel wells. Smooth rubber tires with no axle spacers. TOOTSIETOY CHICAGO U.S.A. CHEV CAMEO CARRIER.

	G	E	LN
(A) Two-tone paint with painted features.	15	23	25
(B) Painted features.	12	18	20
(C) Painted features; patterned rubber tires, no axle spacers.	12	18	20
(D) Same as (C), patterned plastic tires.	10	15	18
(E) Same as (D), body and features same color.	10	13	15

CHAPTER 6

Three-Inch Cars, Jeeps, and Trucks

The 3-inch series contains forty-one different models. In some of the early catalogues, 3-inch vehicles were advertised as "pocket sized," reflecting the fact that they could be carried around quite easily in a child's pocket. These should not be confused with a series of HO-scale vehicles that were introduced in 1962 and called the Pocket (HO) Series, which is described in Chapter 10.

Because of their size, the quality of the details in the 3-inch series varies greatly from toy to toy, depending of course on the vehicle modeled. Because of this variation in detail, it often seems that the prices asked at shows for these toys run unusually high. In many cases they seem to be highly priced regardless of body condition, especially the reissued Mack fire trucks, the 1937 International Wagon, the 1939/1940 Four-Door Sedan, the 1939/1940 Coupe, and the Single-Seat Convertible. Perhaps this tendency is a carryover of perceived value from the 4-inch series, although 3-inch vehicles are much more easily found than 4-inch vehicles. Even in light of their availability, some 3-inch vehicles can be elusive. The most difficult pieces to locate are the 1954 Nash Metropolitan Convertible, the 1947 Studebaker, and the earlier Mack fire trucks. The 1952 Ford Sedan and the 1960 Ford Wagon follow in scarcity. Surprisingly, most of the reissued prewar cars are not difficult to find!

Unlike the 4-inch or 6-inch series, many 3-inch vehicles were paired with other units like the auto transport trailer truck. These pairs were then used within assorted sets, which makes finding 3-inch vehicles from the 1949 to 1969 period somewhat easier. The company included road signs with some 3-inch vehicles in blister packs; road signs can also be found with the 4-inch series and the larger box sets. See Chapter 11 for additional accessory items.

One of the difficulties in describing the prewar reissued 3-inch vehicles has been in properly identifying the models. Their smaller size placed limitations on their design, so it appears that certain style changes were made without too much concern for accuracy in representing the prototypes. This design constraint frequently resulted in rather generic-looking vehicles—cars and trucks that resembled a number of other actual cars and trucks in various ways. For example, the Four-Door Sedan reissued from 1947 to 1952 has been identified by different authors and collectors as a Nash, a Studebaker, and a LaSalle, since it has some features that resemble each of those models. A number of the prototypes were extremely similar in appearance, like the Four-Door Sedan, the Coupe, the Convertible, and the Station Wagon. Each collector may feel a particular vehicle looks more like one prototype than another, yet not be able to find it as such in this guide. These toys will be listed according to the names given in the catalogues, if any. The various possible model types are included in their listings.

The problem is not as prevalent with true *postwar* designs, since prototype vehicles after the war had a boxier style which was much easier for the company to copy. Despite the lack of specific details, the toys can fairly represent these prototypes because of basic differences in design.

There are two types of tires seen in this series. Type 1 is a smooth black rubber tire, ½" in diameter. Type 2 is a black plastic Tootsietoy tire, ½" in diameter. The wheel assembly does not utilize an axle spacer, which is used in the 4-inch and

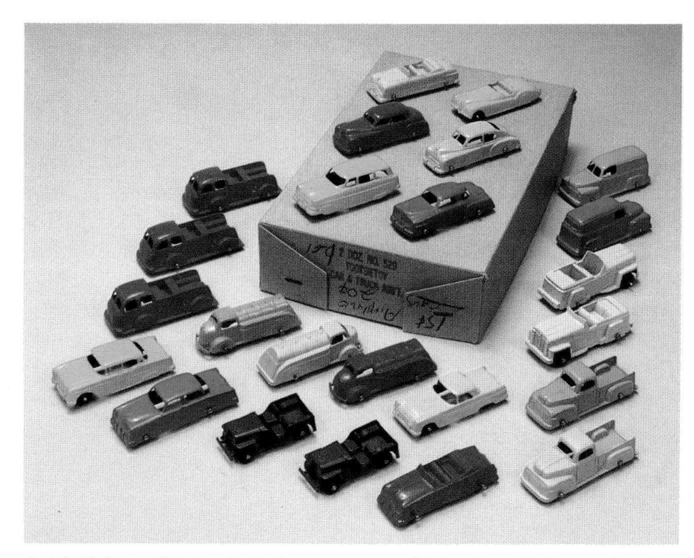

A 1949 No. 529 Dealer's Assortment of 3-inch vehicles, valued at $625. J. Gibson Collection.

6-inch series. Instead, a single steel pin is used to connect a set of wheels to the body casting.

The series must have sold well because, by 1969, the company still produced seven different 3-inch vehicles: the 1960 Studebaker Convertible, 1960 Ford Falcon, 1954 Volkswagen, Hot Rod Model B, 1957 Plymouth, 1956 Triumph TR-3, and 1957 Ford Pickup Truck.

The following vehicles are listed by model year and model name, with prewar reissued vehicles listed first. Special units with uncertain prototype model years appear at the end of the listings. A set of 3-inch cars and trucks that was used as a promotional item for Cheerios® cereal is described at the end of the chapter. Based on historical data, catalogues, advertisements, and data obtained from other collectors, the best known information on production years for each piece is included in the listings. Cast-in information on the underside of each vehicle appears last in each listing.

G E LN

FIRE LADDER TRUCK: (1942/1946) Ladder truck resembling a Mack fire truck; prewar reissued vehicle. Body painted red; silver-painted features include front bumper, grille, headlights, and top of body from behind seat to the rear of truck. Body casting includes a ladder on each side; fireman as driver; spotlight on front hood; headlights mounted to the side of the front grille extending onto front fenders; large horizontal grille; grille-style running board between the front and rear fenders; open wheel wells in front and rear; smooth black rubber tires. TOOTSIETOY MADE IN UNITED STATES OF AMERICA.

	G	E	LN
(A) Painted features.	10	20	30
(B) Body and features same color.	10	20	30

FIRE HOSE TRUCK: (1947-1948) Hose truck resembling a Mack truck; prewar reissued vehicle. Body painted red; silver-painted features include front bumper, grille, headlights, and hose cannon. Body casting includes hose cannon on top of truck over rear wheels; fireman as driver in seat; spotlight on front hood; headlights mounted to side of front grille extending onto front fenders; large horizontal grille; running board between front and rear fenders. Open wheel wells in front and rear; smooth black rubber tires. TOOTSIETOY MADE IN UNITED STATES OF AMERICA.

	G	E	LN
(A) Painted features.	10	20	30
(B) Body and features same color.	10	20	30

FIRE PUMPER AND HOSE TRUCK: (1947-1948) Pumper also known as an Insurance Patrol Truck resembles a Mack truck; prewar reissued vehicle. Body painted red; silver-painted features include front bumper, grille, headlights, and hose reel. Body casting includes large hose reel; spotlight on rear; fireman as driver in seat; bell on hood; headlights mounted to side of front grille extending onto front fenders; large horizontal grille; running boards between front and rear fenders. Open wheel wells on front and rear; smooth black rubber tires. TOOTSIETOY MADE IN UNITED STATES OF AMERICA.

	G	E	LN
(A) Painted features.	10	20	30
(B) Body and features same color.	10	20	30

SINGLE-SEAT CONVERTIBLE: (1947-1952) Prewar reissued vehicle. The intended prototype of this unit is unknown. Body and features painted red, yellow, blue, orange, or green. Body casting includes single seat; cast windshield; long hood; front fenders set back from front of hood; headlights protruding from front fenders; curved front bumper; taillights; license plate over left taillight; rear bumper; running boards between front and rear fenders. Body casting extends over wheel wells; axles protrude through body sides; smooth black rubber tires. TOOTSIETOY MADE IN UNITED STATES OF AMERICA 233.

Fire Ladder Truck and 1940 Convertible. J. T. Riley Collection.

	G	E	LN
(A) As described above.	15	20	25
(B) Silver-painted features, including front and rear bumpers, and grille.	15	20	25

1937 GMC TANK TRUCK: (1947-1954) Redesigned prewar tank truck. Body and features painted red, yellow, orange, blue, or green. Body casting includes one-piece windshield and large door windows; no rear window due to tank; three running lights on the cab roof; short front hood with large front grille; headlights on front fenders; front and rear bumpers. Tank has three cross straps, four filler ports, and double rear doors in casting. Body of tank extends up to cab roof; casting extends over wheel wells; axles protrude through sides of body; smooth black rubber tires. TOOTSIETOY MADE IN THE U.S.A. **15 20 25**

1937 INTERNATIONAL WAGON: (1947-1952) Four-door station wagon sometimes referred to as a Ford; prewar reissued vehicle. Body and features painted orange, green, or red. Body casting includes simulated wooden side panel from back of front fender to rear of wagon; two-piece front windshield; three windows on each side; two-piece rear window; front and rear bumpers; rounded front grille; rounded front fenders with large oversized headlights. Casting extends through wheel wells; axle extends through body sides; smooth black rubber tires. TOOTSIETOY MADE IN UNITED STATES OF AMERICA 239.

	G	E	LN
(A) As described above.	15	20	25
(B) Two-tone paint in orange and maroon.	15	25	30
(C) Same as (A) with silver roof.	15	25	30
(D) Two-tone paint in green and yellow.	15	25	30

1938 FEDERAL TRUCK: (1947-1948) Short-sided, open-body truck; prewar reissued vehicle. Body and features painted silver, red, yellow, blue, green, or orange. Body casting includes two-piece windshield; single door windows; no rear cab window; short round hood with large front grille; protruding front fenders with headlights; front bumper; no rear bumper. Back of truck is slightly lower than main truck sides; body extends over wheel wells; axles protrude through body sides; smooth black rubber tires. TOOTSIETOY MADE IN UNITED STATES OF AMERICA 234. **15 20 25**

G E LN

1939/1940 FOUR-DOOR SEDAN: (1947-1952) Resembles a Nash, LaSalle, or Studebaker sedan; prewar reissued vehicle. Body and features painted red, green, orange, or blue. Body casting includes two-piece windshield; two side windows on each side; single oval-shaped rear window; long V-shaped hood; large round fenders; front grille on fenders and front of hood; headlights on fenders; front and rear bumpers; small rear trunk with license plate in center. Body extends over wheel wells; axles extend through body casting; smooth black rubber tires. TOOTSIETOY MADE IN UNITED STATES OF AMERICA.

(A) As described above. **15 20 25**

(B) Silver-painted features, including front and rear bumpers and grille. **15 20 25**

1939/1940 COUPE: (1947-1952) Resembles a Chevrolet or Buick two-door coupe; prewar reissued vehicle. Body and features painted red, green, blue, or orange. Body casting includes two-piece windshield; large door window with small side window; large rear window; front V-shaped hood; large round front fenders; grille at front of hood extending to fenders; headlights in middle of fender; front and rear bumpers; large rear trunk with license plate; two rear taillights; small running boards between front and rear fender. Body extends over wheel wells; axles extend through body sides; smooth black rubber tires. TOOTSIETOY MADE IN UNITED STATES OF AMERICA 231.

(A) As described above. **15 20 25**

(B) Silver-painted features, including front and rear bumpers and grille. **15 20 25**

1940 CONVERTIBLE: (1942/1946) Resembles a Buick Phaeton two-seat convertible; prewar reissued vehicle. Body and features painted blue, green, red, yellow, or orange. Body casting includes front and rear seats; windshield; long front hood with large front grille extending onto front fenders with headlights; short rounded rear trunk; rear bumper; running board between front and rear fenders. Body casting extends through wheel wells; axles extend through body sides; smooth black rubber tires. TOOTSIETOY MADE IN UNITED STATES OF AMERICA 232. **15 20 25**

1947 STUDEBAKER CHAMPION: (1949) Two-door coupe; body and features painted green, blue, or red. Body casting includes one-piece windshield; large door window; four-piece rear window; sloping roof and trunk; rear fenders protruding slightly from side; front fenders even with car sides; headlights located in front fenders; front and rear bumpers with bumper guards. Body casting extends over wheel wells; axles extend through body sides; smooth rubber tires. TOOTSIETOY MADE IN U.S.A.

(A) All-red body. **25 40 50**

(B) All-green or all-blue body. **20 40 50**

1948 WILLYS JEEPSTER: (1949-1952) Two-door convertible; body and features painted red, yellow, or blue. Body casting includes front and rear seats; tour cover behind rear seat; windshield with long square hood; small air vent between hood and windshield; small narrow front fenders; large vertical grille with headlights; front and rear bumpers; open front wheel wells. Casting covers rear wheel wells; axles protrude through body sides; smooth rubber tires. TOOTSIETOY MADE IN U.S.A. **15 20 25**

G E LN

1949 AMERICAN LAFRANCE FIRE TRUCK: (1949-1959) Pumper truck with red body. Cab-forward design featuring two-piece windshield; two cab windows on each side; large single rear cab window; three warning lights on cab roof; headlights; front bumper; rear step with hose reel; protruding front and rear fenders. Body casting covers wheel wells; open rear truck body contains storage boxes and flooring with cross support; two cast fire extinguishers in front of rear fender on driver side.

(A) Smooth rubber tires; axles extend through body sides. MADE IN U.S.A. TOOTSIETOY. **15 22 25**

(B) Smooth rubber tires; axles mounted inside of body casting. TOOTSIETOY CHICAGO U.S.A. **15 22 25**

(C) Same as (B) with patterned plastic tires. TOOTSIETOY CHICAGO U.S.A. **10 18 20**

1949 CHEVROLET PANEL TRUCK: (1949-1959) Body and features painted green or blue. Body casting includes two-piece windshield; side door windows; two small rear door windows; front and rear bumpers; protruding front and rear fenders with running boards between fenders on each side; large rounded front hood; horizontal-style front grille; headlights in top of fenders which are lower than hood; style line in center of hood and around panel body just below windows; large covered side panels; roof; two rear doors. Smooth rubber tires.

(A) Body casting extends over front and rear wheel wells; axles extend through body sides. TOOTSIETOY MADE IN U.S.A. **15 22 25**

(B) Open front wheel wells; covered rear wheel wells; rear axle mounted inside truck body. TOOTSIETOY CHICAGO U.S.A. **17 23 25**

(C) Same as (A) with solid rear windows. TOOTSIETOY MADE IN U.S.A. 2. **15 22 25**

(D) Same as (B) with solid rear windows. **15 22 25**

1949 COACH BUS: (1949-1950) City transit bus; body and features painted red, orange, blue, yellow, or green. Body casting includes two-piece front and rear windows; six windows on double-door side, eight windows on other side; three running lights on roof, front and back; two additional side lights in rear; three air vents on roof; front and rear bumpers; front headlights. Body sides cover wheel wells; axles extend through body sides; smooth rubber tires. TOOTSIETOY MADE IN U.S.A. **20 28 30**

1949 FORD CONVERTIBLE: (1949-1954) Two-door convertible; body and features painted red, yellow, green, blue, or cream. Body casting includes front and rear seats; cast windshield; rear tour cover; front and rear bumpers with bumper guards; wide, flat front hood and fenders; short rounded rear trunk; front grille extending up at center of hood and sloping down at fenders; headlights in top of fender; narrow taillights in center of rear fenders. Body casting extends over front and rear wheel wells; axles protrude through body sides; smooth rubber tires. TOOTSIETOY MADE IN U.S.A. **10 15 20**

1949 FORD CUSTOM: (1949-1954) Four-door sedan; body and features painted blue, green, red, yellow, or cream. Body casting includes two-piece windshield; two windows on each side and single rear window; front and rear bumpers with bumper guards; wide, flat front hood and fenders; short rounded rear trunk; front grille extending up at center of hood

Back row (from left to right): *1938 Federal Truck, Fire Hose Truck, Fire Pumper and Hose Truck, 1937 International Wagon, 1937 International Wagon in two-tone paint; S. Butler Collection.* **Front row:** *1937 GMC Tank Truck, Single-Seat Convertible, 1939/1940 Coupe, 1939/1940 Four-Door Sedan. S. Butler Collection.*

Clockwise from lower left: *1949 Ford Pickup Truck with open tailgate; 1949 Ford Pickup Truck with solid tailgate; 1950 Plymouth Deluxe; 1949 Ford Custom; 1950 Chevrolet Fleetline Deluxe, S. Butler Collection; 1948 Willys Jeepster; 1949 Ford Convertible.* **Center:** *1947 Studebaker Champion; 1947 Studebaker Champion in rare red color, S. Butler Collection.*

G E LN

and sloping down at fenders; headlights in top of fender; narrow taillights in center of rear fenders. Body casting extends over front and rear wheel wells; axles protrude through body sides; smooth rubber tires. TOOTSIETOY MADE IN U.S.A. 2.
10 15 20

1949 FORD PICKUP TRUCK: (1949-1960) Pickup truck cast with or without rear tailgate. Body and features painted green, red, blue, orange, yellow, or white. Body casting includes protruding fenders in front and rear; front hood with a raised panel through the center; small air vents at front of hood on each side of hood panel; oval-shaped front grille with headlights; one-piece windshield; door windows; rear window; front and rear bumpers; running boards between front and rear fenders. Body casting extends over front and rear wheel wells; smooth rubber tires.

(A) Rear tailgate; axles extend through body sides. TOOTSIETOY MADE IN U.S.A. **15 20 25**

(B) Same as (A) with no rear tailgate. **12 20 25**

(C) No rear tailgate; axles inside truck casting. TOOTSIETOY CHICAGO U.S.A. (U.S.A. behind rear axle). **10 20 25**

Clockwise from lower left: *Civilian Jeep; 1952 Ford Sedan; 1949 Chevrolet Panel Truck with open front wheel wells; 1949 Coach Bus; 1954 Ford Ranch Wagon; 1949 Chevrolet Panel Truck with closed front wheel wells; 1954 MG, S. Butler Collection; 1954 Jaguar.* **Center:** *1955 Ford Thunderbird; 1954 Nash Metropolitan, S. Butler Collection.*

Top: *1949 American LaFrance Fire Truck in two axle variations.* **Middle:** *1956 Triumph TR-3, 1957 Ford Fairlane 500 Convertible, and 1957 Formula D Jaguar.* **Bottom:** *1955 Ford Tanker Truck, 1955 Ford Custom, 1955 Chevrolet Bel Air, and 1957 Plymouth Belvedere, S. Butler Collection.*

	G	E	LN
(D) Same as (C) except TOOTSIETOY CHICAGO U.S.A. in front of rear axle.	10	20	25

1950 CHEVROLET FLEETLINE DELUXE: (1951-1954) Two-door sedan; body and features painted blue, gray, yellow, or red. Body casting includes a sloping roof which, with trunk line, resembles a "fastback"; two-piece front windshield; two side windows on each side, single rear window; long protruding rear fenders with taillights; trunk handle above rear bumper; front bumper with bumper guards; horizontal-style grille; Chevrolet emblem above grille on front hood; headlights on top of fenders; front fenders matching body sides. Body covers front and rear wheel wells; axles extend through body sides; smooth rubber tires. TOOTSIETOY MADE IN U.S.A.

G	E	LN
12	18	20

G E LN

1950 PLYMOUTH DELUXE: (1951-1954) Four-door sedan; body and features painted red, blue, green, orange, or gray. Body casting includes a two-piece front windshield; side windows for each door, small rear window; front fenders matching body sides; front hood that is higher than front fenders; emblem on hood; horizontal grille extends into front fenders; headlights in top of fender; front and rear bumpers with bumper guards; round-shaped trunk with emblem; protruding rear fenders which follow trunk line. Body sides cover wheel wells; axles extend through body sides; smooth rubber tires. TOOTSIETOY MADE IN U.S.A. **12 18 20**

1952 FORD SEDAN: (1953-1954) Four-door sedan; body and features painted blue, red, yellow, or green. Body casting includes one-piece windshield; two side-door windows, single large rear window; box-style body without protruding fenders; rear fenders following contour of rear trunk, front fenders following contour of front hood; large ornament and small Ford emblem on hood; headlights in fenders with directional lights below; front grille extending the width of hood; front and rear bumpers; Ford emblem on trunk; license plate above rear bumper; round taillights in fender. Body sides cover front and rear wheel wells; axles extend through body sides; smooth rubber tires. TOOTSIETOY MADE IN U.S.A. **12 18 22**

1954 FORD RANCH WAGON: (1955-1960) Four-door station wagon; body and features painted red, blue, or green. Body casting includes large single front windshield; three windows on each side; single rear window; rear door with Ford emblem; round taillights in fender; front and rear bumpers with bumper guards; style line extending length of smooth body sides; headlights in top of front fenders; large hood with hood ornament and Ford emblem; front grille, with directional lights, extending body width. Body sides cover wheel wells; axles are mounted inside body casting; smooth rubber tires. TOOTSIETOY CHICAGO U.S.A. FORD. **10 15 18**

1954 JAGUAR: (1955-1960) Single-seat convertible sports car or roadster; body and features painted green, blue, red, or yellow. Body casting features detailed interior including seat, dashboard display, and steering wheel; long, sloping rear trunk; large fender skirts; large, long, and sloping front fenders extending through side doors to rear fenders; narrow horizontal grille between headlights on inside of front fenders; front bumper does not extend through front grille; small rear bumper with guard on each side; license plate above bumper; taillights on each side of trunk. Rear axle mounted inside of body casting; smooth rubber tires. JAGUAR TOOTSIETOY CHICAGO U.S.A.

(A) As described above. **10 15 18**

(B) With patterned plastic tires. **10 12 15**

1954 MG: (1955-1960) Single-seat convertible sports car; body and features painted red, yellow, green, or blue. Body casting includes detailed dash with steering wheel and large flat tour cover behind seat; long sweeping front fenders extending to protruding rear fenders; gas tank and continental kit at rear; front and rear bumpers with small bumper guards; large headlights in front fender; large vertical grille in center; long hood with air vents on each side; top of doors are lower

G E LN

than front hood and rear deck area; open wheel wells front and rear.

(A) Smooth rubber tires; underbody frame extends through back of wheel housing. TOOTSIETOY MG CHICAGO USA. **12 15 18**

(B) Patterned plastic tires; open wheel housing. MG TOOTSIETOY MADE CHICAGO U.S.A. **8 12 15**

1954 NASH METROPOLITAN: (1955) Small single-seat convertible; body and features painted red, blue, yellow, or green. Body casting includes detailed interior with open seat, steering wheel, dash display, and windshield; smooth body sides covering front and rear wheel wells; front hood with large air vent; oval-shaped grille; headlights in fender with directional lights below; front and rear bumpers with bumper guards; doors featuring a simulated, pleated panel at top; protruding lower body panel between bumpers; rear trunk with a continental kit. Axles extend through body sides; smooth rubber tires. TOOTSIETOY MADE IN U.S.A. NASH METRO.

(A) Red or blue body. **20 40 50**

(B) All other colors. **25 45 55**

1954 VOLKSWAGEN: (1960-1964, 1968-1969) Two-door vehicle: body and features painted copper, red, yellow, or green. Body casting includes sloping roof to rear bumper; one-piece windshield; two side windows on each side; single rear window; sloping front hood from windshield to front bumper; large headlights in protruding front fenders; styled body panels on front trunk and on rear of car; taillights in protruding rear fenders; open wheel wells front and rear. Patterned plastic tires. TOOTSIETOY CHICAGO 24 U.S.A.

(A) As described above. **10 13 15**

(B) Same as (A); no casting identification. **10 13 15**

1955 CHEVROLET BEL AIR: (1956-1958) Four-door sedan; body and features painted red, yellow, blue, or green. Body casting includes one-piece windshield; two side-door windows with small back window; front vent window on each side; one-piece rear window; large flat front hood; Chevy emblem on hood and trunk; open front wheel wells; wide narrow front grille does not extend into front fenders; headlights on front fenders; front bumper with bumper guards; directional lights below headlights; style line from rear door to back of rear fender; taillights at top of rear fender; rear bumper with two bumper guards; fender skirt over rear wheels. Smooth rubber tires. TOOTSIETOY CHICAGO U.S.A. CHEVROLET.

(A) As described above. **12 18 20**

(B) Patterned plastic tires. **10 15 18**

1955 FORD CUSTOM: (1955-1958) Two-door sedan; body and features painted red, blue, green, or yellow. Body casting includes one-piece, large front windshield; two side windows with front vent window on each side; single rear window; style line extending length of sides; front bumper with bumper guards; Ford emblem on hood and trunk; front grille extending width of car with directional lights; headlights in fender; large round rear taillights; open front wheel wells; fender skirt over rear wheels; rear bumper. Rear wheels mounted inside body casting; smooth rubber tires. TOOTSIETOY CHICAGO U.S.A. FORD.

(A) As described above. **15 18 20**

(B) Patterned plastic tires. **12 15 18**

	G	E	LN

1955 FORD THUNDERBIRD: (1955-1960) Two-door coupe; body and features painted red, blue, yellow, cream, or green. Body casting includes large front windshield; single door window on each side; large rear window; large hood with air vent; oval-shaped front grille; headlights in fender; top of rear fenders with narrow fin; round taillights below fender fin; Ford emblem on trunk; front and rear bumpers; style line from behind front open wheel wells to rear of car; large rear support post for roof. Open rear wheel well; smooth rubber tires. FORD THUNDERBIRD TOOTSIETOY CHICAGO U.S.A.

	G	E	LN
(A) As described above.	15	18	20
(B) Patterned plastic tires.	12	15	18

1955 FORD TANKER TRUCK: (1955-1960) Body and features painted red, yellow, or blue. Cab casting includes one-piece windshield; side door windows but no rear cab window; rounded front hood with Ford emblem; protruding front fenders below hood with headlights and horizontal front grille; directional lights between front bumper and headlights; small running boards at side doors; open front wheel wells; tanker body covering rear wheels. Tank has three fuel ports on top; simulated handrail on both sides of tank; double rear doors and taillights; rear bumper; tank support body with three equipment doors on each side. Rear axle mounted inside of truck body; smooth rubber tires. CHICAGO TOOTSIETOY U.S.A.

	G	E	LN
(A) As described above.	10	18	20
(B) Patterned plastic tires.	10	15	18

1956 TRIUMPH TR-3: (1963-1969) Two-seat sports car; body and features painted green, red, blue, yellow, or orange. Body casting includes a detailed interior with twin bucket seats, steering wheel, dashboard without windshield, and open area behind seats; long sloping front and rear fenders with open wheel wells; front headlights protruding from inside of front fenders; oval-shaped front grille; thin front bumper with bumper guards; large rear trunk with TRIUMPH below. Patterned plastic tires. TOOTSIETOY TRIUMPH TR-3 CHICAGO 24 U.S.A.
12 15 18

1957 FORD FAIRLANE 500 CONVERTIBLE: (1959-1969) Two-door convertible; body and features painted red, blue, or green. Body casting includes molded front windshield; detailed interior; front and rear seats; tour cover behind rear seat; steering wheel; sweeping style line from front fender through side door and up along top of rear fender fin; headlights in front fenders between front grille; front bumper extending around front of car to front wheel wells; large round taillights; rear bumper with cutout for license plate; open wheel wells in front and rear. Patterned plastic tires. TOOTSIETOY CHICAGO 24 FORD USA. 10 18 20

1957 FORD PICKUP TRUCK: (1959-1964, 1968-1969) Body and features painted yellow, green, or orange. Body casting includes cab with large wraparound windshield; side door window each side; molded or open rear cab window; open wheel wells; wide, flat front hood with seven style lines across top; front fenders with headlights between front grille; hood rest on top of fenders; front bumper; styled side rear body with closed rear tailgate; back bumper; wheel wells inside of truck bed. Smooth rubber tires. FORD TRUCK TOOTSIETOY CHICAGO 24 USA.

	G	E	LN
(A) As described above; open rear window.	8	12	15
(B) Patterned plastic tires; molded rear window.	6	8	12

1957 FORMULA D JAGUAR: (1959-1960) Single-seat sports car; body and features painted green. Body casting includes detailed interior with open driver's seat on right side of car, detailed seat, headrest, steering wheel, and molded windshield around driver's compartment; long wide front hood with fenders protruding out of hood; four small air vents on top of hood; rounded front headlights in smooth body front; no bumper; rounded rear of car, with headrest extending from back of driver's seat to rear of car; open wheel wells. Patterned plastic tires. TOOTSIETOY CHICAGO 24 USA JAGUAR.
10 18 20

1957 PLYMOUTH BELVEDERE: (1959-1969) Two-door hardtop; body and features painted blue or red. Body casting includes one-piece windshield; large side windows; single rear window; wide, flat front hood and trunk; wide front fenders with parking lights and headlights; horizontal grille between fenders; slanting style line on car sides from front fenders to end of rear tail fin; rear fenders containing a raised fin; thin cast bumpers on front and rear. Open wheel wells in front and rear; patterned plastic tires. TOOTSIETOY PLYMOUTH USA CHICAGO 24.
10 18 20

1960 STUDEBAKER LARK CONVERTIBLE: (1960-1964, 1968-1969) Two-door open convertible; body and features painted teal green, green, yellow, blue, or red. Body casting includes front and rear seat; steering wheel and molded front windshield; tour cover behind rear seat; square-style hood with large horizontal front grille; headlights in fender behind front grille; front and rear bumpers with bumper guards; license plate in front and rear; square-style rear trunk which does not extend over rear of car. Open front and rear wheel wells; patterned plastic tires. TOOTSIETOY CHICAGO 24 U.S.A. LARK. 10 15 18

1960 FORD FALCON: (1961-1964, 1968-1969) Two-door sedan; body and features painted red, blue, or orange. Body casting includes one-piece windshield; two side windows on each side; single rear window; wide flat hood with raised panel in the middle; headlights in fender; wide patterned front grille between headlights; two style lines along body sides; sloping rear trunk and rear fenders; small round taillights; rear bumper with license plate. Open wheel wells front and rear; patterned plastic tires. TOOTSIETOY CHICAGO 24 U.S.A. FALCON.
7 10 12

1960 FORD RANCH WAGON: (1962-1964, 1967) Four-door station wagon; body and features painted blue. Body casting includes one-piece windshield; three side windows with air vent window on each side; single rear window; front and rear bumpers with license plates numbered 1969; dual headlights in patterned front grille; FORD on rear tailgate. Open wheel wells front and rear; rear wheel supports visible through side windows; patterned plastic tires. TOOTSIETOY FORD RANCH WAGON CHICAGO 24 U.S.A. 10 15 18

HOT ROD MODEL B: (1961-1964, 1968-1969) Hot rod body probably a 1931 or 1932 Ford. Body and features painted red, blue, or green. Body casting includes a detailed motor; single seat; steering wheel; dash display; protruding square front grille; protruding headlights; half front fenders; no rear

Top: *Indianapolis Racer, S. Butler Collection; 1954 Volkswagen; and 1957 Ford Pickup Truck with molded rear window.* **Middle:** *1960 Ford Ranch Wagon; 1960 Studebaker Lark Convertible; and 1957 Ford Pickup Truck with open rear window.* **Bottom:** *1960 Ford Falcon and Hot Rod Model B.*

	G	E	LN
fenders; spare tire molded in rear trunk; small rear bumper. Patterned plastic tires. TOOTSIETOY CHICAGO U.S.A. MODEL B.	10	13	15

INDIANAPOLIS RACER: (1949-1954) "Indy 500" racing car; body and features painted orange, silver, red, blue, or green. Body casting includes driver's seat; two rows of lower vents along top of engine cover in front of seat; rounded front with horizontal grille; numeral 3 cast behind driver's seat on each side; air vents in lower body panel between front and rear wheels on both sides. Smooth rubber tires outside of racer body. TOOTSIETOY MADE IN U.S.A. 15 22 25

CIVILIAN JEEP: (1952-1955, 1958-1961) World War II Willys-style Jeep; body and features painted red, orange, or yellow. Body casting includes detailed interior with two front seats, steering wheel, and dashboard details; no windshield; five-point star in a circle on hood, with star pointing toward seats; large vertical grille with headlight on each side under hood area; small front fenders open at front of jeep; open wheel wells in front and rear; front protruding bumper; no rear bumper. Smooth rubber tires. TOOTSIETOY JEEP CHICAGO U.S.A.

	G	E	LN
(A) As described above.	8	12	15
(B) Same as (A); patterned plastic tires.	8	10	12

In 1957, General Mills ran a promotional campaign featuring Tootsietoy vehicles from the 3-inch series of cars and trucks. On specially marked boxes of Cheerios® cereal, the company featured five different "Cheerios City" buildings including a drive-in, supermarket, school, City Hall, and gas station. Inside the box, a sheet of directions was included to explain how to obtain special sets of four 3-inch Tootsietoy vehicles with a metal road sign and instructions for making streets, fences, hedges, lawns, and trees for the city. Interested parties could send fifty cents, the words "The oat cereal ready to eat" from a Cheerios box top, and their names and addresses to the address provided. Each set came in a plain brown cardboard box. The sets photographed for this volume contained the following: the first set had two 1949 American LaFrance Fire Trucks, one 1949 Coach Bus, and one 1955 Thunderbird. The second set had two 1949 Chevy Panel Trucks, one 1955 Thunderbird, and one 1955 Ford. The third had two 1949 Coach Buses and two Civilian Jeeps. The fourth had two 1949 Ford Pickup Trucks and two 1955 Tanker Trucks. The sets sold for $80 to $105 each in 1992.

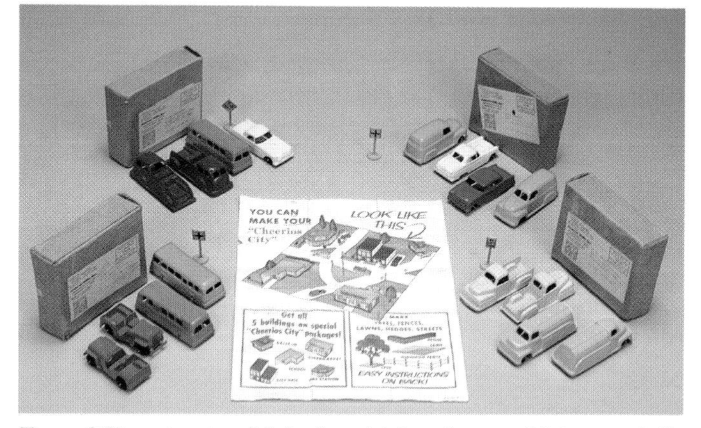

Four different sets of 3-inch vehicles that could be specially ordered from General Mills in 1957, with the layout instruction sheet included with each set. J. Gibson Collection.

CHAPTER 7

Tractor Trailer Trucks

The Tootsietoy truck and trailer series are perhaps the finest in quality of all the series created during the postwar years. The quality of the trailers is especially excellent throughout the many years of production. Not until the mid-sixties—when plastic trailers were introduced—was there any type of reduction in the overall quality of these fine pieces.

The company began the series with the Diamond T Tractor Truck, which was offered with four different trailers after World War II—an auto transport, a shipping van, a machinery trailer, and a utility trailer. In the past, the Diamond T Tractor Truck has been identified by various collectors and publications as a 1940 International Truck. (See Chapter 3 for further information.) While the trucking manufacturers were designing a more modern-looking truck with flush-mounted headlights, most continued to use protruding headlights on their tractor trucks through 1949. It is therefore difficult to determine an exact model year for the Tootsietoy version with flush-mounted headlights. The other features incorporated by Dowst on this tractor truck that resemble a Diamond T are its low profile, the roof design, the roof running lights, and the overall cab appearance. The real 1940 International Tractor Truck does not contain any of these features. The year 1947 has been assigned to these Diamond T trucks since it was the year established for this first 6-inch tractor trailer series. It is not necessarily the correct model year for this truck; a year could not be verified. The Diamond T units are catalogued as part of the 6-inch series, though the actual length of the trucks and trailers is close to 9 inches combined.

The two types of trailer connection.

All of these toys are fairly common at this time, though the van and the machinery trailers may be more difficult to locate. The auto transport is difficult to find with all of the original 3-inch vehicles. (See Chapter 11 for all the known variations of vehicles included in boxed sets with this piece.)

In the early fifties, a 1947 Mack trailer truck was introduced, and the company then offered both the 1947 Diamond T trailer series and the 1947 Mack trailer series for a number of years. The Mack series differed from the Diamond T series in a number of ways. It offered the first tanker trailer truck as well as a stakeside trailer, a hook and ladder fire trailer, and a log and pipe trailer, but it did not include an auto transport trailer. The utility trailer, the van trailer, and the machinery trailer were a bit larger than those in the Diamond T series, although similar in design and detailing. The method for hooking the trailer to the tractor truck was redesigned in 1947 Mack so that the two pieces could be locked together.

The stakeside trailer contains five removable side sections, making this unit difficult to find intact and, consequently, a wonderful find. The hook and ladder trailer may have actually had its origins in the 1947 Diamond T tractor trailer series. A 1947 Diamond T Hook and Ladder Truck is shown on the gift box cover for set No. 5211 and is featured in the 1955 dealer catalogue. However, in order for this unit to have been manufactured, changes in the trailer or truck connection and in the truck wheels were necessary, since the 1947 Diamond T truck tires are much smaller than those on the hook and ladder trailer. It is interesting to note that the picture in the 1955 catalogue shows oversized tires on the 1947 Diamond T Tractor Truck; however, to date, collectors have not reported finding one with these.

The 1947 Mack series also contained a number of difficult-to-find variations. The tanker trailer was made with a rear ladder cast in and without one. A Pure Oil tanker trailer pulled by a 1947 Mack truck was made, though many collectors are not aware of it, and therefore it should be considered rare.

The shipping van trailer truck for this series was first developed as a two-piece casting without any rear trailer doors. The van trailer was later redesigned with a removable tin top, cast body, and operating rear doors. Unfortunately, when the tin top is slid forward, these rear door units can be removed and easily misplaced. Thus, all van trailers with operating rear doors should be considered more collectible. Possibly as a cost-savings measure, the company also produced the tin-top version without the rear doors. Some van trailers feature a removable tandem wheel assembly made for the Bild-A-Truck gift set. This van, more than any other, was used with promotional advertising for various companies.

The 1947 Mack Log Trailer and Pipe Trailer were both featured in the catalogue. The log trailer was developed with both a fixed and a removable rear wheel assembly. Log trailers with the fixed assembly are not very difficult to find; pieces with the removable assembly pieces are usually only found in gift sets or single boxed units. The pipe trailer remains an unconfirmed item. The information included on it was provided by several collectors.

By the late fifties, the company introduced two new lines of tractor trucks: a 1955 Mack Tractor Truck and a 1955 International Tractor Truck. The 1947 Diamond T trucks were phased out, but the 1947 Mack line was featured off and on into the sixties. The last 1947 Mack trailer truck appeared in 1967 before being phased out. With the development of the new trucks, different trailer connections were incorporated. The 1955 Mack trailer trucks utilized the 1947 Mack connection, while the 1955 International Trailer Truck used the older 1947 Diamond T pin connection.

The 1955 Mack trailer series featured almost all of the trailers developed for the 1947 Mack series with the exception of the stakeside trailer and the van trailers with operating doors. It did not feature any new designs. All of the 1947 Mack trailers are interchangeable for use behind a 1955 Mack truck.

The 1955 International trailer series featured a number of new trailers, since none of the older 1947 Diamond T trailers were used. The most important of these new trailers is an auto transport trailer which took the place of the 1947 Diamond T model. The new all-metal trailer included a loading ramp for the first time and was produced in two variations: with tandem single wheels and with a single wheel axle assembly. This pressed tin trailer remained in production until the early sixties when it was replaced with a plastic trailer. The 1955 International series contained a newly designed machinery trailer; it is smaller than the trailer used in the Mack series. All of the units in this series are not difficult to find, and the challenge to a collector is only to find the auto transports *with* the loading ramp! The company used this series of trailers for the military trailer trucks, such as the rocket launcher, the machinery trailer, and an as-yet unconfirmed but advertised Army auto transport trailer. For further information on military trailer trucks, see Chapter 8.

The company later made a slight change in the casting of the 1955 International tractor truck: the design for the single front headlights was modified to a wide flat panel, and dual headlights were painted on it. This change may have reflected the use of dual headlights on many 1958 prototype cars and trucks. For this reason, these toys are identified as 1958 International Tractor Trucks in this chapter, and each listing includes whether the truck is found with or without painted headlights. This truck was offered with all of the trailer units and military units in the 1955 International series. When this modification actually occurred is not known since the company continued to show the 1955 model in its catalogues.

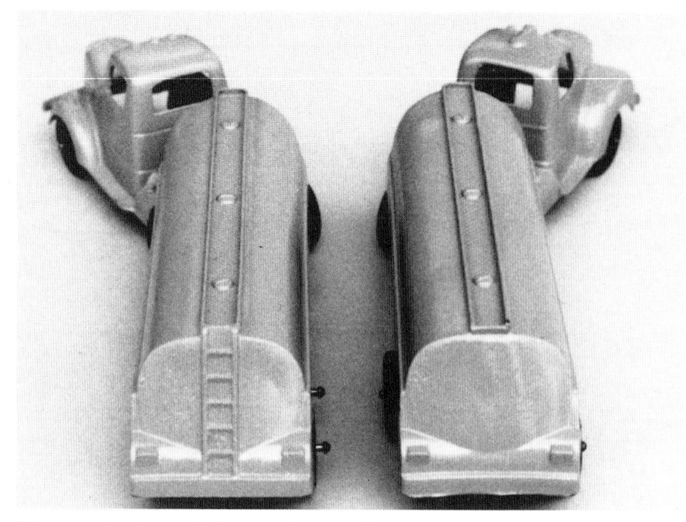
Two variations of the tanker trailer.

In 1965 and 1966, Strombecker introduced a completely new tractor truck which is identified here as a 1959 Chevrolet. It must have been dropped because it does not appear in the 1967 catalogue. Some collectors believe this very short production run was caused by problems with the new casting. This tractor truck is one of the most difficult items in the tractor-trailer-truck series to find today. The 1955 International truck with the machinery trailer was the only other trailer truck offered in 1966.

In 1967 Strombecker went back to producing the 1955 Mack, 1955 International, and 1947 Mack tractor trucks to pull various trailers. Although the 1955 Mack was primarily featured, the 1947 Mack included the hook and ladder fire trailer, and the 1955 International was offered with a moving van that had a plastic body on a metal frame and contained a single operating rear door.

In 1968, however, the hook and ladder fire trailer and the log and tanker trailers were again packaged with the 1955 Mack trailer truck. The 1955 International was used with an auto transport and a boat transport trailer, both of which were made in plastic. The Mack and the International trucks were only featured in red without painted features. By 1969 the tractor trailer series was reduced to one 1955 Mack truck pulling a Mobil tanker trailer. It was only issued in red and did not have painted features.

For ready reference, a chart has been included in this chapter to quickly identify the various types of trailers paired with the proper tractor truck. In the listings, each different series of tractor truck is identified in detail first before the descriptions of the various trailers that were paired with them. Some tractor trucks were produced with different tires and cast-in identification variations. Each truck variation has been identified as a Type I, II, III, etc., in a sequence based on actual production. For the most part, these variations in the tractor truck have not accounted for great differences in value. Collectors should first look for the difficult-to-find units described above, and then for all units containing stickers that have not

Tractor Truck and Trailer Combinations

Trailers	Tractor Trucks 1947 Diamond T	1947 Mack	1955 International	1955 Mack	1958 International	1959 Chevrolet
Utility Trailer	1	2	2	2	2	—
Transport Trailer	1	—	1, 3, b, p, r	1, b, p	1, b, p	1, b, p
Van Trailer	1	2, a	1, p	2	1, p	1
Tanker Trailer	—	2	2	2	2	2
Fire Ladder Trailer	1, u	1	—	1	—	1
Stakeside Trailer	—	2, a, s	—	—	—	—
Log Trailer	—	2, a	—	2	—	2
Pipe Trailer	—	2, a, u	—	2, u	—	—
Machinery Trailer	2	2	t	2	t	—

Trailer Codes

1–single-axle wheels
2–double-axle tandem wheels
3–double-axle wheels
a–adjustable trailer and wheel assembly
b–boat/car load
p–plastic trailer with ramp
r–metal trailer with loading ramp
s–removable sides
t–single tandem wheels
u–unconfirmed

been removed. In some cases, color variations can be important; the 1947 Mack Hook and Ladder Truck has been found in mint condition with silver-painted running boards on the truck and on the trailer. Since the most common version of this unit is red, this piece is a valuable find.

Determining both production years and variations for each of these trailer truck toys is difficult. As various changes were being made to trailer use and load, the catalogues frequently did not show the changes; the same picture was depicted over and over. Consequently, a number of variations are known to exist but the year of manufacture is uncertain. Since so many of these units are interchangeable, different combinations continue to surface. Cast-in information on the underside of each vehicle appears last in each listing.

1947 Diamond T Tractor Trucks

The 1947 Diamond T Tractor Trucks can be found in three variations:

Type I is cast with a large flat front bumper, a semi-rounded hood and front fenders, headlights flush with the face of the fender, a running light on top of each fender, air vents on each side of the truck hood, front hood trim, a two-piece windshield, oversized side windows and a rear window, three running lights on the cab roof, and running boards under the side doors. The body covers the front wheel wells. The front axle extends through the body casting and the rear single axle extends through the body frame. The trailer connection is a short pin. It has smooth black rubber tires with axle spacers. TOOTSIETOY MADE IN U.S.A. is cast underneath the truck hood, and 1 is under the roof.

Type II is the same as Type I except that the trailer connection is a long pin and 2 is under the roof.

Type III is the same as Type I, with a short pin as the trailer connection and 2 under the roof.

1947 DIAMOND T FIRE LADDER TRAILER TRUCK: (1953-1955) This truck is shown on the box cover of set No. 5211, which was featured in a 1955 dealer's catalogue; the ladder trailer appears to be the same as one that comes with the 1947 Mack trailer truck. The rear tires of the trailer, however, are too large for the tractor truck and the pin connection on the tractor truck is not compatible with the ladder trailer. It may not have been manufactured in this configuration. **NRS**

	G	E	LN

1947 DIAMOND T MACHINERY HAULER: (1949-1958) 9" unit. Two-piece Type I or III tractor truck with machinery hauler; trailer also known as a low-boy or gooseneck trailer. Tractor truck is painted red, orange, blue, or green with silver-painted front bumper, grille, and headlights. Machinery trailer is painted red, orange, blue, or green. Units can be found with different truck and trailer colors or both painted the same color. The trailer's very low profile causes the bed to be lower than the truck and trailer connection. The raised trailer connection contains a hole near the front of the trailer that fits over the truck pin. The main part of the trailer bed is cast to simulate wood plank flooring. Dual tandem rear wheels; small smooth rubber tires with axle spacers. TOOTSIETOY MADE IN U.S.A.

	G	E	LN
(A) Type I truck and trailer same color.	30	50	55
(B) Type I truck and trailer different colors.	25	50	55
(C) Type III truck and trailer same color.	25	50	55
(D) Type III truck and trailer different colors.	25	50	55

1947 DIAMOND T SHIPPING VAN: (1949-1958) 9" unit. Two-piece shipping van with Type I or Type III tractor truck and trailer floor-and-frame piece painted red or green; silver-painted front bumper, grille, and headlights; trailer sides-and-roof piece is painted green or silver. Trailer has no rear doors; single rear axle; smooth rubber tires with axle spacer. TOOTSIETOY TRUCK LINE on van sides. Trailer van held to trailer body by six slots with tabs. TOOTSIETOY MADE IN U.S.A..

	G	E	LN
(A) Type I truck with trailer.	30	45	50
(B) Type III truck with trailer.	30	45	50

1947 DIAMOND T TRANSPORT TRAILER TRUCK: (1949-1958) Two-piece transport trailer truck; Type II tractor truck painted red with silver-painted front bumper, grille, and headlights. Double-deck vehicle transport trailer painted yellow, light yellow, or orange. Trailer has a one-piece stamped

Top: *1947 Diamond T Transport Trailer Truck (auto transport) with its original box, S. Butler Collection.* **Upper left:** *1947 Diamond T Shipping Van.* **Upper right:** *1947 Diamond T Auto Transport, S. Butler Collection.* **Middle:** *1947 Diamond T Utility Trailer Truck.* **Bottom:** *1947 Diamond T Machinery Hauler.*

Variations of the 1947 and 1955 Mack Tractor Truck.

G E LN

and folded tin body and holds up to four 3" vehicles. Trailer front has a solid flat protruding tongue with hole which slips over truck pin. Trailer floor has punched-out tabs on top and bottom to hold vehicles in place or to attach a loading ramp. No loading ramp is known to have been included. Single rear axle; smooth rubber tires with axle spacer. No company markings on trailer. See Chapter 11 for a listing of 3" vehicles used with this trailer, and the value of the toy with those loads.

(A) Yellow transport trailer with oval-shaped openings on sides; without vehicle load. **30 50 55**

(B) Orange transport trailer with diagonally shaped openings on trailer sides; without vehicle load. **30 50 55**

1947 DIAMOND T UTILITY TRAILER TRUCK: (1949-1958) 9" unit. Two-piece Type I or III trailer truck; trailer is sometimes identified as a stakeside, low-side, or grain trailer. Tractor truck painted red, green, orange, blue, or yellow with silver-painted front bumper, grille, and headlights. Trailer painted red, green, orange, blue, or yellow. Units can be found with the truck and trailer painted same or different colors. One-piece molded trailer body has rounded front; hole in floor fits over

Top: *1947 Mack "Coast To Coast" Van Trailer Truck and 1947 Mack "Middle States Motors" Van Trailer Truck with their original boxes, S. Butler Collection.* **Middle:** *1947 Mack Stakeside Trailer Truck and 1947 Mack Fire Ladder Trailer Truck with their original boxes, S. Butler Collection.* **Bottom:** *1947 Mack Utility Trailer Truck.*

tractor truck pin; single axle assembly; smooth rubber tires with axle spacer. TOOTSIETOY MADE IN U.S.A.

	G	E	LN
(A) Type I truck and trailer same color.	30	45	50
(B) Type I truck and trailer different colors.	25	40	45
(C) Type III truck and trailer same color.	20	35	40
(D) Type III truck and trailer different colors.	20	35	40

1947 Mack Tractor Trucks

The 1947 Mack Tractor Truck is available in six variations:

Type I is cast with running lights on the roof and front fenders; headlights protruding from the fenders on either side of large vertical front grille; two-piece front windshield; cab side windows and rear cab window; open front wheel wells; gas tanks behind the truck cab; raised round opening with a notch on each side of the opening for the trailer connection; 1 cast under the roof and TOOTSIETOY MADE IN U.S.A. under rear of truck body. It has black rubber tires with a tread pattern on the sidewalls only, and axle pins with axle spacers. Dual rear wheels are made up of two individual tires for each tire set.

Type II has the same features as Type I except for larger window areas on the truck; 2 cast under the truck roof; slightly larger Tootsietoy tires with tread; and rear wheels molded to simulate dual tires.

Type III also has the same features as Type I except 3 cast under the truck roof and TOOTSIETOY CHICAGO U.S.A. under the rear of the truck body.

Type IV is the same as Type III except for a 4 cast under the truck roof. Its axle and tires are the same as Type II.

Type V is a variation developed for the hook and ladder trailer. This truck features a single rear tire assembly, no roof running lights or gas tanks, and no casting identification. A single warning light is cast into the roof with a running light on each front fender. The axles contain pins and axle spacers. The Tootsietoy tires are the larger rubber type with tread. All other body features remained unchanged.

Type VI is the same as Type V except there are no axle spacers; thin plastic tires; TOOTSIETOY CHICAGO 24 U.S.A. cast under the hood.

1947 MACK FIRE LADDER TRAILER TRUCK: (1956-1961, 1963-1965, 1967) 8¾" unit. Two-piece fire truck remained in production until 1967. Truck and trailer are both painted red with silver front bumper, grille, and ladder assembly on trailer. Tractor truck is a 1947 Mack Type V or VI above. Trailer features

G E LN

fenders with open wheel wells; two-piece ladder assembly; single axle and tire assembly; TOOTSIETOY MADE IN U.S.A. cast underneath. Ladder assembly on trailer may be rotated or moved up or down. Ladder base is part of trailer connection to tractor truck; it contains a small spring extending from ladder base to tractor truck axle when connected. This causes tension on ladder assembly and allows ladder to be moved to any upright position.

(A) Type V truck; trailer with patterned rubber Tootsietoy tires and axle spacers. **55 75 85**

(B) Type VI truck; trailer with patterned plastic Tootsietoy tires, no axle spacers. **50 70 80**

(C) Same as (A) or (B) but missing ladder extension piece. **45 60 65**

(D) Same as (A) with silver-painted running boards. Rare. S. Butler Collection. **60 80 90**

1947 MACK LOG TRAILER TRUCK: (1955-1959, 1961, 1963-1965) 9" unit. Tractor truck painted red or green. The trailer is a steel flat rod which connects the front trailer connection with the rear dual tandem wheel assembly. All metal parts are unpainted. It is common to find a mint trailer with some rust on the steel rod. The front trailer connection piece has a flat surface and is about 1¼" in width; at each end is a short pin which helps hold the log load on the trailer. The rear truck assembly also contains a short pin on each side of the assembly. Just beyond these pins is a groove to hold a rubber band which secures six 6" wooden logs. There is no casting identification on the trailer.

(A) A combination of the Type I and Type II tractor truck. 1 cast under cab roof; TOOTSIETOY MADE IN U.S.A. under rear body. Patterned rubber Tootsietoy tires on front with axle spacers; patterned rubber rear dual tires without "Tootsietoy" on sidewall; dual tires are a one-piece molded unit. Trailer contains single patterned rubber tires held by pins and axle spacers making up the tandem wheel assembly. Trailer is adjustable; front and rear assembly can be removed from steel rod. Rear wheel assembly held by a removable pin; steel rod contains four adjustment holes to change location of rear wheel assembly. **50 70 75**

(B) Type II truck; log trailer is not adjustable; rear wheel assembly attached to flat rod; no adjustable holes in flat rod. Front trailer connection is pressed into L-shaped flat rod. Trailer has patterned rubber Tootsietoy tires molded to simulate dual wheels, with axle spacers. **45 60 65**

1947 MACK MACHINERY TRAILER TRUCK: (1956-1960) Two-piece unit produced in a variety of color combinations. Truck and trailer painted red, green, or orange. Trailer sometimes identified as a low-boy or gooseneck trailer. Trailer contains a long depressed section between trailer connection and rear wheel assembly; dual tandem rear wheels are smaller than tractor truck tires; smooth rubber tires, no axle spacers. TOOTSIETOY CHICAGO U.S.A.

(A) Type I truck and trailer same color. **50 75 80**

(B) Type II truck and trailer same color. **50 75 80**

(C) Type IV truck and trailer different colors. **40 70 75**

1947 MACK PIPE TRAILER TRUCK: (Date unknown) 9" unit. Tractor truck painted red or green. Trailer body is a steel flat rod which connects the front trailer connection with

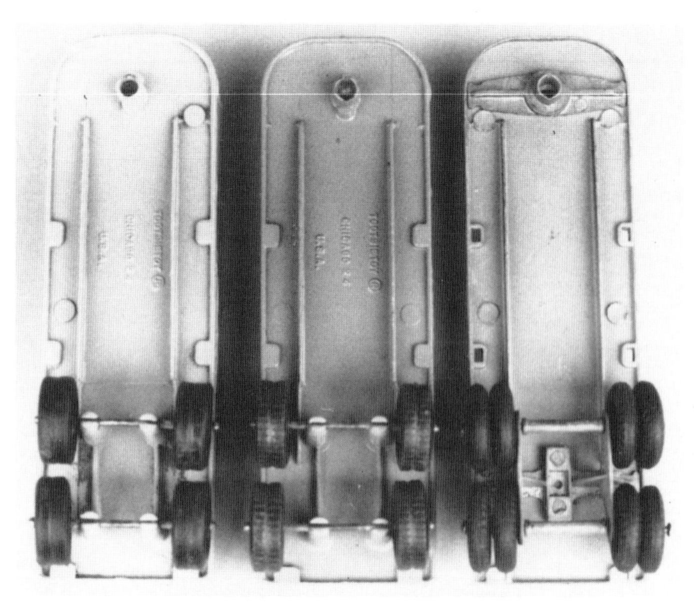

Variations of the utility trailer wheel assembly and trailer connection. The version on the left was made in Mexico.

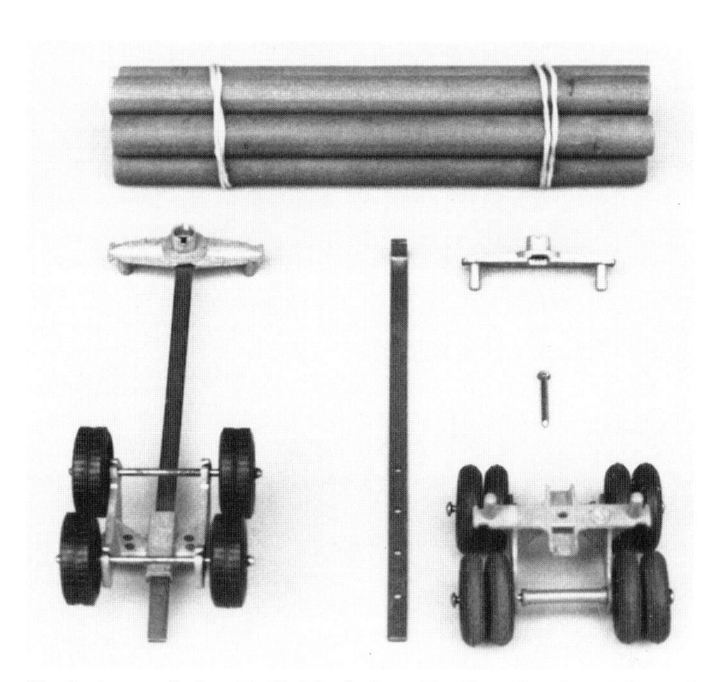

Variations of the 1947 Mack Log Trailer Truck, with and without an adjustable assembly.

G E LN

the rear dual tandem wheel assembly. All metal parts are unpainted. It is common to find a trailer in untouched condition with some rust on the steel rod. The front trailer connection has a flat surface about 1¼" in width. A pin at each end helps hold the pipe load on the trailer. A groove next to each pin holds a rubber band to secure the load of pipes. Six silver-gray plastic 6" pipes. No casting identification on trailer.

(A) Type II truck and pipe trailer with patterned rubber tires and axle spacers. Trailer is adjustable: front and rear cross frame can be removed from main body rod. Rod contains four

	G	E	LN
holes to change location of rear wheel assembly, which is held by a pin.	45	85	95
(B) Type II truck; pipe trailer is not adjustable; trailer tires are patterned rubber Tootsietoy tires; simulated molded dual tires with axle spacers.	45	70	80
(C) Same as (A) but missing pipe load.	30	50	60
(D) Same as (B) but missing pipe load.	25	45	50

1947 MACK STAKESIDE TRAILER TRUCK: (1954-1959) 9″ unit. Two-piece stakeside truck; Type I tractor truck painted red or green with silver-painted features including front bumper and grille. Stakeside trailer painted green; trailer has a short front section of solid siding included with floor casting and five pieces of removable stakeside panels, two on each side and one at back of trailer painted green or natural cast-metal finish; dual tandem wheels with axle spacers. Each dual wheel is made up of two separate tires. U.S.A.

	G	E	LN
(A) Type I truck; trailer contains removable rear wheel assembly and removable trailer connection. From No. 7600 Bild-A-Truck Set. Rare.	60	100	120
(B) Type III truck; trailer contains pressed connections for rear wheel assembly and trailer connection.	55	100	115
(C) Same as (A) or (B) but missing stakeside panels.	35	50	55

1947 MACK TANKER TRAILER TRUCK: (1954-1959) 9″ unit. Two-piece tanker trailer with variations. Tractor truck painted red, blue, black, orange, or green with silver front bumper and grille. Tanker body painted red, silver, orange, blue, or green. One-piece tanker trailer casting includes a walkway along the entire length of the top of the tank with three filler ports in the walkway. Some units include a rear ladder. Dual tandem wheels.

	G	E	LN
(A) Type II truck painted black; trailer painted orange with a see-through TOOTSIETOY LINE SERVING YOUNG AMERICA sticker in black lettering; rear ladder. TOOTSIETOY CHICAGO 24 U.S.A.	45	65	75
(B) Type II truck painted red; trailer painted red with blue and white MOBIL sticker on tanker sides and rear; no rear ladder. TOOTSIETOY CHICAGO 24 U.S.A.	55	75	85
(C) Type II truck; truck and trailer painted red, orange, or green; trailer includes rear ladder. TOOTSIETOY CHICAGO 24 U.S.A.	45	60	65
(D) Same as (C) without rear ladder.	35	50	60
(E) Type III truck; trailer has blue PURE OIL COMPANY paper sticker on tank sides; truck and trailer painted blue. Included in No. 7600 Bild-A-Truck Set. Rare.	55	80	90

1947 MACK UTILITY TRAILER TRUCK: (1960-1963) 9″ unit. Two-piece utility trailer produced in a variety of color combinations. Tractor truck painted red, yellow, orange, blue, or green; utility trailer painted red, yellow, orange, blue, or green. Trailer also known as a low-side, stakeside, or grain trailer. Trailer open in the rear; sides contain four supports in solid casting; front of trailer rounded at the corners; rear dual tandem tires. TOOTSIETOY CHICAGO 24 U.S.A.

	G	E	LN
(A) Type II truck and utility trailer painted same color; patterned rubber tires with no axle spacers; simulated dual Tootsietoy tires.	25	45	55

Variations of the 1955 and 1958 International Tractor Truck.

	G	E	LN
(B) Type IV truck and utility trailer same color; trailer same as (A) above.	25	45	55
(C) Same as (A) except truck and trailer different colors.	20	40	50
(D) Same as (B) except truck and trailer different colors.	20	40	50

1947 MACK VAN TRAILER TRUCK: (1954-1959) 9½″ unit. Two-piece van trailer with many variations. All types of tractor truck can be found with the van trailer except for Type V and VI. Two-piece trailer body design with or without operating rear doors. The first version of trailer has one piece cast for the sides and roof and a second piece cast for the trailer frame and flooring; no rear doors. The next version has a one-piece cast frame and van sides; a stamped-tin van roof which slipped over a ridge at the top of the van sides; rear doors. Some pieces have been found without the doors. Dual tandem wheels with axle spacers.

	G	E	LN
(A) Type I truck; trailer with one-piece cast sides and roof and cast trailer frame. Truck painted red, trailer frame painted red, roof and trailer sides painted silver; no rear doors; SERVING YOUNG AMERICA on clear sticker on each side of trailer.	55	70	75
(B) Type I truck; trailer has one-piece frame and sides, tin top. Truck painted red, frame and sides painted silver, top painted red. TOOTSIETOY COAST TO COAST cast in on both sides; rear doors.	60	75	80
(C) Type II truck; trailer has one-piece frame and sides, tin top. Truck painted red; frame, sides, and top painted silver; GERARD MOTOR EXPRESS sticker on van sides; rear doors.	70	85	90
(D) Type II truck; trailer same as (B) above.	55	70	75
(E) Type III truck; trailer same as (B) above.	60	75	80
(F) Type IV truck; trailer same as (B) above.	55	70	75
(G) Same as (B) without rear doors.	40	55	60
(H) Same as (C) without rear doors.	55	70	75
(I) Same as (C) except no lettering or advertisement on van sides.	55	75	80

(Above) **Top:** *1947 Mack Log Trailer Truck with its original box; 1947 Mack "Libbys" Van Trailer Truck with its original box, K. Jestes Collection.* **Middle:** *1947 Mack "Serving Young America" Van Trailer Truck, K. Jestes Collection; 1947 Mack Tanker Trailer Truck with original box, S. Butler Collection.* **Bottom:** *1947 Mack "Serving Young America" Tanker Trailer Truck.*

(Below) **Top:** *1955 International Auto Transport with tandem trailer wheels and its original box, S. Butler Collection.* **Bottom:** *1955 International Auto Transport with single trailer wheels, S. Butler Collection.*

Top: *1955 International Tanker Trailer Truck.* **Middle:** *1955 International Utility Trailer Truck.* **Bottom:** *1955 International Machinery Trailer Truck with dozer, S. Butler Collection, and 1947 Mack Machinery Trailer Truck with dozer.*

G E LN

(J) Same as (B) but contains removable tandem wheel assembly and trailer connection. From No. 7600 Bild-A-Truck Set. Rare. **60 95 100**

(K) Same as (A) except truck is black and trailer is orange with TOOTSIETOY LINE SERVING YOUNG AMERICA on clear sticker on sides of van trailer. **55 70 75**

(L) Same as (C) with MIDDLE STATES sticker on silver van trailer truck; truck cab is green. S. Butler Collection. **55 85 90**

(M) Same as (C) with LIBBY'S FROZEN FOOD sticker in red and blue lettering on a light blue cloud background on each side of trailer. Trailer painted silver with red top and truck. K. Jestes Collection. **55 85 90**

(N) Silver truck; same as (C) with OLSON TRANSPORTATION COMPANY SERVING WISCONSIN / GREEN BAY / CHICAGO sticker in black lettering; cab painted red. D. Campbell Collection. **55 85 90**

1955 International Tractor Trucks

The 1955 International Tractor Truck came in three variations:

The body casting of **Type I** features a short front hood with a lower grille; air vents above the grille; narrow front fenders with headlights; an International Harvester emblem on the hood; a one-piece windshield; a door window and a rear cab window; small running boards with a step behind each front fender; open front wheel wells; dual gas tanks behind the truck cab; and a protruding pin for the trailer connection. Patterned rubber Tootsietoy tires are on the front; the rear tires are one piece molded as two tires with no markings on the sidewall; there are no axle spacers, and no running lights on the roof or fenders. TOOTSIETOY CHICAGO 24 U.S.A. is cast underneath. It has silver-painted features, but no other markings.

Type II is the same as Type I except a 2 is cast under the front hood, and TOOTSIETOY CHICAGO 24 U.S.A. is cast under the rear body.

Type III is the same as Type I except that the front wheels are patterned plastic Tootsietoy tires, the rear tires are molded dual plastic Tootsietoy tires, and there are no axle spacers. The body and features are painted same color.

G E LN

1955 INTERNATIONAL MACHINERY TRAILER TRUCK: (1963-1966) Two-piece unit produced in a variety of color combinations; tractor truck red, yellow, blue, orange, or green. Some units have silver-painted features including the front bumper, lower grille, and headlights. Long flat trailer with simulated wood flooring painted red, yellow, blue, orange, or green. Raised trailer connection with hole in casting for tractor truck pin. Raised box on each side of rear of trailer over dual wheels. Molded dual tires; no axle spacers; tires same size as tractor truck tires. TOOTSIETOY CHICAGO 24 U.S.A. P-10334.

(A) Type I truck and trailer same color with painted features. **35 65 75**

(B) Type III truck and trailer same color; no painted features. Trailer has molded dual plastic Tootsietoy tires, no axle spacers. **30 60 70**

(C) Same as (B) except truck and trailer different colors; no painted features. **30 60 70**

1955 INTERNATIONAL TANKER TRAILER TRUCK: (1962) Two-piece unit produced in various color combinations; tractor truck red, yellow, blue, orange, or green. Silver-painted features include the front bumper, lower grille, and headlights. Tanker body includes a walkway along the entire length of the

G E LN

top of the tank with three filler ports located in the walkway. One-piece tanker trailer painted red, yellow, blue, orange, or green; dual tandem wheels. TOOTSIETOY CHICAGO 24 U.S.A.

(A) Type I truck and tanker trailer painted same color; painted features; molded dual tandem wheels; patterned rubber tires, no axle spacers. **25 50 60**

(B) Type I truck and tanker trailer painted red with blue and white MOBIL sticker on tanker sides and rear. Molded dual tandem wheels; patterned rubber Tootsietoy tires, no axle spacers; painted features. **30 60 70**

(C) Same as (A) with Type II tractor truck. **25 50 60**

(D) Type III truck and tanker trailer with molded dual tandem wheels; patterned plastic Tootsietoy tires; molded ladder on rear of tanker. Truck and trailer painted same color or mixed colors. **20 45 50**

1955 INTERNATIONAL TRANSPORT TRAILER TRUCK: (1959-1961) 9" unit. Vehicle transport trailer with two-piece tin trailer. Bottom piece is folded to form lower bed floor and side walls of trailer body. Top piece is pressed over body sides to form upper level of trailer. Tractor truck painted red, blue, or green with silver-painted features including front bumper, lower grille and headlights. Trailer painted yellow or dark yellow, single tire on axle, no axle spacer; no casting identification on trailer. Top level contains four stamped-out slots to hold two 3" vehicles. Rear slots also support removable loading ramp in play. Lower level contains two rear slots for vehicle tires or loading ramp, and a hole in front floor for tractor truck pin. Three large openings on each side.

(A) Type I truck; transport trailer with patterned rubber Tootsietoy tires, no axle spacers; loading ramp; 3" 1957 Ford Convertible, 3" 1955 Ford Two-Door Sedan; 3" 1949 Ford Pickup Truck. **75 115 125**

(B) Same as (A) with Type II truck. **75 115 125**

(C) Type III truck; truck body and features same color. Transport trailer with patterned Tootsietoy tires, no axle spacers; loading ramp. **45 65 70**

(D) Same as (A) or (B) without loading ramp and 3" vehicles. **35 45 50**

(E) Same as (C) without loading ramp. **30 40 45**

(F) Type I truck with patterned rubber Tootsietoy tires, no axle spacers; loading ramp; 3" 1949 American LaFrance Fire Truck; 1955 Ford; 1957 Jaguar. **75 110 120**

(G) Type II truck with patterned plastic Tootsietoy tires, no axle spacers; loading ramp; 3" 1955 Ford; 1954 Jaguar. **65 90 95**

(H) Tandem wheel trailer; tractor truck painted red or blue; patterned rubber tires, no axle spacers; loading ramp; 3" 1949 Ford Pickup Truck, 3" 1954 Ford Station Wagon; 3" Ford Sedan. No casting markings on trailer. S. Butler Collection. **75 115 125**

(I) Same as (H) without vehicles. **35 60 75**

(J) Same as (I) without loading ramp. **30 60 65**

1955 INTERNATIONAL UTILITY TRAILER TRUCK: (1962) Trailer sometimes called a stakeside, a low-side, or a grain trailer. Truck and trailer painted red, yellow, orange, medium green, green, or blue. Silver-painted features include front bumper, lower grille, and headlights. Solid-side trailer, open in rear; front of trailer rounded at each corner; molded dual tandem tires, no axle spacer. TOOTSIETOY CHICAGO 24 U.S.A.

G E LN

(A) Type I or II tractor truck with utility trailer, painted features; patterned rubber Tootsietoy tires, no axle spacers. **25 50 55**

(B) Type III tractor truck; molded patterned plastic Tootsietoy tires on trailer, no axle spacers; no painted features on truck. **25 45 50**

1955 INTERNATIONAL VAN TRAILER TRUCK: (1963-1964) See description for the 1958 International Moving Van. **30 60 65**

1955 Mack Tractor Trucks

The 1955 Mack Tractor Truck came in three variations:

Type I features large rounded front fenders, a large vertical front grille, headlights in the center of the front fenders, a one-piece windshield, and side and rear windows. The roof of the cab has two running lights with a molded air horn. The body also has running boards and dual gas tanks, open front wheel wells, and a raised open hole trailer connection. It rides on patterned rubber Tootsietoy tires, no axle spacers; molded dual rear rubber tires with no axle spacers. Its silver-painted features include the front bumper, grille, and headlights. TOOTSIETOY CHICAGO 24 U.S.A. is under the cab roof; 1 is under the rear.

Type II is the same as Type I except for patterned plastic Tootsietoy tires with no axle spacer in the front and molded dual rear plastic tires with no axle spacer. The body and features are painted the same color.

Type III is the same as Type II except for molded dual Tootsietoy tires in the rear; 2 under the rear of the truck.

1955 MACK AUTO TRANSPORT TRUCK: (1967) 9" unit. Type III tractor truck painted red; molded plastic transport trailer in blue or yellow with plastic loading ramp; TOOTSIETOY CHICAGO 24 U.S.A. P-10391 under trailer. Unit includes two 3" vehicles: a 1956 Triumph and a Hot Rod Model B.

(A) As described above. Rare. **45 75 80**

(B) Same as (A) but missing ramp. **30 60 70**

(C) Same as (A) but missing ramp and vehicles. **20 35 40**

1955 MACK BOAT TRANSPORT: (1967) 9" unit. Type III tractor truck painted red; molded plastic transport trailer in blue or yellow; TOOTSIETOY CHICAGO 24 U.S.A. P-10391 under trailer. Unit includes two plastic boats in brown and white.

(A) As described above. Rare. **50 75 80**

(B) Same as (A) but missing boat load. **20 35 40**

1955 MACK FIRE LADDER TRAILER TRUCK: (1968) 8½" unit. Truck and ladder trailer painted red; ladder painted silver on all units. Some units have silver-painted front bumper, front grille, and headlights. Ladder assembly on trailer may be rotated or moved up or down. Ladder base is part of trailer connection to tractor truck and contains a small spring which extends from ladder base to truck axle when connected. This connection causes tension on ladder assembly, and allows ladder to be held in any upright position. Trailer has a rear single axle and tire assembly; fenders with open wheel well; and two-piece ladder assembly which can be extended; TOOTSIETOY MADE IN U.S.A.

(A) Type I truck with painted features; fire ladder trailer containing single rear patterned rubber tires, no axle spacer. **40 65 75**

G E LN

(B) Type II truck with fire ladder trailer containing single rear patterned plastic tires, no axle spacer. Painted features limited to ladder assembly. **35 60 70**

(C) Type III truck with fire ladder trailer containing single rear patterned plastic Tootsietoy tires, no axle spacer. Painted features limited to ladder assembly. **35 60 70**

(D) Same as (A) but missing ladder extension piece. **30 55 60**

(E) Same as (B) or (C) but missing ladder extension piece. **30 50 55**

1955 MACK LOG TRAILER TRUCK: (1960, 1967-1968) 9″ unit. Tractor truck painted red or green. Unpainted trailer made of a single steel flat rod connecting the front trailer connection with the rear dual tandem wheel assembly. The front trailer connection has a flat surface about 1¼″ in width. At each end of this piece is a short molded pin which helps hold the log load on the trailer. The rear truck assembly also contains a short cast pin on each side of the assembly. Just beyond these pins is a groove to hold a rubber band to secure the log load. Six 6″ wooden logs. No casting identification on the trailer.

(A) Type I tractor truck; molded dual tandem patterned rubber tires; no axle spacers. **30 55 60**

(B) Type II tractor truck; molded dual tandem plastic tires; no axle spacers. **30 50 55**

(C) Type III tractor truck; molded dual tandem plastic Tootsietoy tires; no axle spacers. **30 50 55**

(D) Same as (A) except log load is missing. **25 45 50**

(E) Same as (B) or (C) except log load is missing. **25 40 45**

1955 MACK MACHINERY TRAILER TRUCK: (1961-1962) The machinery trailer in this unit is identical to the unit described with the 1947 Mack Tractor Truck. Trailer painted red, green, or orange.

(A) Type I truck; machinery trailer with painted truck features. **40 70 80**

(B) Type II or III truck; machinery trailer, truck body, and features same color. **40 65 75**

1955 MACK MOBIL TANKER TRAILER TRUCK: (1960-1961, 1963-1965, 1967-1969) 9″ unit. Tanker trailer painted red with blue and white MOBIL stickers on tanker sides and rear. Type I tractor truck with silver-painted features. One-piece tanker trailer includes a walkway along the entire length of the tanker top; three filler ports located in the walkway; no rear step ladder; dual tandem wheels; molded rubber patterned tires, no axle spacers. TOOTSIETOY CHICAGO 24 U.S.A. P-01035 2.

(A) As described above. **35 60 70**

(B) Same as (A) except Type II tractor truck; trailer has molded tandem dual patterned plastic Tootsietoy tires, no axle spacers. **30 50 60**

(C) Same as (A) with Type III tractor truck. **30 50 60**

(D) Type I tractor truck; tanker trailer and truck painted medium green, orange, or red; also red or green truck with silver tanker trailer. Trailer has molded tandem dual patterned rubber tires, no axle spacer. TOOTSIETOY CHICAGO 24 U.S.A. With or without rear ladder cast in. **35 50 55**

(E) Same as (C) with Type II tractor truck; trailer wheels same as (A). **30 45 50**

G E LN

(F) Black truck and orange tanker with TOOTSIETOY LINES / SERVING YOUNG AMERICA sticker; painted features. **30 55 70**

(G) Same as (A) with MOBILGAS sticker on tanker sides and rear. Rare. S. Butler Collection. **30 60 85**

1955 MACK PIPE TRAILER TRUCK: (Date unknown) 9″ unit. Tractor truck painted red or green. Trailer is the same as the one described with the 1955 Mack Log Trailer Truck; trailer load contains five or six plastic 6″ silver-gray pipes.

(A) Type I tractor truck with pipe trailer; molded tandem dual rubber tires, no axle spacers; painted features. **35 60 65**

(B) Type II tractor truck with pipe trailer; molded tandem dual plastic tires, no axle spacers; truck body and features painted same color. **30 55 60**

(C) Type III tractor truck with pipe trailer; molded tandem dual plastic Tootsietoy tires, no axle spacers; truck body and features painted same color. **30 55 60**

(D) Same as (A) except pipe load missing. **30 45 50**

(E) Same as (B) or (C) except pipe load missing. **30 40 45**

1955 MACK UTILITY TRAILER TRUCK: (1960-1961, 1963) 9″ unit. Two-piece trailer truck produced in a variety of color combinations. Trailer also known as a low-side, stakeside, or grain trailer. Tractor truck painted red, yellow, orange, blue, or green. Utility trailer painted red, yellow, orange, blue, or green. Trailer open in rear; sides contain four molded side supports; front of trailer rounded at each corner; rear dual tandem wheels; TOOTSIETOY CHICAGO 24 U.S.A.

(A) Type I truck; painted features; trailer with molded patterned dual tandem rubber Tootsietoy tires, no axle spacers. **25 40 45**

(B) Type II truck; body and features same color; trailer with molded patterned dual tandem plastic Tootsietoy tires, no axle spacers. **25 35 40**

(C) Type III truck; trailer same as (B). **25 35 40**

1955 MACK VAN TRAILER TRUCK: (1959) 9″ Black tractor truck and orange one-piece trailer with TOOTSIETOY LINES / SERVING YOUNG AMERICA sticker; no doors. **50 75 85**

1958 International Tractor Trucks

The 1958 International Tractor Truck came in three variations:

Type I features a short front hood, a lower front grille, an air vent above the grille, narrow front fenders with a large flat panel in the fender face for dual headlights, an International Harvester emblem on the hood, a one-piece windshield, a door window, and a rear cab window, small running boards with a step behind the front fenders, dual gas tanks behind the cab, and a protruding pin for the trailer connection. It has patterned plastic Tootsietoy tires in front with no axle spacer, and molded pattern plastic dual Tootsietoy tires in the rear with no axle spacer. TOOTSIETOY CHICAGO 24 U.S.A. is cast underneath.

Type II is the same as Type I except that the casting identification includes a 2 under the truck hood.

Type III is a transition piece between the 1955 International tractor truck and the 1958 Type I version. It has dual headlights painted over the light panel on the 1955 unit which is designed for a single headlight. How extensive this was done

(Above) **Top:** *1955 Mack Utility Trailer Truck; 1955 Mack "Serving Young America" Van Trailer Truck, S. Butler Collection.* **Middle:** *1955 Mack Mobilgas Tanker Trailer Truck, S. Butler Collection; 1955 Mack Mobil Tanker Trailer Truck.* **Bottom:** *1955 Mack "Serving Young America" Tanker Trailer Truck, S. Butler Collection.*

(Below) **Top:** *1955 Mack Machinery Trailer Truck with Dozer.* **Middle:** *1955 Mack Fire Ladder Trailer Truck.* **Bottom:** *1955 Mack Log Trailer Truck.*

Top: *1958 International "Dean Van Lines" Moving Van.* **Middle:** *1958 International Boat Transport, S. Butler Collection; 1958 International Vehicle Transport.* **Bottom:** *1958 International Boat Transport, K. Jestes Collection.*

G E LN

prior to the modification in the light panel in the casting for the 1958 model is unknown.

1958 INTERNATIONAL BOAT TRANSPORT: (1962-1964, 1968) 9" unit. Two-piece tractor trailer; tractor truck painted red with yellow trailer, blue with yellow trailer, red with blue trailer, or yellow with blue trailer. Silver-painted features include front bumper, lower grille, and dual headlights. Boat transport trailer is same one used with the 1958 International Vehicle Transport. TOOTSIETOY CHICAGO 24 U.S.A. P-10391.

(A) Type I tractor truck; painted features with three small plastic boats in blue and white or brown and white. 45 55 60

(B) Same as (A) with Type II tractor truck. 45 55 60

(C) Same as (A) without painted features. 40 50 55

(D) Same as (B) without painted features. 40 50 55

(E) Same as (A) or (B) without three small boats. 15 22 25

(F) Same as (C) or (D) without three small boats. 15 30 35

(G) Same as (A) or (B) with two small plastic boats. 30 45 50

1958 INTERNATIONAL MACHINERY TRAILER TRUCK: (1963-1966) Truck and trailer painted red, yellow, orange, green, or blue; silver-painted features including front bumper, lower grille, and dual headlights. Long flat trailer with raised floor section at front of trailer for trailer connection. Hole in casting for truck pin. Rear of trailer has a raised box on each side of trailer over rear dual wheels. Simulated wood flooring, molded dual plastic Tootsietoy tires, no axle spacer. TOOTSIETOY CHICAGO 24 U.S.A. P-10334.

(A) Type I tractor truck; painted features. 30 60 65

(B) Type II tractor truck; painted features. 30 55 60

G E LN

(C) Same as (A) or (B) without painted features. 25 50 55

1958 INTERNATIONAL MOVING VAN: (1963-1964, 1967) 9" unit. Tractor trailer truck lettered for Dean Van Lines, Inc. Type I tractor truck and van trailer painted white; blue-painted features including front bumper, lower grille, and dual headlights. Two-piece van trailer has a molded plastic shell which snaps into a die-cast body; operating one-piece double rear door; dual patterned plastic Tootsietoy tires, no axle spacer. Van sides and rear contain clear DEAN VAN LINES INC. WORLD WIDE MOVING stickers in red and blue. TOOTSIETOY CHICAGO 24 U.S.A. P-10304. 35 55 65

1958 INTERNATIONAL UTILITY TRAILER TRUCK: (1962) Tractor truck and trailer painted red, yellow, orange, green, or blue. Some units have silver-painted features including front bumper, lower grille, and dual headlights. Trailer unit also called a stakeside, a low-side, or a grain trailer. Solid sides and rounded front corners; rear is open; molded tandem dual tires, no axle spacer. TOOTSIETOY CHICAGO 24 U.S.A.

(A) Type I truck with painted features; utility trailer with molded dual tandem plastic Tootsietoy tires, no axle spacers. 30 38 40

(B) Same as (A) with Type II tractor truck. 30 38 40

(C) Same as (A) or (B) without painted features. 25 32 35

1958 INTERNATIONAL VEHICLE TRANSPORT: (1962-1964, 1968) Two-piece tractor trailer unit; tractor truck painted red with blue or gray trailer, red with yellow trailer, blue with yellow trailer, or white with blue trailer. Silver- or blue-painted features include front bumper, lower grille, and dual headlights. Highly-detailed plastic, double-deck trailer molded in two pieces: trailer sides-and-body piece has a single rear wheel and axle; top piece slides through channels at the

	G	E	LN

top of trailer sides. Trailer will hold up to four 3" vehicles. Loading ramp included. Patterned plastic Tootsietoy tires, no axle spacer. TOOTSIETOY CHICAGO 24 U.S.A. P-10391.

	G	E	LN
(A) Type I tractor truck, painted features; 1956 Triumph and 1960 Ford Falcon.	45	60	70
(B) Same as (A) with Type II tractor truck.	45	60	70
(C) Same as (A) without painted features.	35	50	60
(D) Same as (B) without painted features.	35	50	60
(E) Same as (A) or (B) without 3" vehicles and ramp.	15	30	35
(F) Same as (C) or (D) without 3" vehicles and ramp.	15	30	35

1959 Chevrolet Tractor Trucks

The 1959 Chevrolet Tractor Truck has a cab-over-front wheel design. The **Type I** truck cab is painted red or white with a silver- or blue-painted front bumper and grille. The body casting includes a one-piece windshield; door windows and a rear cab window; a narrow front grille with headlights extending the width of truck cab; dual gas tanks behind the cab; a pin or open slotted trailer connection, patterned plastic Tootsietoy tires with no axle spacers in front and a dual rear wheel assembly; and TOOTSIETOY U.S.A. cast underneath. **Type II** is the same as Type I without painted features.

1959 CHEVROLET AUTO TRANSPORT: (1965-1966) 9" unit. Tractor truck painted red or white; molded plastic, double-deck, transport trailer painted in silver or blue. Highly detailed trailer has room for up to four 3" vehicles. Two pieces to trailer: one piece makes up trailer sides and body, top piece slides through channels at the top of trailer sides; loading ramp; single rear wheel and axle assembly; patterned plastic Tootsietoy tires; no axle spacer. TOOTSIETOY CHICAGO 24 U.S.A. P-10391.

	G	E	LN
(A) Type I trailer truck with loading ramp; 1956 Triumph; 1960 Ford Falcon. Rare.	50	85	110
(B) Same as (A) with Type II trailer truck. Rare.	50	85	110
(C) Same as (A) or (B) without ramp and vehicles.	30	55	60

1959 CHEVROLET BOAT TRANSPORT: (1965-1966) 9" unit. Tractor truck painted red or white; two-piece, molded plastic transport trailer in gray, yellow, or blue. Highly detailed double-deck trailer features a single rear wheel and axle assembly. Two pieces include the trailer sides and body and a top section which slides through channels at the top of the trailer sides. Trailer holds up to three two-piece plastic boats having brown tops with white bottoms; patterned plastic Tootsietoy tires, no axle spacer. TOOTSIETOY CHICAGO 24 U.S.A. P-10391.

	G	E	LN
(A) Type I tractor truck; two boats. Rare.	50	75	100
(B) Type II tractor truck; two boats. Rare.	50	75	100
(C) Same as (A) or (B) without boats.	30	55	60

1959 CHEVROLET HOOK AND LADDER FIRE TRUCK: (1966) 9" unit. Tractor truck and trailer painted red; ladder assembly on trailer painted silver. Trailer has a single rear axle and tire assembly with fenders and open wheel wells.

A rare 1959 Chevrolet Tractor Truck Cab. I. Davis Collection.

	G	E	LN

Two-piece ladder assembly can be extended, rotated, or moved up or down. Ladder base is connected to tractor truck with a spring which extends to truck axle. TOOTSIETOY MADE IN U.S.A.

	G	E	LN
(A) Type I tractor truck with ladder assembly complete. Rare.	70	115	125
(B) Type II tractor truck with ladder assembly complete. Rare.	70	115	125
(C) Same as (A) or (B) but missing ladder extension.	60	100	115

1959 CHEVROLET LOG TRAILER TRUCK: (1966) 9" unit. Truck cab painted red. Trailer is made of a single steel flat rod that connects the front trailer connection to the rear dual tandem wheel assembly; no axle spacers. Unpainted trailer comes with five wooden logs held on by two elastic rubber bands. No markings on the trailer.

	G	E	LN
(A) Type I tractor truck with trailer and logs. Rare.	55	65	90
(B) Type II tractor truck with trailer and logs. Rare.	55	65	90
(C) Same as (A) or (B) without logs.	45	55	60

1959 CHEVROLET MOBIL OIL TANKER: (1966) Tractor truck painted red; trailer painted red with blue and white MOBIL stickers on each side of tanker body and rear of trailer. One-piece trailer has a walkway along the tanker top extending its full length; three filler ports located in the walkway; no rear step ladder. Dual tandem wheels, molded plastic Tootsietoy tires, no axle spacers. TOOTSIETOY CHICAGO 24 U.S.A. P-01035 2.

	G	E	LN
(A) Type I tractor truck with trailer. Rare.	60	75	95
(B) Type II tractor truck with trailer. Rare.	60	75	95

1959 CHEVROLET MOVING VAN: (1965-1966) 9" unit. Tractor trailer truck lettered for Dean Van Lines. Tractor truck painted red or white; trailer painted white. Two-piece trailer design has a molded plastic shell which snaps into a die-cast body; operating one-piece rear door; dual patterned plastic Tootsietoy tires, no axle spacer. Van sides and rear contain a clear sticker with DEAN VAN LINES INC. WORLD WIDE MOVING in red and blue. TOOTSIETOY CHICAGO 24 U.S.A. P-10304.

	G	E	LN
(A) Type I tractor truck with trailer. Rare.	45	70	95
(B) Type II tractor truck with trailer. Rare.	45	70	95

CHAPTER 8

Military Vehicles

A wide variety of Tootsietoy military vehicles and equipment produced after the war successfully modeled vehicles used during both World War II and the Korean War. The quality of the materials, detailing, features, and scale incorporated into the 4-inch and 6-inch vehicles is excellent. This chapter presents only the 3-inch, 4-inch, and 6-inch vehicles and associated equipment. Military ships and airplanes can be found in Chapter 9.

The 4-inch series contains the largest number of military pieces. Many of the 4-inch models were offered in boxed sets and have recently become some of the most desirable pieces in the entire Tootsietoy line. The 4-inch series also contains two reissued prewar pieces: the No. 4635 Army Armored Car and the No. 4634 Army Supply Truck. The Supply Truck with postwar black tires is rare. The Armored Car was used from 1946 to 1948 as a load for the popular A. C. Gilbert No. 715 Flatcar for S Gauge train layouts. Gilbert also used two 4-inch Army Jeeps as a flatcar load from 1959 to 1961.

The Tootsietoy military series also includes the rare Atomic Cannon/155 mm Howitzer featured in set No. 4398 and the 1955 International Tractor Truck with and without adjustable Rocket Launcher, Trailer, and Rocket. Because the launcher unit could be removed from the trailer, this toy is very difficult to find intact in either Air Force or Army version. The rocket is frequently found broken, cracked, and warped.

Although military vehicles are popular for collectors, the company must not have found them profitable. By 1965 the company no longer offered any military vehicles.

Based on historical data, catalogues, advertisements, and data obtained from collectors, the best known information of production years is included in each listing. Cast-in information on the underside of each vehicle appears last in each listing.

G E LN

4634 ARMY SUPPLY TRUCK: (1942/1946) 4-inch series. Prewar reissued Mack truck; very difficult to find with black tires. Body painted tan; casting includes a tin cover over truck body behind open driver seat; fenders over front and rear wheels; headlights in front fender; and driver resembling a fireman. Same truck body was used for the 4" Fire Truck (see Chapter 5 on the 4-inch series). Smooth rubber tires with axle spacers. TOOTSIETOY MADE IN THE UNITED STATES OF AMERICA.

(A) As described above. **40 60 65**

G E LN

(B) Camouflaged in tan and black or olive drab paint; no driver. **50 65 75**

(C) Camouflaged in brown and gray; no driver. **50 65 75**

4635 ARMY ARMORED CAR: (1942/1946, 1947-1948) 4-inch series. Resembles an armor-plated vehicle. Body painted gray with brown camouflage; brown with green camouflage; gray; or olive drab. Casting includes headlights; slanted front, no grille; four small cab windows; U.S. ARMY on vehicle sides; upper turret with three small windows; red or silver guns protruding from cab's right front window and rear of turret. Wheels outside of vehicle body; smooth rubber tires, no axle spacers. TOOTSIETOY MADE IN THE UNITED STATES.

(A) As described above. **35 42 45**

(B) Same as (A) without gun in cab or turret. **30 38 40**

ARMY CANNON TRAILER: (1958-1960) 4-inch series. Three variations of anti-aircraft/field cannons mounted on four- or six-wheel trailers exist. Each has a well-detailed olive-drab cannon cast in a fixed position. Trailer frame has a hook and eyelet at either end to attach or pull other units.

(A) The smallest of the three variations; trailer has a depressed design with the small cannon mounted in the center of trailer body; four wheels and smooth rubber tires mounted outside of cannon body on full length axles. TOOTSIETOY MADE IN U.S.A. **14 20 25**

(B) Large cannon unit; cannon barrel extends beyond end of trailer body. Trailer depressed at one end; four wheels; smooth rubber tires mounted by a separate pin through each tire; axle housing above trailer body. TOOTSIETOY CHICAGO 24 U.S.A. **14 20 25**

(C) Large cannon unit mounted on a six-wheel trailer; cannon barrel extends beyond end of trailer body. Trailer depressed at the rear; two sets of wheels in front and one set in rear; smooth rubber tires mounted outside of cannon body by a separate pin through each tire, no axles; axle housing is above trailer body. TOOTSIETOY CHICAGO 24 U.S.A. **14 20 25**

ARMY FIELD CANNON: (1942/1946) 4-inch series. Long-range cannon; olive-drab barrel with tan support structure and front shield. Body features include spring lever that permits firing of cannon and cannon barrel that moves up or down. Large rubber tires; MADE IN U.S.A. **15 18 20**

Top: *Army Searchlight Trailer (4-inch); No. 4635 Army Armored Car (4-inch); No. 4634 Army Supply Truck (prewar version); Army Jeep (3-inch) with steering wheel.* **Bottom:** *Army Field Cannon (4-inch); Army Half Track (4-inch); Army Tank (4-inch); Army Jeep (3-inch) without steering wheel.*

	G	E	LN

ARMY FIELD CANNON: (1958-1960, 1963-1965) 4-inch or 6-inch series. Artillery field cannon made of two-piece metal casting; body painted olive drab. Cannon barrel contains a spring-and-lever assembly to shoot six small red plastic shells. Cannon barrel is cast in a fixed position; end of cannon support frame includes a tow hook. Overall length of unit is over 6". Thick hard rubber tires mounted through lower cannon frame by single thick axle. TOOTSIETOY CHICAGO 24 U.S.A. inside cannon support frames on both sides.

	G	E	LN
(A) As described above.	15	18	20
(B) Without shells.	10	13	15

ARMY JEEP: (1947, 1949, 1955, 1958-1960, 1963-1965) 4-inch series. World War II Willys body painted olive drab. Body casting includes front and rear seats; steering wheel; windshield in down position; five-point star in circle on hood; large front grille; headlights on fenders; open wheel wells; eyelet type of trailer hitch; front bumper; no rear bumper. Smooth rubber tires with axle spacers.

	G	E	LN
(A) As described above; star on hood points toward front. TOOTSIETOY MADE IN U.S.A. JEEP.	15	22	25
(B) Same as (A) but no axle spacers; star on hood points toward windshield. TOOTSIETOY MADE IN THE U.S.A. JEEP.	15	18	20
(C) Same as (B) but patterned rubber tires.	15	18	20
(D) Same as (B) but patterned plastic tires.	12	17	18
(E) Same as (A) or (C) with red, white, and blue paper star on hood.	20	28	30

ARMY JEEP: (1949, 1951, 1955) 6-inch series. World War II Willys body painted olive drab. Body contains separate cast windshield and slender three-spoke steering wheel in natural metal finish; hood with molded star in a circle and W-2017590 in front of the star; headlights on front fenders; U-shaped trailer hitch on rear body panel. Smooth black rubber tires with axle spacers. TOOTSIETOY MADE IN U.S.A. 4.

	G	E	LN
(A) As described above.	17	22	25
(B) Same as (A) but cast steering wheel has three thick spokes and large center hub painted silver. Patterned rubber tires with axle spacers; no casting identification.	15	20	22
(C) Same as (A) with steering wheel and windshield same as body color. S. Butler Collection.	17	25	30

ARMY JEEP: (1955, 1958-1959, 1961, 1965) 3-inch series. World War II Willys body and features painted olive drab. Body casting contains a five-point star in circle on front hood; no windshield; detailed dash without steering wheel; two front seats; front fenders; open wheel wells; large front grille area with headlights; front bumper. Smooth rubber tires, no axle spacers; no casting identification.

	G	E	LN
(A) As described above.	15	22	25
(B) Same as (A) except for variation in dash display with a steering wheel; patterned plastic tires, no axle spacers. TOOTSIETOY JEEP CHICAGO U.S.A.	13	17	20

ARMY JUMBO FOUR-PIECE SET: (1956) Set featured on cardstock in a cellophane package includes one 6" olive-drab 1956 Army CJ5 Jeep, one miniature silver pistol, one miniature silver bugle, and one 1" silver foot soldier. See listing in this chapter for additional information on the Jeep. All three pieces are cast metal. Jeep has a cast windshield and steering wheel. **40 48 50**

ARMY JUMBO FIVE-PIECE SET: (1959, 1964) Blister pack containing one 4" World War II Army Jeep, one 4" or 6" Army Field Cannon, three plastic soldiers, and six red plastic shells. All pieces including the three soldiers are olive drab. See the descriptions in this chapter for the Army Jeep and

Army Radar Trailer (4-inch). E. Poole Collection,

A rare 155 mm Howitzer (6-inch). R. Johnson Collection.

G E LN

Field Cannon. The three plastic soldiers are approximately 2½″ high. Two are holding pistols and the third is throwing a hand grenade. DOWST MANUFACTURING CO. CHICAGO 24 IL U.S.A. **40 60 65**

ARMY RADAR TRAILER: (1959-1960) 4-inch series. Rare trailer and radar unit actually models a sound detector used as a prewar radar aircraft-detector device; body painted olive drab. Trailer contains a center post which holds three cone-shaped radar units. Four-wheel trailer has smooth rubber tires mounted to the outside of body on separate pins. TOOTSIETOY CHICAGO U.S.A. E. Poole Collection. **25 32 35**

ARMY SEARCHLIGHT TRAILER: (1958-1960) 4-inch series. All-metal casting with chrome reflector as searchlight; light suspended by bracket that allows it to swing or tilt. Trailer and searchlight housing painted olive drab; short trailer body has hook on one end and eyelet on the other to pull another vehicle. Four-wheel trailer has smooth rubber tires held on by separate pin for each wheel. TOOTSIETOY CHICAGO U.S.A. **20 28 30**

G E LN

ARMY TANK: (1958-1960) 4-inch series. Resembles an early World War II tank; body painted olive drab. Body casting has extensive details including tank tracks; small turret on top with short cannon; lower tank body with a short cannon on center of tank and a small cannon/machine gun set back from front cannon on right side; simulated armor plating along tank sides; smooth body front and rear. Smooth rubber tires with axle spacers; axles extend through body sides. TOOTSIETOY MADE IN THE U.S.A. **12 18 22**

ATOMIC CANNON/155 MM HOWITZER: (1958-1960) 5¼″ in length. Rare unit painted olive drab; casting features a revolving turret and tank body extending over tank tracks. Turret gun moves up or down; operating rubber tank tracks; two hatches on turret top with five-pointed star. Featured in No. 4398 Combat Set. Information from C. Breslow and R. Johnson. **50 85 90**

1938 FEDERAL TRUCK: (1948) 4-inch series. Open high-sided truck; body and features painted tan with green camouflage. Body casting includes a two-piece windshield; single-window doors, no rear window; protruding fenders on front and rear; hood and front grille protruding from front windshield; headlights behind front grille between hood and front fenders; front of truck bed extends to top of cab. Body extends over wheel wells; axles extend through body sides; smooth black rubber tires with axle spacers. TOOTSIETOY MADE IN UNITED STATES OF AMERICA NO. 1010. **25 35 45**

1941 ARMY HALF TRACK: (1960) 4-inch series. Body painted olive drab; casting contains detailed armor plating with simulated canvas cover over rear of vehicle; machine gun on front hood; front fenders with headlights; front grille; U.S.A. W-60118 located above rear track assembly on both sides of vehicle body; bumper with center winch; simulated rear tracks; slot in rear for pulling other units. Axles extend through body sides. Smooth rubber tires; no axle spacer for front wheels, short spacer for rear wheels. TOOTSIETOY MADE IN THE U.S.A. **15 20 25**

1941 INTERNATIONAL ARMY AMBULANCE: (1949) 4-inch series. Panel truck painted green or tan. Body casting includes Red Cross symbol on roof; warning light on roof and front hood; two-piece front windshield; two small rear windows; headlights in fenders; front bumper; casting extending over wheels; axles extending through body sides; smooth rubber tires with axle spacers; TOOTSIETOY MADE IN U.S.A.

(A) Body and features same color except for Red Cross symbol. **25 38 40**

(B) Same as (A) with silver-painted features, front grille, and headlights. **25 38 40**

1949 CHEVROLET ARMY AMBULANCE: (1958-1960) 4-inch series. Panel truck painted olive drab; casting includes Red Cross symbol on roof and emergency light; two-piece windshield; two rear windows molded in body; front and rear bumper; narrow fenders both in front and rear; headlights in fenders between horizontal front grille; small air vent behind front fender each side; casting extending over wheel wells; axles extending through body sides; smooth rubber tires with axle spacers. TOOTSIETOY MADE IN THE U.S.A.

(A) Molded rear windows. **20 32 35**

A selection of 4-inch military vehicles. **Top:** *1949 Chevrolet Army Ambulance; 1941 International Army Ambulance, C. Jones Collection.* **Middle:** *Army Cannon Trailer, large version; Army Cannon Trailer, large version with two sets of front wheels; Army Cannon Trailer, small version.* **Bottom:** *1954 Oldsmobile Army Officers Car, K. Jestes Collection; Army Jeep.*

	G	E	LN
(B) Same as (A) with silver-painted grille, front bumper, and headlights; two small rear windows are open.	25	35	40

1950 CHEVROLET ARMY SEDAN: (Dates unknown) 3-inch series. Chevrolet Fleetline two-door sedan painted olive drab; body and features painted same color. See chapter on 3-inch series for additional information. Smooth rubber tires, one-piece axles. TOOTSIETOY MADE IN U.S.A. **12 20 25**

1955 FORD ARMY TANKER: (Dates unknown) 3-inch series. Tanker truck painted olive drab; truck body and features painted same color. See Chapter 6 on 3-inch series for additional information. Smooth black rubber tires, one piece axles. TOOTSIETOY CHICAGO U.S.A. **15 18 20**

1955 INTERNATIONAL ARMY TRAILER TRUCK WITH JEEP: (1965) Tractor truck, low-boy trailer, and 3-inch Jeep painted olive drab. Tractor truck has short hood and lower front grille; air vent above grille; narrow front fender with headlights; International Harvester emblem on hood; one-piece windshield; side windows and rear cab window; running boards with step behind fender; dual gas tanks; pin for trailer connection. Patterned plastic Tootsietoy tires; molded dual rear tires, no axle spacers; TOOTSIETOY CHICAGO 24 U.S.A. Low-boy trailer with raised front trailer connection; hole in casting for truck pin; a raised box over each rear dual wheel; molded dual plastic Tootsietoy tires, no axle spacer. TOOTSIETOY CHICAGO 24 U.S.A. P-10334 on trailer. Willys Army Jeep has detailed dash display and steering wheel; star in circle on hood; patterned plastic tires, no axle spacers. TOOTSIETOY JEEP CHICAGO U.S.A.

	G	E	LN
(A) As described above.	55	80	90
(B) Without 3" Jeep.	50	70	80

1955 INTERNATIONAL ARMY TRANSPORT: (Dates unknown) 6-inch series. Tractor truck with auto transport; trailer painted olive drab; truck features painted same color as truck and trailer. Tractor truck has a short front hood; lower front grille; air vent above grille; narrow front fenders with headlights; International Harvester emblem on hood; one-piece windshield; door windows; rear cab window; small running board with step behind front fender; dual gas tanks; protruding pin for trailer connection; patterned plastic Tootsietoy tires; no axle spacers; TOOTSIETOY CHICAGO 24 U.S.A. Transport trailer is a two-piece tin stamped trailer with single axle assembly; no axle spacer; U.S. ARMY underneath. **NRS**

1955 INTERNATIONAL ARMY TRUCK WITH ROCKET LAUNCHER: (1958-1960) 6-inch series. Tractor truck with low-boy trailer painted olive drab; truck features painted same color as truck and trailer. Tractor truck has short front hood; lower front grille with air vent above grille; narrow front fenders with headlights; International Harvester emblem on hood; one-piece windshield; door window and rear cab window; small running boards with step on each side behind front fender; dual gas tanks behind truck cab; protruding pin for trailer connection. Patterned plastic Tootsietoy tires, molded dual rear plastic Tootsietoy tires, no axle spacers; TOOTSIETOY CHICAGO 24 U.S.A. Trailer for rocket launcher includes a step-up connection with a hole for tractor truck pin; trailer flooring is cast to simulate wood planking; a box on each side over dual wheel assembly in rear; special slot in floor; extended bracket between boxes. Metal rocket launcher and plastic red, white, and blue rocket. Dual molded plastic Tootsietoy tires, no axle spacer; TOOTSIETOY MADE IN U.S.A. CHICAGO 24.

	G	E	LN
(A) With paper star on roof.	80	135	150
(B) Without paper star.	80	130	140
(C) Same as (A) in Air Force Blue. Rare.	95	150	175
(D) Same as (A) or (B) with mechanized launching unit; plastic red-and-white rocket with blue rubber tip; slots to hold rocket on launcher. Rare. S. Butler Collection.	95	150	175

Back: *Army Jeep (4-inch) with modern field cannon, original box; 1955 International Army Truck with Rocket Launcher, original box.* **Front:** *Army Jeep (3-inch). J. Gibson Collection.*

G E LN

1954 OLDSMOBILE ARMY OFFICERS CAR: (1958-1960) 4-inch series. Two-door Oldsmobile 98 Holiday hardtop painted olive drab with five-point red, white, and blue paper star sticker on roof. Silver-painted features include front and rear bumpers, grille, headlights, and taillights. Body has a boxy design with side vent windows; style line along body sides extends from front fender to beyond door; smooth rubber tires.

(A) Body sides extend over wheel wells; axles extend through body sides with axles spacers; painted features; silver star. TOOTSIETOY MADE IN U.S.A. OLDS 98 HOLIDAY. **25 35 40**

(B) Open wheel wells; no axle spacers; painted features; paper star. TOOTSIETOY CHICAGO U.S.A. HOLIDAY OLDS 98. **25 35 40**

(C) Same as (A) without star. **25 32 35**

(D) Same as (B) without star. **20 30 35**

(E) Same as (C) body and features same color. **20 30 35**

(F) Same as (D) body and features same color. **20 30 35**

1955 THUNDERBIRD ARMY OFFICERS CAR: (Dates unknown) 4-inch series. Two-door coupe; body and features painted olive drab; paper star on roof. Casting contains open wheel wells; vent scoop on hood; Ford emblem on front and rear; front and rear bumper guards; rear fenders with fins and round taillights; smooth rubber tires; no axle spacers. TOOTSIETOY CHICAGO U.S.A. FORD THUNDERBIRD. H. Van Curler Collection.

(A) As described above. **30 42 45**

(B) Same as (A) with patterned rubber tires. **NRS**

(C) Same as (A) with axle spacers and silver-painted features. TOOTSIETOYS MADE IN U.S.A. FORD THUNDERBIRD. **NRS**

(D) Same as (A) with patterned plastic tires. **NRS**

1956 ARMY CJ5 JEEP: (1956-1959) 6-inch series. Body painted olive drab; cast windshield and steering wheel painted silver. Body casting includes detailed interior; open wheel wells; U-shaped trailer hitch; USA 20965148 on left and right of front hood in small print; headlights on flat front grille; narrow front fenders; seat backs extending above sides of Jeep. Patterned rubber Tootsietoy tires, no axle spacers. TOOTSIETOY CHICAGO U.S.A. 1/4 TON M38 ARMY JEEP 1.

(A) As described above. **15 22 25**

(B) Same as (A) with plastic Tootsietoy tires, no axle spacers. **15 22 25**

1956 ARMY CJ5 JEEP: (1961) 6-inch series. Body and features painted olive drab. Body casting includes windshield molded in down position; detailed molded interior including steering wheel and seats; open wheel wells and trailer hitch; headlights and front grille on flat panel between narrow front fenders. Patterned rubber Tootsietoy tires, no axle spacers. TOOTSIETOY CHICAGO 24 U.S.A. 3.

(A) As described above. **10 18 20**

(B) Same as (A) with patterned plastic Tootsietoy tires, no axle spacers. **10 18 20**

1956 ARMY CJ5 JEEP WITH PLOW: (1961) 6-inch series. Body and features painted olive drab; plow painted yellow; cast windshield and steering wheel painted silver. Body casting includes detailed interior; open wheel wells; U-shaped trailer hitch; USA 20965148 in small print on left and right of front hood; flat front grille with headlights; narrow front fenders; seat backs extending above sides. Patterned rubber Tootsietoy tires; no axle spacers. TOOTSIETOY CHICAGO U.S.A. 1/4 TON M38 ARMY JEEP 1. Plow assembly mounted to body behind front wheel wells with pin through body sides.

(A) As described above. **20 40 45**

(B) Same as (A) with plastic Tootsietoy tires; no axle spacers. **20 40 45**

Top: *1955 International Army Truck cab in Air Force colors; 1955 International Army Truck with Rocket Launcher, K. Jestes Collection; 1955 International Army Truck with Jeep load.* **Middle:** *1956 Army CJ5 Jeep (6-inch); 1956 Army CJ5 Jeep with Plow (6-inch); Army Jeep (6-inch).* **Bottom:** *Army Jeep (4-inch) with modern Field Cannon.*

G E LN

1956 FORD ARMY ANTI-AIRCRAFT TRUCK: (1959, 1963-1965) 6-inch series. Ford F-700 flatbed truck; body painted olive drab. Body casting includes wraparound windshield; large front grille with headlights, V-8 emblem located in center; protruding front fenders with open wheel wells; running boards under side doors behind front fender and extending back to flatbed; open truck bed with no sides extending over dual rear wheels; box on truck bed behind cab; circular area in center of flatbed casting. Hole in the center of circle contains mounting bracket for the anti-aircraft gun. Gun assembly contains two guns with sight scopes on outer sides; assembly snaps onto pins on each side of mounting bracket. Bracket assembly can be turned in any direction; gun assembly can be tilted up or down. Patterned rubber Tootsietoy tires on front, no axle spacer; dual molded rear wheels, no axle spacer.

(A) As described above with a red, white, and blue paper star on roof; bracket and anti-aircraft gun are cast metal painted olive drab. TOOTSIETOY CHICAGO 24 U.S.A. 2. **35 65 75**

(B) No star on roof; bracket for anti-aircraft gun is metal; anti-aircraft gun is molded plastic and painted olive drab. TOOTSIETOY CHICAGO 24 U.S.A. **30 60 70**

(C) No star on roof; bracket and anti-aircraft gun are molded yellow or white plastic. TOOTSIETOY CHICAGO 24 U.S.A. **30 55 65**

Variation of the Army trailer for the Rocket Launcher assembly and the standard low-boy trailer.

G E LN

(D) Same as (A) except for casting identification: TOOTSIETOY CHICAGO 24 U.S.A. 1. **35 60 75**

(E) Same as (B) except bracket is olive drab, anti-aircraft gun is yellow. **30 60 70**

(F) Same as (C) with plastic Tootsietoy tires. **30 60 65**

(G) Same as (F) with white plastic gun assembly. **30 60 65**

1956 FORD ARMY RADAR TRUCK: (1958-1959, 1963-1965) 6-inch series. Ford F-700 flatbed truck; body painted

Back: *Variations of the 1956 Ford Army Anti-Aircraft Truck; variations of the 1956 Ford Army Radar Truck.* **Front:** *1956 Ford Army Searchlight Truck; 1956 Ford Army Stakeside Truck with tin top, K. Jestes Collection.*

	G	E	LN

olive drab. Body casting includes wraparound windshield; large front grille with headlights, V-8 emblem located in center; protruding front fenders with open wheel wells; running board under side doors behind front fender and extending back to flatbed; open truck bed with no sides extending over dual rear wheels; box on truck bed behind cab; circular area in center of bed casting. Hole in center of circle includes a mounting bracket for radar screen. Elongated radar screen is molded plastic. Metal bracket assembly can be turned in any direction; radar screen can be tilted up or down. Patterned rubber Tootsietoy tires on front, no axle spacers; molded dual rear wheels, no axle spacers.

	G	E	LN
(A) Truck, bracket, and radar screen painted olive drab or shiny metal (silver) finish; red, white, and blue paper star on roof of truck. TOOTSIETOY CHICAGO 24 U.S.A. 1.	40	65	70
(B) Same as (A) except radar screen is molded yellow plastic.	40	60	65
(C) Same as (A) except TOOTSIETOY CHICAGO 24 U.S.A. 2.	40	65	70
(D) Same as (C) except radar screen is molded yellow plastic.	40	60	65
(E) Bracket and radar screen molded yellow plastic; TOOTSIETOY CHICAGO 24 U.S.A.	40	55	60
(F) Same as (E) with plastic Tootsietoy tires.	40	55	60

1956 FORD ARMY SEARCHLIGHT TRUCK: (1959) 6-inch series. Ford F-700 flatbed truck; body painted olive drab. Casting includes a wraparound windshield; a large front grille with headlights, V-8 emblem located in center; protruding front fenders with open wheel wells; running boards under side doors behind front fender and extending back to flatbed; open truck bed with no sides extending over dual rear wheels; box on truck bed behind truck; circular area in center of bed. Hole in center of circle contains mounting bracket for searchlight unit. Round cast-metal searchlight painted olive drab with chrome reflector as light; small handle in rear; indentation on each side for pins in mounting bracket. Bracket assembly can be turned in any direction; searchlight can be tilted up or down. Patterned rubber Tootsietoy tires on front, no axle spacer; molded dual rear wheels, no axle spacer.

	G	E	LN
(A) Metal truck, bracket, and searchlight painted olive drab; red, white, and blue paper star on truck roof. TOOTSIETOY CHICAGO 24 U.S.A. 1.	40	75	85
(B) Same as (A) without paper star.	40	70	80
(C) Same as (A) except for TOOTSIETOY CHICAGO 24 U.S.A. 2.	45	75	85
(D) Same as (C) without paper star.	40	70	80

1956 FORD ARMY STAKESIDE TRUCK: (1958-1960) 6-inch series. Ford F-700 flatbed truck with solid simulated stakesides; open tailgate at rear of truck; body painted olive drab. Truck cab includes wraparound windshield; large front grille with headlights, V-8 emblem located in center; protruding front fenders with open wheel wells; running boards under each side door behind front fender and extending back to stakeside body; truck bed extending over dual rear wheels. Patterned rubber Tootsietoy tires on front, no axle spacers; molded dual rear wheels, no axle spacers.

	G	E	LN
(A) Body and features olive drab with red, white, and blue paper star on cab roof. TOOTSIETOY CHICAGO 24 U.S.A. FORD F-700.	45	53	55
(B) Same as (A) without paper star.	40	48	50
(C) Same as (A) with olive-drab tin cover; large white star on top; U.S. ARMY on each side.	50	70	80
(D) Same as (C) without paper star.	50	70	75

1959 CHEVY ARMY TRAILER TRUCK WITH JEEP: (1965) Same as 1955 International except with Chevy tractor truck. Rare.

	G	E	LN
(A) As described above.	65	110	125
(B) Without 3″ Jeep.	50	100	110

CHAPTER 9

Civilian and Military Airplanes and Ships

Airplanes

An impressive variety of Tootsietoy airplanes was produced during the postwar years. For the most part, the early models are excellent replicas of the real planes, thanks in part to accurate details achieved by the two-piece design used to form the fuselage. One or both of these parts included the wings, tail assembly, and landing gear. Newer models had a single cast body which included the wings, tail section, and landing gear; the bottom was left open. This may have been done due to the shortages of zinc in the fifties. The small propeller planes came in two styles. The first featured open windows in the body, an axle spacer, and a propeller mounted to the plane by a separate pin. The later design did not have open windows or axle spacers; the propeller was mounted using a pin molded as part of the body. The propeller was placed over the pin and the pin was crimped to hold it in place.

The DC-2, P-40, DC-4, DC-4 Army Transport, Lockheed Electra 10A, U.S. Army Plane, Aero-Dawn, and the Aero-Dawn Seaplane are reissued prewar pieces; many of them around today could have been store stock pieces available during and shortly after the war. These pieces are given the variable date of issue of 1942/1946; they are all somewhat difficult to find, but the most desirable and the most difficult are the P-40 and the DC-4 Army Transport.

The Waco "Bomber" is also a prewar piece with an interesting story. Although Waco made light bombers only for export, this particular model of biplane was never made into an actual bomber. Occasionally, Waco cabin planes were used as light military transports. According to collector Robert Straub, the Tootsietoy version is a "beautiful replica of the Waco C-6 private plane of 1936, but the bombs are inaccurate additions."

In the postwar series, the P-38 Lightning Fighter, the P-39 Airacobra, the Lockheed Constellation, the Convair 240, and the Boeing Stratocruiser are very desirable. While most Tootsietoy airplanes were not scaled to each other, the Constellation, Convair, Stratocruiser, and Boeing 707 are in approximate scale. In the military series, the P-39 and P-38 propeller fighters are both very much sought after by collectors, but they are not as rare as the U.S. Coast Guard Amphibian. The P-39 has a stamped tin wing; it is a closer replica to the actual P-39 than its Hubley counterpart. The Sikorsky S-58 Helicopter is a difficult piece to obtain; it can be classified as either a military or as a civilian piece.

Dowst produced this piece in 1939 and designated it in the catalogue as a DC-4. The first real DC-4 was made in 1938 and had a triple-fin tail assembly, yet this very large airplane never went into production for passenger service; the airlines felt it was too large. The plane was modified to the smaller DC-4 that is more familiar today with its single large tail; it went into full service in 1942.

There are several other instances where a reissued prewar Tootsietoy plane was called by a later (postwar) version's name. This may have been a way to capitalize on either the popularity or the familiarity of the postwar versions. For instance, the U.S. Coast Guard Amphibian was called a "PBY Flying Boat" in the 1950 catalogue and a "Coast Guard PBY" in an ad which ran in the April 1950 *Playthings* magazine. However, this Tootsietoy seaplane models the real prewar Sikorsky S-43 Amphibian (1938-1941). The S-43 was dropped from service during the war and replaced by the war-worthy, popular PBY made by Consolidated. Dowst's prewar Amphibian had "Sikorsky" cast under the wing. A good clue to identify the seaplane is that both the actual S-43 and the Tootsietoy version have pontoons attached to the plane. The actual S-43 pontoons extend down from the wings, while the toy's extend out from the body, an easier and cheaper die-casting design. However, the real PBY had pontoons that were retractable during flight coming off the wing tips. The toy more closely resembles the shape of the S-43 than the PBY. Since the PBY was very popular during the war, Dowst may have wanted to use a name children were more familiar with; however, it is also possible that the advertising department made an error in identification.

Further instances of these misnomers include the reissued P-40, which has been called a "Warhawk" by most postwar collectors, the name by which the real wartime P-40 fighter made by Curtiss was known. However, the Tootsietoy more closely resembles the prewar prototype P-40. The Piper Cub Tootsietoy airplane closely models the Skysedan made by Piper.

Underside of the P-39 Airacobra Fighter Plane showing the wing attachment. R. Johnson Collection.

A rare P-39 Airacobra Fighter Plane. R. Johnson Collection.

The Cub, by far more famous, would have been very difficult to cast.

Collectors may be interested in knowing that the Navy nomenclature used in the cast-in identification under each plane is accurate. It was used by the Navy to designate the plane's type, issue, and maker. For an example, see the note following the listing for the Cutlass "Army" Jet.

Most of the planes issued by Tootsietoy utilized the propeller connection which was first used on the Aero-Dawn in the thirties: a separate propeller connected by a pin to the plane. Others have propellers pushed onto a cast-in pin which was then crimped. The P-40, however, has blades cast onto a painted nose piece, which is an accurate replica of the real one; see its listing for a complete description.

There are two types of tires used in the Airplane Series. The first is a cast-metal ⅜-inch diameter tire carried over from prewar production, and found only on a limited number of models. The second is a smooth black rubber tire, 7⁄16 inch in diameter, that was used on almost all of the postwar aircraft models. The airliners do not have an axle spacer; instead, they have sets of double wheels on a strut that fit into slots in the casting. These wheels could be removed in play to simulate an airliner in flight with its wheels retracted.

By 1969, the company still offered six different planes: the Sabre, Panther, Cutlass, Starfire, and Skyray jets, and the Beechcraft Bonanza Airplane. All were issued in a variety of colors.

Based on historical data, catalogues, advertisements, and data obtained from other collectors (with special thanks to Robert Straub), the best known information on production years for each piece is included in the listing. Sizes given are the measurements of the wing span. Cast-in information on the underside of each vehicle appears last in each listing, unless otherwise indicated.

AERO-DAWN: (1942/1946) 4" wing span, top wing. Reissued prewar airplane, which was a crude replica of Charles Lindbergh's "The Spirit of St Louis". Hollow cast body painted red, blue, yellow, or silver with unmarked stamped tin wing; single propeller painted same as plane; exposed piston motor; UX214 on each side of fuselage. White rubber tires with single, one-piece axle. TOOTSIETOY on inside of fuselage. **G** 20 **E** 25 **LN** 30

AERO-DAWN SEAPLANE: (1942/1946) Same as Aero-Dawn above; body painted blue, green, or red. Pontoon assembly mounted to wheel struts by pin extending through wheel struts. **25 40 45**

BEECHCRAFT BONANZA: (1948-1969) 4¼" wing span. One-piece hollow casting of a private four-seat, single engine, low-wing plane. Casting painted red, yellow, orange, green, silver, or blue with a blue, orange, or silver propeller. Body casting includes an open two-piece windshield, two windows on each side, two open air vents in front of engine housing, and a V-shaped rear tail assembly. Propeller connected to plane with pin; wheel assembly includes small rubber tires with axle spacer connected to a single strut under each wing. TOOTSIETOY MADE IN USA BEECHCRAFT BONANZA.

	G	E	LN
(A) As described above.	12	18	20
(B) Same as (A) except solid windows.	10	16	18
(C) Same as (B) except for no front engine vent holes; body casting includes a pin for propeller; wheel struts moved to plane body; no axle spacer. TOOTSIETOY U.S.A. BEECHCRAFT BONANZA.	8	13	15

BOEING 707 JET AIRLINER: (1958-1961, 1964-1966) 6" wing span. Three-piece plane; two-piece fuselage and tail assembly painted blue; wings painted silver. Top piece includes the rear tail assembly; bottom section contains slots for wheels. Wing assembly is held between the two body sections. Swept-back wing has four jet engines cast in. Front wheel and main wheels have twin rubber tires; each wheel unit fits into a slot in body or wing casting which allows them to be removed to simulate a plane in flight with wheels retracted. Simulated windows and other body details are poor in quality and difficult to see. TOOTSIETOY CHICAGO 24 USA BOEING 707.

	G	E	LN
(A) As described above.	25	45	50
(B) All-silver body and wings.	30	60	65

BOEING STRATOCRUISER AIRLINER: (1951-1954, 1959) 6½" wing span. Pan American World Airways plane

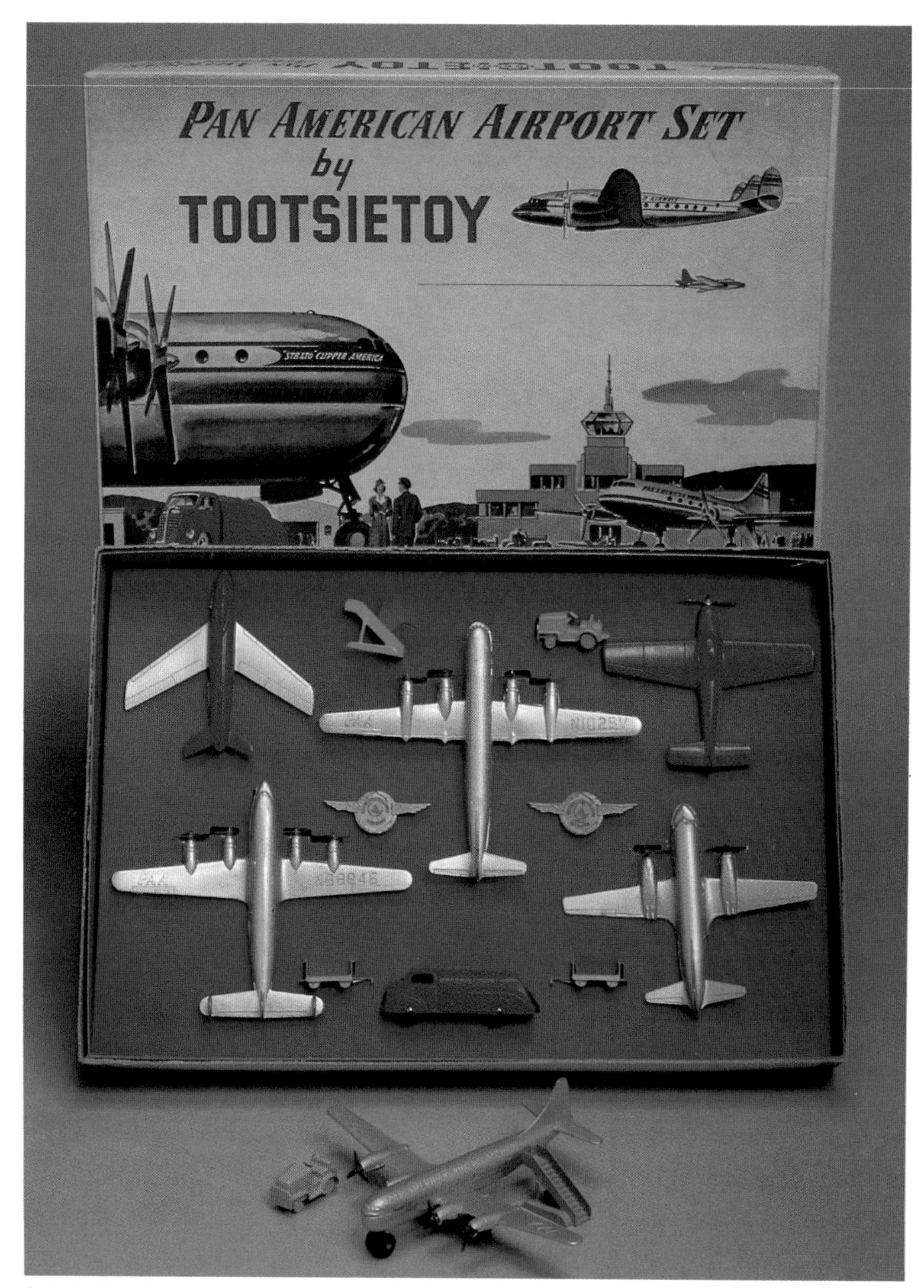

A 1951 No. 6500 Pan American Airport Set features the following planes: **Bottom left:** *Lockheed Constellation.* **Middle and in front of box:** *Boeing Stratocruiser Airliner.* **Bottom right:** *Convair 240 Airliner. The two remaining airplanes are shown again later in this chapter. Note the loading ramp and baggage truck with carts, the pilot and stewardess wings, and the 3-inch gas truck. S. Butler Collection.*

Top: *Panther.* **Middle:** *Skyray "Army"; Cutlass "Army"; Starfire.* **Bottom:** *F-86 Sabre; two Delta Jets in color variations; P-80 Shooting Star.*

	G	E	LN

painted silver with blue propellers. Casting consists of a two-piece hollow fuselage with simulated windows: lower section includes wings; upper section contains rear tail section. Authentic lettering, including PAA on left wing; N1025V on right wing; and PAN AMERICAN WORLD AIRWAYS on both sides of upper airplane body. Two motors on each wing have three-blade propellers. Front and main wheels have twin rubber tires modeling the actual plane; each wheel unit fits into a slot in casting which allows them to be removed to simulate a plane in flight. TOOTSIETOY MADE IN U.S.A. **60 115 125**

CONVAIR 240 AIRLINER: (1950-1954, 1958-1959) 5" wing span. Two-piece airplane painted silver with blue propellers. Hollow body; lower piece includes wings; upper piece contains tail section. No airline markings on fuselage or wing; single motor on each wing with three-blade propellers. Front and main wheels have twin rubber tires; each wheel unit fits into a slot in casting which allows for removal to simulate a plane in flight. TOOTSIETOY U.S.A.

	G	E	LN
(A) As described above.	50	85	95
(B) Red body and silver wings. Rare.	75	115	125

CUTLASS "ARMY" JET: (1958-1960) 3½" wing span. One-piece casting of an F7U3 Vought Cutlass that is clearly marked as a Navy plane but was featured in Army Set No. 3198. Body and features painted olive drab. Large wing with large fins on each side. Wide body with cockpit in front of body and wing; simulated jet engine intake on each side in front of wing; two air outlets at rear of body. Two red, white, and blue star decals are positioned on the top of each large wing. Apparently cast from the same mold as the Cutlass "Navy" Jet, the top of the right wing was modified by eliminating the word NAVY, though NAVY is still present on the underside of the wing. Wheel assembly includes small rubber tires with single axle through struts cast on each side of jet body. TOOTSIETOY U.S.A. F7U3 CUTLASS. **Note:** F7U-3 is the official Navy designation for the seventh version of fighter (F7) made by Vought (U), and the third modification (3). **17 22 25**

CUTLASS NAVY JET: (1956-1969) 3½" wing span. One-piece casting of Navy's F7U3 Cutlass jet made by Vought painted red, green, blue, silver, or light blue. Large wing with large fins on each side. Wide body; cockpit in front of fuselage and main wing; simulated jet engine intake on each side in front of wing; two air outlets at rear of body. Star insignia on left wing; NAVY cast on right wing; markings are reversed on the bottom of the wings. Wheel assembly includes small rubber tires with single axle through struts cast on each side of jet body. TOOTSIETOY U.S.A. F7U3 CUTLASS; see note for Cutlass "Army" Jet above.

	G	E	LN
(A) As described above.	6	8	10
(B) Two-tone colors.	7	12	15

DC-2 TWA AIRLINER: (1942/1946) 5½" wing span. Prewar reissued plane modeling the Douglas DC-2; may have been carried over from prewar production and available through in store stock. Airplane painted silver, orange, red, green, or silver with red wings; blue or black propellers. Fuselage cast as a two-piece hollow body; left side contains the left wing, engine, single wheel on cast strut, and center fin;

Top: *DC-2 TWA Airliner; DC-4 "Army" Transport; DC-4 United Super Mainliner, C. Jones Collection.* **Bottom:** *Boeing 707 Jet Airliner; Sikorsky S-58 Helicopter; P-38 Lightning Fighter Plane, H. Van Curler Collection.*

Top: *Panther Navy Jet; Skyray Navy Jet; Cutlass Navy Jet.* **Middle:** *F-86 Sabre Jet; Panther Navy Jet, two-tone variation; Skyray Navy Jet, two-tone variation; Cutlass Navy Jet, two-tone variation.* **Bottom:** *Beechcraft Bonanzas in different color variations; Piper Cub; Ryan Navion.*

G E LN

right side contains the right wing, right engine, and single wheel on cast strut; third wheel in back; seven open windows on each side. TWA cast on the left wing, and NC 101Y on the right wing. Twin motors with a three-blade propeller held by a pin into motor casting; metal wheels painted black. TOOTSIETOY MADE IN UNITED STATES OF AMERICA PAT. APL.F.

(A) As described above. **30 50 60**

(B) Two-tone colors. **40 65 75**

DC-4 "ARMY" TRANSPORT: (1942/1946) 5½" wing span. Prewar reissued plane modeling a Douglas DC-4 transport; may have been carried over from prewar production and available through in store stock. Body painted tan with green camouflage; white star with red dot in center of a blue circle on both wings. Fuselage cast as two-piece hollow body divided under the windows: lower section includes wings, stabilizer and tail fins; upper section includes center fin, ten open windows on left side, and eleven windows on right. Two motors on each wing with three-blade black propellers held by pins in motor casting. Three metal wheels with double cast struts for each. ARMY TRANSPORT TOOTSIETOY MADE IN U.S.A. **50 85 95**

DC-4 UNITED SUPER MAINLINER: (1942/1946) 5½" wing span. Reissued prewar piece; may have been carried over from prewar production and available through in store stock. Plane like the DC-4 above except body painted silver, red, or green with blue propellers, or silver with red wings; UNITED on left wing; and NC 20100 on right wing. SUPER MAINLINER / ANOTHER TOOTSIETOY MADE IN U.S.A. **40 65 75**

DELTA JET: (1954-1955) 2¾" wing span. Fighter jet in two-piece casting: lower fuselage section includes the wheel struts; upper section includes a triangular delta wing and tail. Body painted in several combinations: red top with a silver bottom; silver top with a blue bottom; blue top with a silver bottom; and silver top with a red bottom. Wing casting includes a star insignia. Small rubber tire mounted on a pin in wheel struts under wing. TOOTSIETOY MADE IN U.S.A. DELTA. **15 22 25**

F-86 SABRE JET: (1950-1955, 1958) 4" wing span. Two-piece casting of a North American fighter jet: lower fuselage section painted silver and includes the main wings; upper body section painted red and includes rear tail assembly. Single wheel assembly under each wing; small rubber tires with an axle spacer on each. Jet engine exhaust opening at rear of fuselage. TOOTSIETOY MADE IN U.S.A. F-86 SABRE.

(A) As described above. **15 22 25**

(B) Blue upper body. **NRS**

F-86 SABRE JET: (1956-1969) 3¼" wing span. One-piece casting of North American fighter jet painted red, green, blue, silver, light blue, or olive green. USAF and star insignia on right wing. No casting identification. **6 8 10**

HILLER HELICOPTER: (1968-1969) Similar to the Sikorsky S-58 Helicopter but has skids to rest on; no wheels. HILLER 12c cast into tail boom; body painted blue. (Robert Straub Collection and information.) **NRS**

LOCKHEED ELECTRA 10A PLANE: (1942/1946) Reissued prewar plane; may have been available through in-store stock. One-piece hollow twin-engine airplane with forward cockpit. Body painted silver, green, orange, or yellow with blue three-blade propellers; simulated side windows; small twin-tail assembly; EAL on left wing and NC 1011 on right wing. Smooth black rubber tires with single, through struts cast into bottom of plane axle. **20 30 35**

LOCKHEED CONSTELLATION PAA AIRLINER: (1951-1953, 1958) 6" wing span. Two-piece Pan American Airways plane painted silver with a hollow fuselage: lower section includes wings; upper section contains triple fins on tail section. PAN AMERICAN WORLD AIRWAYS cast on both sides of fuselage above windows; PAA on left wing; N88846 on right wing; two motors on each wing with three-blade blue propellers. Front and main wheels have twin rubber tires; each wheel unit fits into a slot in casting. **75 115 135**

P-38 LIGHTNING FIGHTER PLANE: (1950) 5⅛" wing span. One-piece twin-engine model of a Lockheed P-38 painted silver with blue propellers. Center nacelle does not extend behind the wing. Each of the two motor housings extend to the rear of the plane to support the long stabilizer and twin fins. U.S.A. on left wing; P-38 on right wing; two three-blade propellers held by pins into casting. Two rubber tires, axle spacer, and pin through cast-in struts. TOOTSIETOY MADE IN USA. **45 80 100**

P-39 AIRACOBRA FIGHTER PLANE: (1947) 5" wing span. Rare single-propeller fighter modeling the P-39 made by Bell; die-cast silver body and tail section; protruding air vent behind raised cockpit; stamped-tin wing painted red includes the wheel strut tabs; held in place by tabs cast into body. Red, silver, and blue star insignia with bars and black flap lines painted on each wing. Black rubber tires with axle spacer. Featured in gift set No. 7100. TOOTSIETOY under nose of plane; MADE IN U.S.A. under tail section. R. Johnson Collection. **55 100 125**

P-40 FIGHTER PLANE: (1942/1946) 5" wing span. Extremely rare plane; may have been a reissued prewar P-40; may have been carried over from prewar production and available through in store stock. Two-piece single-engine fighter plane painted silver-gray; upper body section includes the wings and rear tail assembly; bottom piece is the lower body of the airplane. Cockpit sits over main wing and extends back to tail. Nose of airplane is pointed; two simulated guns cast behind nose on top of engine cover. Unusual propeller design; the blades are cast into a painted spinner (or nose-piece) which follows the contours of the nose of the plane. Peg on spinner is clamped in place by the two halves of the fuselage. The bottom section of the fuselage is riveted to the upper section, which is very unusual for Tootsietoys; four rivets are visible on the outside of the toy. TOOTSIETOY cast under the middle of the left wing; MADE IN U.S.A. cast under the middle of the right wing; CURTIS P-40 PURSUIT PLANE is cast down the length of the inside of the fuselage. **55 100 200**

P-80 SHOOTING STAR JET: (1948-1955) 4⅜" wing span. Two-piece fighter jet modeling the Lockheed P-80; lower section painted red or blue includes the wheel assembly and wing; upper section includes a silver-painted fuselage, and tail assembly. Cockpit cutouts simulate the bubble on the real plane; air intake openings on each side of body above wing and

G E LN

at rear. Wing extends straight out from body; insignia cast into each wing features a star in a circle with a bar on each side. Wheel assembly has rubber tires on axle with spacer between cast-in struts. TOOTSIETOY MADE IN U.S.A. 485004.
15 30 35

PANTHER JET: (1953-1955) 3¾″ wing span. Two-piece Grumman Panther jet painted blue. Lower body section includes wheel assembly; upper body section includes wing and tail assembly. Casting includes fuel tank on wing tips; star on left wing; two bars on each side of star; three rockets cast-in on underside of wing; pierced cockpit openings to simulate bubble; and engine intake on each side of body. Rubber tire mounted on cast pins extending out from sides of cast strut. TOOTSIETOY MADE IN U.S.A. **25 35 40**

PANTHER NAVY JET: (1956-1969) 3½″ wing span. One-piece Grumman Panther jet painted red, green, silver, metallic blue, or blue. Tail extends beyond jet body; tail assembly is connected to section beyond jet body. Star insignia on left wing; NAVY on right wing; markings are reversed on the bottom of the wing. Fuel tank at the end of each wing. Wheel assembly includes small rubber tires with single axle through a single strut from each side of jet body. TOOTSIETOY U.S.A. F9F-2.

(A) As described above. **6 8 10**

(B) Same as (A) except wing fuel tanks and rear tail section painted silver. **10 13 15**

PIPER CUB: (1948-1952) 4⅛″ wing span. One-piece single engine, low-wing plane is a good replica of an experimental Piper Skysedan. Hollow main body painted red, orange, blue, green, or silver with a blue, orange, or silver propeller. Casting includes a rib to make an open two-piece windshield; a two-piece round rear window; two windows on each side; and air vents on front of engine housing. Propeller connected to plane with pin. Wheel assembly includes rubber tires with axle and spacer through a single strut from under each wing. TOOTSIETOY PIPER CUB MADE IN USA.

(A) As described above. **15 18 20**

(B) Front and rear windows cast open. **15 22 25**

RYAN NAVION: (1948-1953) 4⅜″ wing span. One-piece single engine, low-wing plane. Casting painted red, yellow, orange, silver, or blue with a blue, orange, or silver propeller. Casting includes an open two-piece windshield; two windows on each side; single rear window; rounded engine front. Cockpit extends above body. Propeller connected to plane with pin. Wheel assembly includes small rubber tires with axle and spacer through a single strut die-cast under each wing. TOOTSIETOY MADE IN USA NAVION.

(A) As described above. **15 18 20**

(B) Windows are not open; MADE IN U.S.A. NAVION.
12 16 18

SIKORSKY S-58 HELICOPTER: (1958-1969) 3½″ Rare; silver-painted four-blade main rotor and three-blade rear rotor; 3½″-long body painted blue. S-58 in side of body casting; solid cast landing gear and wheels painted same as body. TOOTSIETOY USA CHICAGO 24.

(A) As described above in blue and silver. **30 55 75**

The U.S. Coast Guard Amphibian closely resembles the Sikorsky S-43 issued before the war. This postwar toy was called a "PBY" in company ads, probably in acknowledgment of the war-time popularity of the PBY made by Consolidated. E. Poole Collection. R. Straub information.

G E LN

(B) Same as (A) except body painted in olive drab; shiny metal (silver) propeller. **30 55 75**

SKYRAY "ARMY" JET: (1958-1960) 3″ wing span. One-piece Douglas F4D Skyray jet clearly marked as a Navy jet but featured in Army Set No. 3198; body painted olive-drab. Cockpit at front of jet body; large triangular wing extending from cockpit to rear of plane; small jet intake behind cockpit and in front of wing. Star insignia on left wing; NAVY on right wing. Markings are reversed on the bottom of the wing. Unlike the Cutlass "Army" Jet, there were no casting changes to eliminate the word NAVY on the wing surface. Single narrow tail extends from jet body. Wheel assembly uses single axle through a single strut at each side of jet body; small rubber tires. TOOTSIETOY U.S.A. F4D SKYRAY. **15 18 20**

SKYRAY NAVY JET: (1956-1969) 3″ wing span. One-piece Douglas F4D Skyray jet; casting painted red, green, blue, silver, or light blue. Cockpit at front of body; large triangular wing extending from cockpit to rear of plane; small jet intake behind cockpit and in front of wing. Star insignia on left wing; NAVY on right wing. Markings are reversed on the bottom of the wing. Single narrow tail extends from body. Wheel assembly uses single axle to a single strut from each side of body; small rubber tires. TOOTSIETOY U.S.A. F4D SKYRAY.

(A) As described above. **6 8 10**

(B) Two-tone colors. **7 12 15**

STARFIRE JET: (1956-1969) 3½″ wing span. One-piece Lockheed Starfire jet painted red, green, blue, olive drab, silver, or light blue. Casting includes wing with fuel tank on each tip; small swept back tail; simulated rocket launcher or radar pod on front of main wing between fuel tank and body. USAF on right wing and star insignia on left wing. Markings cast underneath in same locations. Wheel assembly includes small rubber tires with single axle through a single strut under each wing. TOOTSIETOY U.S.A. F-94 STARFIRE.

(A) As described above. **6 9 10**

(B) Two-tone colors. **7 12 15**

U.S. ARMY PLANE: (1942/1946) Reissued prewar plane; may have been available through in-store stock during the war. One-piece, small single-engine plane. Body painted sil-

G E LN

ver, green, yellow, gold, or silver with red wing. Black, blue, or silver three-blade propeller. Body casting includes a very large engine cowl, forward wing with set-back cockpit located in front of a large rear tail assembly. Five-point star in circle on each wing; US cast into left wing, ARMY cast in right wing. Smooth white rubber tires with single, one-piece axle, through a strut under each wing. **15 25 30**

U.S. COAST GUARD AMPHIBIAN: (1950) 5½" wing span. Rare two-piece twin-engine seaplane resembling a Sikorsky prewar S-43 but called a "PBY" in company advertising. Painted all-silver, all-blue, red with a silver wing (located above the body), or silver with a red wing. Top of wing contains two prewar insignias with blue circle, white star, and red dot in center. One-piece hollow body; separate wing attached with rivets to bent tabs on body. Cast-in pontoons extending out from lower sides of body. COAST GUARD cast on wing between the motors with black three-blade propellers. Single casting of axle and wheels fits into lugs inside hull similar to wheels on Tootsietoy ships. E. Poole, R. Johnson, and R. Straub Collections. **80 130 200**

WACO "BOMBER": (1942/1946) 5" wing span. Prewar biplane reissued in postwar sets or may have been carried over from prewar production and available through in store stock. A good replica of the real Waco C-6 cabin biplane transport for private purchase. Details are very accurate, other than those necessitated by casting such as the windows where the two halves meet, and the omission od wing struts. Two-piece casting similar to the DC-4; top half includes top of fuselage and top wing; bottom section includes bottom of fuselage and lower wing. Usually sold in civilian colors of red or blue top with silver bottom. U.S. NAVY on wing of blue models. Later version in camouflage colors. Halves joined under open windows. Dividing line climbs over top of nose to allow a front flat radial engine to be cast with cowling and cylinders accurately reflecting a plane of that period. Gun cast in top of cabin fuselage behind U.S. NAVY on wings. Bombs cast under lower wing. Wheel assembly includes struts with holes for the pin and wheels. **25 40 50**

Ships

Ten different types of ships, both military and civilian pieces, were produced prior to World War II and were probably reissued after the war in 1945 or 1946. Each ship contains one or two sets of small metal undercarriage wheels to permit the unit to be pushed easily along a flat surface. They vary from 4 inches to 6 inches in length. For the most part, there is a significant number of these toys for the collector to choose from. Therefore the prices being asked at most shows are usually quite reasonable. Collectors interested in purchasing these items should be sure there are no broken pieces, such as masts or the guns on war ships. The ships were produced in a wide range of colors, which challenges collectors who wish to find every variation. In addition, many of the ships are painted in at least two different colors. A variety of miniature ships were also produced both before and well after World War II; these may be found on blister packs with other miniature items.

G E LN

The best known information on production years is provided based on historical data, catalogues, advertisements, and information from various collectors. Cast-in information on the underside of each vehicle appears last in each listing.

AIRCRAFT CARRIER: (1942/1946) 6" long with two sets of undercarriage wheels. Open flight deck with superstructure on right side of ship; two single guns on front structure as well as on smaller rear structure; large oval stack between structures; small hoist unit at stern; five airplanes on flight deck; portholes and elevator doors on hull. TOOTSIETOY MADE IN UNITED STATES OF AMERICA NO. 1036.

(A) Silver hull and superstructure; red mast and top of superstructures; blue airplanes. **20 30 35**

(B) Gray hull and superstructure; silver mast and top of superstructures; silver airplanes. **15 22 25**

(C) Same as (B) with blue airplanes. **20 30 35**

BATTLESHIP: (1942/1946) 6" long with two sets of undercarriage wheels. Front and rear of ship have two sets of triple guns each; two single guns on each side at deck level. Large front superstructure behind front guns, followed by a large stack and mast and then a smaller structure. Double row of simulated portholes on each side of hull extending from the bow to the rear guns; single row of windows continues to the stern. TOOTSIETOY MADE IN UNITED STATES OF AMERICA NO. 1034.

(A) Silver hull and main structure; red guns front and rear; red top of superstructure, smokestack, mast, and top of smaller structure. **15 22 25**

(B) Gray hull and main structure; silver guns front and rear; silver top of superstructure, smokestack, mast, and top of smaller structure. **10 18 20**

CRUISER: (1942/1946) 5½" long with two sets of undercarriage wheels. Front of ship contains two sets of double guns, one single rear gun, two single guns in center of ship on each side; large front superstructure with mast; two center stacks; large rear mast; and an airplane between stacks. Double row of portholes on each side from bow to main superstructure, followed by a single row to stern of ship. TOOTSIETOY MADE IN UNITED STATES OF AMERICA NO. 1035.

(A) Silver hull and superstructure; red front guns, top of superstructure, stacks, and mast; blue airplane. **15 22 25**

(B) Gray hull and superstructure; silver front guns; silver top of superstructure, stacks, mast, and airplane. **10 18 20**

(C) Same as (B) with blue airplane. **10 18 20**

DESTROYER: (1942/1946) 4" long with one set of undercarriage wheels. Single deck gun in front and rear; forward superstructure with mast; two small stacks; one lifeboat; rear small structure. Simulated portholes and K880 in large letters near the bow. Hull contains graduated levels increasing in height from the stern to the bow. TOOTSIETOY MADE IN UNITED STATES OF AMERICA NO. 127.

(A) Silver hull and main structure; red front and rear deck guns; red top of stacks, superstructure, and mast. **10 14 15**

(B) Gray hull and main structure; silver front and rear deck guns; silver top of stacks, superstructure, and mast. **10 14 15**

Top: *Yacht; Cruiser; Freighter.* **Middle:** *Battleship; Aircraft Carrier.* **Bottom:** *Transport Ship; Destroyer.*

	G	E	LN
(C) All-silver destroyer.	8	10	12
(D) All-gray destroyer.	8	10	12

FREIGHTER: (1942/1946) 5½" long with two sets of undercarriage wheels. Two individual superstructures in center of ship; rear structure has stack and air vent; small structure at stern. Casting includes a three-piece loading boom on each side of center superstructures and a single row of portholes from bow to stern. TOOTSIETOY MADE IN UNITED STATES OF AMERICA NO. 1038.

(A) Black hull with a blue line; light yellow deck and superstructures; blue stack and loading booms. **15 22 25**

(B) Black hull with a green stripe; white deck and superstructures; red stack; and green loading booms. **15 22 25**

(C) Gray hull, deck, and superstructures; silver stack and loading booms. **10 18 20**

MINIATURE SHIPS: (1942/1946, 1960) Hollow castings include a submarine, cruiser, destroyer, battleship, liner, and aircraft carrier which vary in length from 1¼" to 2½". Bodies painted gray, black, red, blue, yellow, orange, or white. The smaller ships have no casting identifications; larger ships marked TOOTSIETOY USA. **2 4 5**

SUBMARINE: (1942/1946) 4" long with one set of undercarriage wheels. Center superstructure (conning tower); single deck gun in front of conning tower; short mast in front and rear; curved side hull with simulated riveted panels; front torpedo tube. TOOTSIETOY MADE IN UNITED STATES OF AMERICA NO. 128.

(A) Red hull panels; silver hull, conning tower, mast, and gun. **10 14 15**

(B) Red hull panels; silver hull and conning towers; blue mast and gun. **12 16 18**

(C) All-silver submarine. **8 10 12**

(D) All-gray submarine. **8 10 12**

A variation of the Tanker Ship with front gun. Tips of loading booms and underside of hull are painted red. E. Poole Collection.

	G	E	LN
(E) Gray hull and conning tower; silver mast and gun.	8	10	12

TANKER: (1942/1946) 5½" long with two sets of undercarriage wheels. All-gray tanker comes with or without single front deck gun; casting includes center superstructure; stern superstructure with stack; three-piece loading boom on each side of center superstructure; single row of portholes at bow, under middle superstructure, and under stern superstructure; three air vents on stern structure, and two air vents on center structure. TOOTSIETOY MADE IN UNITED STATES OF AMERICA NO. 1039.

	G	E	LN
(A) With front gun.	15	22	25
(B) Without front gun.	10	18	20
(C) Same as (A) or (B) with red and gray hull.	15	22	25

TENDER: (1942/1946) 4" long escort ship with single set of undercarriage wheels. Casting includes main superstructure in center between depressed hull sections; superstructure has a single stack, air vent, and searchlight; three-piece cargo boom in each depressed section; simulated portholes at bow, superstructure, and stern; water line along bottom of hull. TOOTSIETOY MADE IN UNITED STATES OF AMERICA NO. 129.

Top: *Tender escort.* **Bottom left:** *Submarine. An assortment of miniature ships make up the rest of the fleet.*

	G	E	LN
(A) White ship with brown camouflage pattern.	10	18	20
(B) All-gray ship.	10	16	18
(C) Blue and red hull with white superstructure.	15	22	25

TRANSPORT SHIP: (1942/1946) 6" long passenger liner with two sets of undercarriage wheels. Superstructure has four main levels with a fifth forward level. Top of ship has three large stacks and front and rear masts. Lifeboats on both sides of upper structure; double row of simulated portholes in hull from bow to stern. TOOTSIETOY MADE IN UNITED STATES OF AMERICA NO. 1037.

	G	E	LN
(A) Light yellow ship with gray camouflage pattern.	15	22	25
(B) Blue hull; silver superstructure; red and blue stacks and mast.	10	18	20

YACHT: (1942/1946) 4″ long with one set of undercarriage wheels. Gray hull; white superstructure and deck; blue mast front and rear; blue top of stack. Two-tier superstructure with front structure; stack behind front structure; front and rear mast and front jib extension; two lifeboats on each side of lower structure; portholes in hull on both sides. TOOTSIETOY MADE IN UNITED STATES OF AMERICA NO. 130. **12 18 20**

CHAPTER 10

Miscellaneous Vehicles

This chapter presents many different Tootsietoys that do not fall into the previous chapter divisions, including some of the series classified as Postwar First Generation and Postwar Second Generation in Chapter 1. The series in this chapter include construction and farm equipment, the Classic Antique Series, two 7-inch special vehicles, the Pocket (HO) Series, and the Classic Series by Lone Star, as well as race cars, period pieces, space ships, trains, and a kit model. Many of these were sold as individually boxed pieces and will therefore be mentioned in the next chapter. However, the likelihood that they will be encountered without their boxes prompted an inclusion of their descriptions here.

Four of the farm and construction toys are noted for their exceptional play value. They are the Caterpillar Dozer, the Caterpillar Grader, No. 289 Tractor and Disc Harrow, and No. 389 Tractor with Scoop. Both of the Caterpillars contain moving parts which significantly add to their quality and individual value. The Caterpillar Dozer's side lever allows the blade to move up or down, or to rest in two fixed positions. The lever can be broken and should be checked carefully prior to purchase. The Grader has a spring-loaded yet very durable, adjustable scraper blade. The detailing on this piece is not as good as on the Caterpillar Dozer, but nonetheless it is a good reproduction of a grader.

The following listings describe individual toys of varying length produced from the early fifties to the late sixties. Based on historical data, catalogues, advertisements, and data obtained from other collectors, the best known information on production years for each piece is included with its listing. Cast-in information found on the underside of each vehicle appears in small caps as the last item in each listing.

Construction and Farm Equipment

CATERPILLAR DOZER: (1956-1967) 4½" long with blade. Tractor painted yellow with silver-painted exhaust pipe, diesel motor, front blade lever, motor grille, and tread support wheels. Tractor treads are molded black rubber. Casting contains front blade assembly which can be raised, lowered, or held in the up position; highly detailed exposed diesel motor; hood over motor with CATERPILLAR DIESEL on both sides of hood; operator's seat with lever controls in floor platform behind motor; circular tow bar assembly. TOOTSIETOY CHICAGO 24 U.S.A.

	G	E	LN
(A) With front blade assembly.	20	45	55
(B) Without front blade assembly.	15	35	40
(C) Red body with silver features.			NRS

CATERPILLAR SCRAPER: (1956-1967) 5½" long with blade. Road grader painted yellow with a silver-painted motor grille, exhaust pipe, and metal scraper blade. Body contains a rear motor housing; open operator's seat; front frame extending to front wheel assembly and supporting a subframe which contains a circular casting to hold the scraper blade in three different positions. Scraper blade has a center pin which extends through circle casting, a spring, and a lock washer. Motor housing includes large air vents on each side, rear radiator, grille, and exhaust pipe. Subframe is supported by single tandem wheels; front frame by single wheel assembly. Black rubber tires 1" in diameter are held by cast pins in body of scraper. TOOTSIETOY CHICAGO 24 U.S.A.

	G	E	LN
(A) Dark yellow body.	20	35	45
(B) Light yellow body.	20	35	45
(C) Dark yellow with silver features. No subframe supporting scraper blade; top of blade contains a flat extended spacer with a long shaft extending up through a hole in scraper frame; top of shaft contains a cast butterfly to hold unit in place; spring inside frame provides tension for the blade. Blade is made of plastic.	15	30	35
(D) Same as (C) but light yellow color.	15	30	35

FORD FARM TRACTOR: (1952-1969) 4¾" long. Body painted red including exposed motor, transmission, and rear axle assembly; silver-painted motor cover and front grille; black tractor seat and steering wheel. Casting includes a detailed motor; front grille with partial engine cover extending back to steering wheel; FORD on both sides of engine cover; three-spoke steering wheel; rear hitch bracket. Front rubber tires 1¼" in diameter; rear rubber Tootsietoy tires 2" in diameter ("Tootsietoy" is only on the rear tires). No casting identification on body.

	G	E	LN
(A) As described above.	25	45	55
(B) All-red tractor with silver grille.	25	45	55
(C) All-red tractor with molded solid steering wheel and seat; tractor tires are solid plastic.	20	40	50

Top: *Caterpillar Dozer with its original box; S. Butler Collection.* **Bottom:** *Variations of the Caterpillar Scraper. Note the different color and design for the scraper blade and assembly. K. Jestes and S. Butler Collections.*

FORD FARM TRACTOR WITH DISC HARROW: (1952-1969) 7½" long. Two-piece unit painted red; disc on disc harrow painted silver. Tractor body includes a detailed motor; transmission; rear axle assembly; front grille with partial engine cover; solid cast steering wheel; seat; FORD on both sides of engine cover; rear hitch. Front plastic tires 1¼" in diameter; rear Tootsietoy tires 2" in diameter ("Tootsietoy" is only on the rear tires). Disc harrow contains ten discs mounted on two shafts under a V-shaped frame. TOOTSIETOY CHICAGO 24 U.S.A.

	G	E	LN
(A) As described above.	**40**	**65**	**75**
(B) Same as (A); tractor has silver motor cover and front grille.	**45**	**70**	**80**
(C) Disc harrow only.	**10**	**20**	**25**

FORD FARM TRACTOR WITH FERTILIZER SPREADER TRAILER: (1958-1959) 10" long. Two-piece unit; tractor has a red motor, transmission, and rear axle assembly; silver motor cover and front grille; black seat and steering wheel. Farm trailer is red with silver disc and teeth harrow. Tractor body casting includes detailed motor, transmission, rear axle assembly; front grille with partial engine cover extending back to steering wheel; FORD on both sides of engine cover; three-spoke steering wheel; rear hitch; front rubber tires 1¼" in diameter; rear rubber Tootsietoy tires 2" in diameter. No casting identification on tractor body. 6" farm trailer contains a rear disc assembly and teeth harrow mounted on top of the low-side trailer behind the wheels; round disc on outside of trailer connected to the teeth harrow on each side makes contact with the trailer tires and allows teeth harrow to rotate as trailer is pulled; single bar hitch; rubber tires 1¼" in diameter. TOOTSIETOY CHICAGO 24 U.S.A.

	G	E	LN
(A) As described above.	**35**	**65**	**75**
(B) Same as (A) with all-red tractor.	**35**	**65**	**70**
(C) Fertilizer trailer only.	**10**	**20**	**25**

FORD FARM TRACTOR WITH HAUL WAGON: (1953-1958) 14" long. Two-piece unit; tractor is all red with a silver or yellow front scoop and black tractor seat. Haul wagon has a red base with yellow sides; came unassembled. Tractor has a detailed motor, transmission, and rear axle assembly; front grille with partial engine cover extending back to steering wheel; FORD on engine cover; three-spoke steering wheel; rear hitch; and a front scoop which can be moved up or down with a side lever; front rubber tires 1¼" in diameter; rear Tootsietoy tires are 2" in diameter; no casting identification on tractor body. Front scoop assembly connected to tractor frame. Haul wagon has high sides on front and rear; wheel assembly on front and rear; rubber

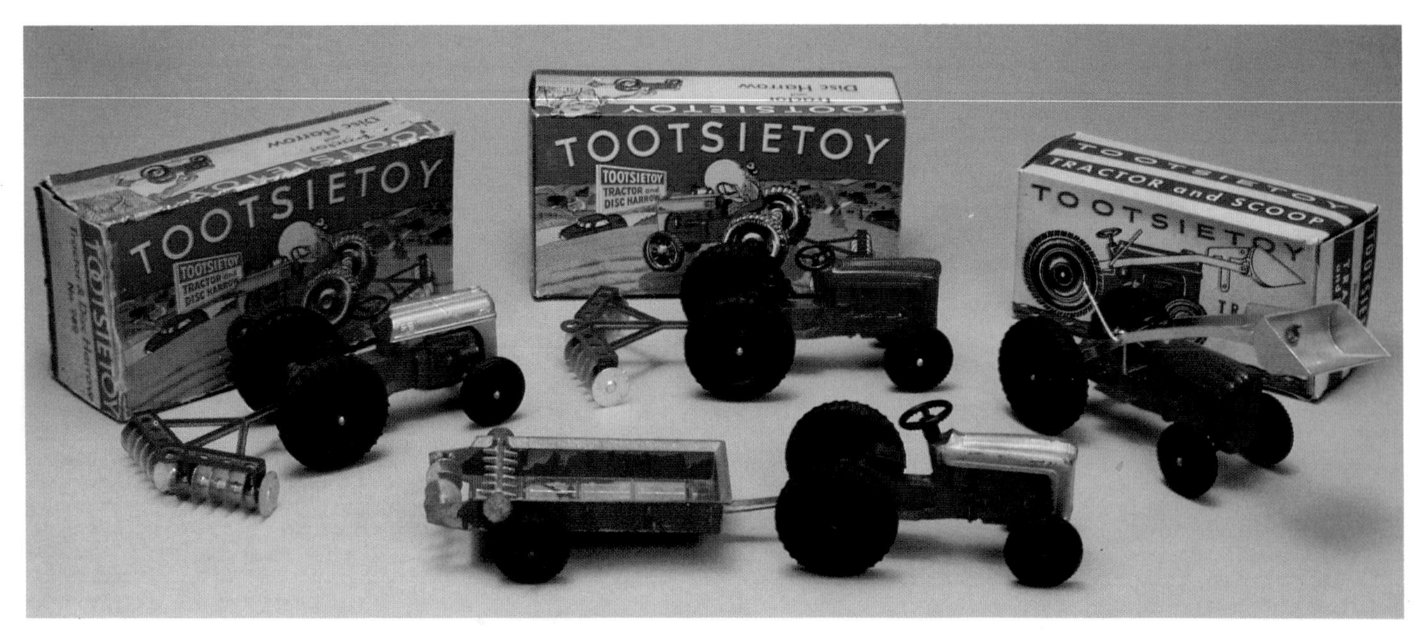

Left: *Ford Farm Tractor with Disc Harrow, an all-red Ford Farm Tractor with Disc Harrow, and a Ford Farm Tractor with Scoop, all with their original boxes. S. Butler and K. Jestes Collections.* **Bottom:** *Ford Farm Tractor with Fertilizer Spreader Trailer.*

Top: *1907 Stanley Steamer Runabout; 1929 Ford Model A.* **Middle:** *1906 Cadillac.* **Bottom**: *1919 Stutz Bearcat; 1912 Ford Model T; 1912 Ford Model T. Strombecker Corporation archives.*

tires 1¼" in diameter. TOOTSIETOY CHICAGO 24 U.S.A. H. Van Curler Collection.

	G	E	LN
(A) As described above.	**50**	**85**	**100**
(B) Haul wagon only.	**25**	**40**	**45**

FORD TRACTOR WITH SCOOP: (1955-1960) 7" long. Tractor body painted red with black seat; silver-painted operating front shovel. Tractor casting includes a detailed motor; transmission; front grille with partial engine cover extending back to steering wheel; FORD on engine cover; three-spoke steering wheel made of plastic; rear hitch bracket; rear axle assembly. Front rubber tires 1¼" in diameter; rear rubber Tootsietoy tires 2" in diameter. Front scoop assembly connected to tractor frame can be raised or lowered by side

G E LN

lever. No casting identification on tractor body. H. Van Curler Collection. **35 60 85**

HARROW PLOW: (1958-1960) Painted red with silver blades; featured as an accessory in No. 4300 Farm Set. Designed to be pulled by the Ford Farm Tractor. **10 20 25**

The Classic Antique Series

From 1960 to 1962, Strombecker offered a group of highly detailed vehicles in "true 1/50 scale" called the Classic Antique Series. The antiques featured in this group are becoming popular among collectors.

3107 1906 Cadillac, 2½"
3109 1907 Stanley Steamer Runabout, 3⅛"
3101 1912 Ford Model T, 3"
3108 1919 Stutz Bearcat, 3⅞"
3111 1922 Mack Truck (1961-1962), 3¾"
3102 1929 Ford Model A, 3¾"

Each of these vehicles originally sold for between fifty-nine and sixty-nine cents and are currently valued from $8 to $20. Boxed set No. 4350 contains five of these vehicles—all but the Mack truck—and is valued at $150 in mint condition.

Collectors may come across a line of classic antique cars and trucks which at first appear to be part of this Classic Antique Series but which were not, in fact, produced by Strombecker. These vehicles are reproductions of prewar Tootsietoy vehicles manufactured by Accucast, a small American firm. The only vehicle that resembles any of the postwar Classic Antique Series cars and trucks is the 1929 Ford Model A. However, the Tootsietoy version is easily distinguished by its four windows, front bumper, and spare tire mounted on the rear trunk. The Accucast model has six windows but none of the other features.

The Austin-Healy Kit Model

1960 AUSTIN-HEALY 3000: (1961) 5" long. Rare kit packaged in a clear plastic cover on a cardboard base (not a typical blister pack). Originally sold for fifty-nine cents. Package front reads AUSTIN-HEALY MODEL SPORTS CAR KIT with eight assembly instructions. Kit contains an unpainted white metal body with front bucket seats and a rear bench seat; four vinyl tires; two steel axles; a decal set; and the following clear plastic pieces: a windshield, a steering wheel with column, the floor gearshift lever, and four hubcaps. The instructions state that plastic parts to be glued onto body. The decal sheet includes four flames in red and white, outlined in black; two 711 numbers in blue; two crossed checkered flags with red CUSTOM underneath; two blue-on-white WILDCAT door panels outlined in black; one black 400 HP for the hood; and one black-and-white decal containing three gauges for the dash. S. Butler Collection. **50 115 125**

The Lone Star Classic Series

From 1960 to 1961, the Tootsietoy company contracted with the Lone Star Company in England to produce a small line of five American cars to be sold in the United States, Canada, and Europe. These vehicles were developed to compete with Dinky Toys and other toys flooding the market; they were marketed as the Classic Series. The detailing is arguably the finest produced in the sixties.

1960 CADILLAC FOUR-DOOR HARD TOP: (1960-1961) 1/50 scale. Highly detailed metal; body painted light blue with a white top with plastic windows and chrome bumpers, grille, and wheel covers; coil springs for suspension, rubber tires, black base plate. TOOTSIETOY CLASSIC SERIES.

	G	E	LN
(A) With detailed interior.	20	35	40
(B) Without detailed interior.	15	30	35

1960 CHEVROLET CORVAIR FOUR-DOOR SEDAN: (1960-1961) 1/50 scale. Same features and materials as Cadillac above; body painted red. TOOTSIETOY CLASSIC SERIES.

	G	E	LN
(A) With detailed interior.	20	35	40
(B) Without detailed interior.	15	30	35

1960 DODGE POLARA: (1960-1961) 1/50 scale. Same features and materials as Cadillac above; colors unknown. TOOTSIETOY CLASSIC SERIES.

	G	E	LN
(A) With detailed interior.	20	35	40
(B) Without detailed interior.	15	30	35

1960 FORD GALAXIE 500 CONVERTIBLE: (1960-1961) 1/50 scale. Same features and materials as Cadillac above; colors unknown. TOOTSIETOY CLASSIC SERIES.

	G	E	LN
(A) With detailed interior.	20	35	40
(B) Without detailed interior.	15	30	35

1960 RAMBLER WAGON: (1960-1961) 1/50 scale. Same features and materials as Cadillac above; body painted green and white. TOOTSIETOY in lowercase letters; CLASSIC SERIES / RAMBLER STATION WAGON / REBEL V-8 ENGINE / SCALE 1/50.

	G	E	LN
(A) With detailed interior.	20	35	40
(B) Without detailed interior.	15	30	35

The Lone Star Company also produced a tanker trailer truck (and possibly some other models) which was similar in size to the Tootsietoy tanker trailer truck in the 6-inch Jumbo Series, but there has not been any evidence that ties any of these larger units with the Tootsietoy manufacturer.

Period Pieces

CIVIL WAR CANNON AND CAISSON: (1961) 10⅜" in length. Five-piece set; die-cast metal cannon; polyethylene caisson with two polyethylene horses; six plastic shells. **20 40 45**

COVERED WAGON: (1961) 7¾" in length. Five-piece set; die-cast metal wagon with polyethylene hitch, cover, and horses. **20 40 45**

The Pocket (HO) Series

In 1962 the company developed a line of HO-scale vehicles called the Pocket Series; they were sold in blister packs for between twenty-nine and forty-nine cents each. Lettering appearing on the side is included.

From left to right: *Ford Sunliner Convertible with Midget Racer and Trailer (Pocket Series); Rambler Station Wagon with Midget Racer and Trailer (Pocket Series); blister pack assortment of miniature ships, airplanes, and vehicles from 1959; 1960 Rambler Station Wagon from the Collector Series produced by Lone Star.*

2325 Car and U-Haul Trailer: 1960 Rambler Station Wagon with U-Haul Trailer, 3⅞"
2465 Metro Van, 2⅜", blue, MERCURY PARCEL SERVICE
2465 Metro Van, 2⅜", white, SUNNYDALE FARMS / FRESH MILK
2465 Metro Van, 2⅜", red, PARIS DRY CLEANERS
2465 Metro Van, 2⅜", olive green, RAILWAY EXPRESS
2465 Metro Van, 2⅜", US MAIL
2465 Metro Van department store delivery, 2⅜"
2490 School Bus, 3¼", yellow with black trim, TOWNSHIP SCHOOL BUS
2425 Car And Boat: Ford Sunliner Convertible with Chris-Craft Boat and Trailer, 5½"
2485 1960 Ford Tow Truck, 2⅝"
2470 1960 Ford Dump Truck, 2⅜"
2460 Two Cars: 1960 Rambler Station Wagon and Ford Sunliner Convertible, 2¾" each
2440 Car and Racer: Ford Sunliner Convertible with Midget Racer and Trailer, 5½"
Cadillac Sedan
Cadillac Sedan with Chris-Craft Boat and Trailer
1960 Rambler Station Wagon
Three Chris-Craft Boats

Depending upon condition and whether or not the package is intact, these HO-scale models can range in value from $10 to over $30 for two-piece units.

G E LN

Race Cars

FERRARI LANCIA RACE CAR: (1964-1967) 5" long. Body is red or dark green with white seat area; silver grille; no racing number. Driver's head made of plastic was often broken off during play or storage. Casting includes driver's upper body and steering wheel; slanted front of racer; front vertical grille partially covered by front of racer; panels protruding from sides of racer between front and rear wheels; protruding panel on top of engine cover; air vents on both sides of panel; protruding headrest above rear of racer body which includes fuel cap; rounded sloping rear. Patterned plastic tires, no axle spacers. FERRARI LANCIA TOOTSIETOY CHICAGO 24 U.S.A.

(A) With racing number on hood and detailed painted head of driver. **20 30 35**
(B) Without hood racing number. **15 25 30**
(C) Same as (A) or (B) with all-white driver. **12 20 25**

MASERATI RACE CAR: (1962-1967) 5" long. Body painted dark green or red with gold seat area; silver grille with black racing number on white background. Racing numbers include 11, 17, 18, or 33. Body casting includes driver's arms, shoulders and top of steering wheel; slanted front end; front grille with no details, covered somewhat by slanted front; air foil behind front wheels; rear of racer with sloping top and sides; fuel port

The underside of the Classic Series Rambler Wagon from 1960. J. T. Riley Collection.

An assortment of Metro Vans. D. Campbell Collection.

	G	E	LN
behind driver. Driver's head made of plastic was often broken off during play or storage. Patterned plastic tires no axle spacers. TOOTSIETOY CHICAGO 24 U.S.A. 01044.			
(A) With detailed painted driver's head.	15	30	35
(B) Without detailed driver's head.	12	20	25

7-inch Specials

The company produced two special 7-inch models from 1956 to 1958: the green or red No. 995 Mercedes Benz 300 and the blue-and-white No. 895 Pontiac Safari Wagon. These highly detailed pieces are difficult to find. They are made of heavy, die-cast metal with rubber tires and special features including operating doors, trunks, and detailed interiors. They were sold as individually boxed items.

895 PONTIAC SAFARI WAGON: (1956-1958) 7" by 3"; GM wagon painted blue and white with extensive silver-painted features; realistic interior; rear door opens. **75 150 200**

995 MERCEDES BENZ 300SL: (1956-1958) 7" by 3"; painted red or green with extensive silver-painted features; gull-wing doors open; realistic light-yellow interior. **100 225 300**

Space Ships and An Airship

BUCK ROGERS SPACE SHIPS: (1953) 4" long. Highly detailed and "brilliantly finished" (catalogue description) reproductions of space ships and a blimp from the original 1937 Buck Rogers series. Originally sold in No. 4025 Tootsietoy Buck Rogers Assortment. Designed to glide along a suspended string, assortment includes a string-and-pulley system like the original series. Two-piece hollow metal castings.

	G	E	LN
(A) Battle Cruiser.	20	40	45
(B) Destroyer.	20	40	45
(C) Attack Ship.	20	40	45
(D) Navy Zeppelin. Silver-painted reproduction of the Navy Zeppelin first offered by Dowst before World War II; U.S.N. LOS ANGELES.	20	45	40

SPACE SHIPS: (1958-1959) 4" long. Silver-painted reintroductions of the 1953 Buck Rogers prewar Battle Cruiser, Destroyer, and Attack Ships. Three body variations, each containing modern U.S. star insignia. Two-piece hollow metal castings. Surprisingly difficult to find and are not widely known by collectors. Mint units in their original blister packs are valued from $60 to $80 each. **25 45 50**

Trains on Wheels

F3 UNION PACIFIC DIESEL: (1955-1958) 4" long. One-piece metal casting painted yellow with silver top; two sets of black rubber tires. Part of boxed set No. 5610. **15 30 35**

BOX CAR: (1955-1958) 3½" long. One-piece metal casting painted green with loop and hook coupler at each end; two sets of black rubber tires. Part of boxed set No. 5610. **10 25 30**

BOX CAR: (1968) Approximately 1¾" long. Yellow plastic body with blue metal frame with hook connection on one end and circle hole connection at the other end; two sets of Tootsietoy tires. **5 7 8**

CABOOSE: (1955-1958) 3½" long. One-piece metal casting painted red; loop and hook coupler at each end; two sets of black rubber tires. Part of boxed set No. 5610. **10 25 30**

CABOOSE: (1968) Approximately 1¾" long. Red plastic body with black metal frame; two sets of Tootsietoy tires; hook connection on one end and circle hole connection at the other end. **5 7 8**

Left: *Pontiac Safari Wagon with its original box.* **Center:** *1960 Austin-Healy 3000 in its original kit package and as a completed model.* **Right:** *Mercedes Benz 300SL with its original box. S. Butler Collection.*

	G	E	LN

CIVIL WAR GENERAL STEAM ENGINE: (1968) Approximately 5½" in length with tender. Red die-cast body with yellow plastic smoke stack, light, and bell; **325** on boiler cab; two sets of Tootsietoy tires extending through lower boiler frame. No casting identification. Tender is dark blue plastic with a black metal frame with two sets of Tootsietoy tires.

	G	E	LN
(A) As described above.	**6**	**12**	**15**
(B) Green plastic tender, blue metal frame.	**6**	**12**	**15**

COAL HOPPER CAR: (1955-1958) 3½" long. One-piece metal casting painted silver; loop and hook coupler at each end; two sets of black rubber tires; load of black coal. Part of boxed set No. 5610. **10 25 30**

GONDOLA: (1968) Approximately 1¾" long. All-black plastic body and metal frame with hook connection on one end and circle hole connection at the other end; two sets of Tootsietoy tires.

	G	E	LN
(A) As described above.	**5**	**7**	**8**
(B) All-blue body and frame.	**5**	**7**	**8**

SINGLE DOME TANK CAR: (1955-1958) 3½" long. Silver one-piece metal casting with loop and hook coupler at each end; two sets of black tires. Part of boxed set No. 5610. **10 25 30**

STOCK CAR: (1955-1958) 3½" long. One-piece metal casting painted red with silver roof; loop and hook coupler at each end; two sets of black rubber tires. Part of boxed set No. 5610. **10 25 30**

CHAPTER 11

Boxed Sets with Individually Boxed Items, Blister Packs, and Accessories

By far, the most valuable postwar collectible Tootsietoys at this time are the wonderful boxed sets, which will be listed first all together because of the great interest they generate among collectors. Because of the rarity of these sets, it has been difficult to determine how many were actually produced. The 4-inch and 6-inch vehicle sets contain the most variations in their contents, and therefore are challenging to document. In addition to the car and truck sets produced with vehicles from the 3-inch, 4-inch, 6-inch series, including sets produced in both civilian and military versions and with at least one airplane, there are tractor trailer sets, airplane sets, train sets, and ship sets, a number of which were prewar sets reissued after 1945. The reissue of prewar boxed sets as postwar sets seems logical, since it is known that the company reissued a number of prewar vehicles with black tires after the war. In addition, based on toy magazine advertisements placed during the war, it is clear that the stores had stocked enough boxed sets manufactured up to late 1941 to provide an adequate supply lasting well past the end of the war. While vehicles with white wheels are easily identified as prewar, it is more difficult to date various train, ship, and airplane sets. The sets that cannot be determined to be only prewar editions will be identified in this chapter by a variable date of issue: 1942/1946.

There are a number of planes and vehicles which are not true postwar toys yet are found in some of these postwar sets. These pieces are: the Waco "Bomber"; the DC-2; the DC-4; the DC-4 Army Transport; the Aero-Dawn; the Aero-Dawn Seaplane; the Lockheed Electra 10A; a P-40; a U. S. Army Plane; a Federal Tank Truck; a Graham Army Ambulance; a 3-inch Ford Wrecker; miniature planes; and 1½-inch soldiers. Individually, many of these may sell for between $30 and $60, with the exception of the Graham Army Ambulance which can sell for as much as $125, the P-40 which has sold for up to $200, and the soldiers and miniature planes which sell for less than $10.

The sets with the variable 1942/1946 date will undoubtedly cause much discussion and debate among collectors who try to classify them as either prewar or postwar. It is a fair assumption that most of these sets were not produced in 1947, the first year of major new production after the war. It is possible, however, that some sets were assembled in either 1945 or 1946 just as they were before the war to help generate business while new castings and sets were being developed. This possibility, plus the possibility that many remained shelf inventory in stores during and after the war, should allow for some flexibility among collectors.

Acquiring a first edition of an early postwar boxed set is often a great challenge to any collector. The earliest editions in complete form are scarce; many of these original-issue sets contain the premium two-tone version of each toy with painted features. It is true with many different kinds of collectibles that the cost of an original set usually exceeds the total value of the individual pieces within it, primarily because of its rarity and the existence of the original box. The condition of the box can be a factor in determining the set's market price, as well.

The values assigned to the boxed sets and boxed toys in this chapter reflect items in Good **(G)**, Excellent **(E)**, and Mint **(M)** condition. It should be remembered that none of the boxes were ever sealed or covered with cellophane at the factory to protect either the boxes or their contents. Therefore, boxes were subject to wear from handling, storage, and inspection by potential buyers. Boxed items in Good condition will have boxes with damaged corners, stains, warped sides and tops, and some fading of the graphics. The box insert, if present, will most likely have soil marks and some tears at the corners of the cutouts. The contents will be in at least Excellent condition, having probably been removed from the box on a number of occasions. The contents are almost always found to be in better condition than the box, and quite frequently are in Mint condition. Boxed sets in Mint condition should not have any soil marks, tears, or warping. Minor wear marks on the box top corners is acceptable due to storage and aging. The box insert must be undisturbed and in Mint condition; it should be carefully inspected for evidence that a toy was once removed and replaced. The toys themselves must be in Mint condition.

Regardless of the amount of research to verify production years for each and every set encountered, it often remains unclear whether sets identified in different catalogue years were always issued without any change in their contents. This practice of using the same catalogue and advertisement depiction could have allowed the manufacturer to introduce of new items in old sets without changing the set number. While this chapter provides a large listing of the various sets, it probably does not contain all of the sets produced by Dowst and Strombecker. To help reference the sets quickly, the following list provides known sets with dates of production according to dealer catalogues.

Airplane Sets

4240 Playtime Airport Set, 1959
4310 Pan American Airways Set, 1958-1959
5698 Airplane Set, 1956-1958
5700 Airplane Set, 1958
6100 Speedy Aeroplane Set, 1942/1946
6150 Aeroplane Set, 1942/1946
6500 Pan American Airport Set, 1951-1953
6500 Pan American Airway Set, 1958
7500 Tootsietoy Plane Set, 1950

Military Sets

179 Mosquito Fleet Set, 1942/1946
189 Air Raiders Set, 1942/1946
650 Army Set, 1942/1946
1404 Land Defense Set, 1942/1946
1405 Fleet Set, 1942/1946
1407 Air Defense Set, 1942/1946
1408 Naval Defense Set, 1942/1946
3198 Land and Air Set, 1958
4210 Land and Air Set, 1959
4215 Army Set, 1963-1965
4320 Rocket Launching Site, 1959
4398 U. S. Army Combat Set, 1958
5220 Army Set, 1942/1946
5700 Navy Fleet Set, 1942/1946
5750 Navy Set, 1942/1946
5900 Convoy Set, 1942/1946

Train Sets

186 Fast Freight Set, 1942/1946, 1949-1950
5450 Diesel Freight Set, dates unknown
5500 Freight Set, dates unknown
5550 Freight Set, 1942/1946, 1950-1954
5600 Freight Set, 1942/1946
5610 Diesel Freight Train Set, 1955-1958
5800 Battery Operated Electric Train Set, 1965-1969
5810 Tootsietoy Cartoon Train Set, 1966
5810 Battery Operated Train Set, 1967
5850 Passenger Limited Set, 1942/1946
5851 Santa Fe Set, 1942/1946
5900 Operating Electric Train Set, 1964-1966

Vehicle Sets

184 Fire Department Set, 1942/1946
199 Playtime Set, 1942/1946
207 Auto Transport Set, 1949-1958
289 Tractor and Disc Harrow Set, 1951-1969
290 Tractor with Shovel and Wagon, 1951-1957
411 Fire Department Set, 1948
525 Rol-Ezy Assortment Set, 1942/1946
550 Fire Department Set, 1942/1946
750 Jumbo Set, 1942/1946
1735 Camping Set, 1966
4110 HO Sport Set, 1960
4200 Service Station Set, 1959-1960
4205 Corral Set, 1963-1965
4225 Raceway Set, 1960
4250 Sportsman Set, 1960, 1963-1965
4250 Playtime Sportsman Set, 1959
4260 Race Team Set, 1964-1965
4300 Farm Set, 1959
4301 Farm Set, 1960, 1963
4330 Construction Set, 1959-1960, 1963-1966
4335 Camping Set, 1960, 1963-1964
4340 Civil War Set, 1960
4350 Classic Antique Set, 1960-1962
4360 American Road Set, 1964
4410 Playtime Village Set, 1960
4500 Turnpike Set, 1958-1959
4545 American Road Set, 1963
4550 Service Station Set, 1963-1964
4600 Playtime Set, 1948
4600 Truck Terminal Set, 1958
4700 Jumbo Set, 1948
4700 Hi-Way Set, 1949
4900 Interchangeable Truck Set, 1949-1958
5000 Motors Set, 1942/1946
5050 Playtime Set, 1942/1946
5100 Playtime Set, 1942/1946
5149 Playtime Motors Set, 1952-1955
5150 Motors Set, 1942/1946
5200 Motors Set, dates unknown
5210 Commercial Set, 1942/1946
5211 Fire Department Set, 1953-1958
5400 Jumbo Set, 1942/1946
5710 Service Station Set, 1958, 1960
5798 Car and Ramp Set, 1956-1958, 1960
6000 Road Construction Set, 1956-1958
6800 Farm Set, 1958
7000 Playtime Set, 1950-1958
7049 Motors Set, 1949
7100 Playtime Deluxe Set, 1942/1946, 1947-1948, 1951
7200 Motors Set, 1947-1948, 1950-1958
7250 Motors Set, 1950-1958
7600 Bild-A-Truck Set, 1954-1958
8000 Playtime Set, 1949

G E M

179 MOSQUITO FLEET SET: (1942/1946) Set contains two Destroyers, two Submarines, and Tender. **65 75 100**

184 FIRE DEPARTMENT SET: (1942/1946) Set contains Mack Hose Truck, Mack Hook and Ladder Truck, Mack Pumper Truck, Federal Tanker Truck, and two ladders. **150 195 250**

Left: *The No. 5100 Playtime Set (1942/1946) was first issued in 1939.* **Right:** *No. 7100 Playtime Set (1942/1946). Strombecker Corporation archives.*

G E M

186 FAST FREIGHT SET: (1942/1946) Set contains a gray 2-6-2 steam engine marked T186 under the side windows; gray Tender marked NEW YORK CENTRAL; orange Boxcar with THE MORE YOU EAT CRACKER JACKS THE MORE YOU WANT and the Cracker Jack boy located on each side; silver Tank Car with Texaco emblem on each side; and red Caboose with N.Y.C.R.R. on each side. Each piece contains two sets of black rubber tires and TOOTSIETOY MADE IN U.S.A. on the underside. S. Butler Collection. **100 175 225**

186 FAST FREIGHT SET: (1949-1950) Five-piece set contains Steam Locomotive and Tender, Boxcar, Single-Dome Tank Car, and Caboose. **NRS**

189 AIR RAIDER SET: (1942/1946) Set contains two Lockheed Electra 10As, two Army Planes, and seven miniature airplanes. **300 325 475**

199 PLAYTIME SET: (1942/1946) Set contains Army Plane, 1939 Convertible, GMC Tanker Truck, 1939 Coupe, and 1939 Sedan (3-inch). **175 200 275**

Note: The following No. 207 Auto Transport Sets are descriptions of known examples. The vehicles included varied according to what was available. The values given are for these known examples; collectors should adjust values for sets they encounter that have items that are different, either more scarce or more common, than those in the listings. Other variations that are not listed should be valued according to the desirability of the 3-inch vehicles included.

G E M

207 AUTO TRANSPORT SET: (1949) Combination 3-inch and 6-inch series. Set contains 1947 Diamond T Tractor Truck with Auto Transport Trailer (no loading ramp), Single-Seat Convertible (3"), 1939 Coupe (3"), 1939 Sedan (3"), and 1937 International Wagon (3"). **150 175 200**

207 AUTO TRANSPORT SET: (1949) Combination 3-inch and 6-inch series. Set contains 1947 Diamond T Tractor Truck with Auto Transport Trailer (no loading ramp), 1947 Studebaker (3"), Single-Seat Convertible (3"), 1939 Coupe (3"), and 1937 International Wagon (3"). **175 200 225**

207 AUTO TRANSPORT SET: (1950) Combination 3-inch and 6-inch series. Set contains Army Jeep (3"), 1949 Ford Pickup Truck (3"), 1949 Ford Convertible (3"), 1950 Plymouth (3"), and 1947 Diamond T Tractor Truck with Auto Transport Trailer (no loading ramp). **150 175 200**

207 AUTO TRANSPORT SET: (1950) Combination 3-inch and 6-inch series. Set contains 1947 Diamond T Tractor Truck with Auto Transport Trailer (no loading ramp), 1949 Ford Pickup Truck (3"), 1949 Ford Sedan (3"), 1950 Chevrolet (3"), and 1949 Chevrolet Panel Truck (3"). S. Butler Collection. **125 160 180**

Top: *No. 5900 Convoy Set (1942/1946).* **Bottom:** *No. 179 Mosquito Fleet Set (1942/1946). S. Butler Collection.*

G E M

207 AUTO TRANSPORT SET: (1951) Combination 3-inch and 6-inch series. Set contains 1947 Diamond T Tractor Truck with Auto Transport Trailer (no loading ramp), Army Jeep (3"), 1949 Chevrolet Panel Truck (3"), 1950 Chevrolet (3"), and 1950 Plymouth (3"). **125 160 180**

207 AUTO TRANSPORT SET: (1952) Combination 3-inch and 6-inch series. Set contains 1952 Ford (3"), 1949 American LaFrance Fire Truck (3"), 1950 Plymouth (3"), 1949 Chevy Panel Truck (3"), and 1947 Diamond T Tractor Truck with Auto Transport Trailer (no loading ramp). **150 175 200**

207 AUTO TRANSPORT SET: (1953-1954) Combination 3-inch and 6-inch series. Set contains 1947 Diamond T Tractor Truck with Auto Transport Trailer (no loading ramp), 1949 Ford Convertible (3"), 1949 Ford Pickup Truck (3"), 1950 Chevrolet Sedan (3"), and 1952 Ford Sedan (3"). **135 165 190**

207 AUTO TRANSPORT SET: (1954) Combination 3-inch and 6-inch series. Set contains 1947 Diamond T Tractor Truck and Auto Transport Trailer (no loading ramp), 1949 Ford Pickup Truck (3"), 1952 Ford Four-Door Sedan (3"), 1954 Nash Metro Convertible (3"), and 1949 American LaFrance Fire Truck (3"). **150 175 200**

207 AUTO TRANSPORT SET: (1955) Combination 3-inch and 6-inch series. Set contains 1947 Diamond T Truck with Auto Transport Trailer (no loading ramp), 1949 Ford Pickup Truck (3"), 1954 Nash Metro Convertible (3"), 1955 Ford Sedan (3"), and 1954 Jaguar (3"). **125 160 180**

207 AUTO TRANSPORT SET: (1956) Combination 3-inch and 6-inch series. Set contains 1947 Diamond T Tractor Truck with Auto Transport Trailer (no loading ramp), 1949 Ford Pickup Truck, 1954 MG, 1955 Thunderbird, and 1955 Chevrolet Sedan. **125 160 190**

207 AUTO TRANSPORT SET: (1957) Combination 3-inch and 6-inch series. Set contains 1947 Diamond T Tractor Truck with Auto Transport Trailer (no loading ramp), 1955 Ford Sedan, 1949 American LaFrance Fire Truck (3"), 1954 Jaguar (3"), and 1949 Chevy Panel Truck (3"). **150 200 225**

Five variations to the No. 207 Auto Transport Set. J. Gibson Collection.

G E M

207 AUTO TRANSPORT SET: (1958) Combination 3-inch and 6-inch series. Set contains 1947 Diamond T Tractor Truck with Auto Transport Trailer (no loading ramp), 1952 Ford (3"), 1950 Plymouth (3"), 1949 Ford Pickup Truck (3"), and 1954 Ford Wagon (3"). **150 200 225**

207 AUTO TRANSPORT SET: (1958) Combination 3-inch and 6-inch series. Set contains 1947 Diamond T Tractor Truck with Auto Transport Trailer (no loading ramp), 1955 Ford (3"), Army Jeep (3"), 1955 Ford Tanker Truck (3"), and 1949 Chevy Panel Truck (3"). **150 200 225**

207 AUTO TRANSPORT SET: (1959) Combination 3-inch and 6-inch series. Set contains 1955 International Tractor Truck with Tandem-Wheel Transport Trailer, loading ramp, 1949 Ford Pickup Truck (3"), 1954 Ford Wagon (3"), and 1955 Ford Sedan (3"). S. Butler Collection. **175 200 250**

289 TRACTOR AND DISC HARROW SET: (1951-1969). 6-inch series. Set contains Ford Tractor and Disc Harrow. **125 150 195**

290 TRACTOR AND WAGON SET: (1951-1957) 6-inch series. Set contains red Ford Tractor with yellow operating shovel; unassembled Haul Wagon with red base, yellow sides; instruction sheet. **125 160 225**

411 FIRE DEPARTMENT SET: (1948) 4-inch series. Set contains 1937 Mack Hook and Ladder Fire Truck, 1937 Mack Pumper Fire Truck, 1937 Mack Hose Fire Truck, four ladders, Junior Fire Chief badge, shovel, and axe. **200 350 425**

G E M

525 ROL-EZY ASSORTMENT SET: (1942/1946) 3-inch series. Set contains 1939 Sedan, 1939 Coupe, 1939 Roadster, Federal Truck, GMC Tanker Truck, 1937 International Wagon, and Ford Wrecker. **175 225 300**

550 FIRE DEPARTMENT SET: (1942/1946) 3-inch series. Set contains Mack Hook and Ladder Truck, Mack Hose Truck, and Mack Pumper. **125 150 200**

650 ARMY SET: (1942/1946) 4-inch series. Set contains Army Supply Truck, Armored Car, Field Cannon, Waco "Bomber", and nine 1½" soldiers. **250 300 375**

750 JUMBO SET: (1942/1946) 6-inch series. Set contains Jumbo Convertible, Jumbo Sedan, Jumbo Coupe, Trans-American Bus, and Waco "Bomber." **295 375 450**

1404 LAND DEFENSE SET: (1942/1946) Set contains ten 1½" Soldiers. **60 75 100**

1405 FLEET SET: (1942/1946) Set contains nine miniature battleships in assorted colors. **50 75 125**

1407 AIR DEFENSE SET: (1942/1946) Set contains ten miniature bombers in assorted colors. **50 60 75**

1408 NAVAL DEFENSE SET: (1942/1946) Set contains six miniature battleships and eight other assorted ships (Destroyer, Carrier, Cruiser, Tug, Submarine) in an assortment of colors. **65 90 125**

1735 CAMPING SET: (1966) 6-inch series. Set contains 1960 Chevrolet El Camino, 1959 Oldsmobile Convertible, 1962

No. 5750 Navy Set (1942/1946) and No. 411 Fire Department Set (1948). Strombecker Corporation archives.

G E M

Ford Wagon, Race Car and Trailer, U-Haul Trailer, Chris-Craft Boat and Trailer, and 1960 4" Chrysler Convertible. **150 175 275**

3198 LAND AND AIR SET: (1958) 4-inch series. Set contains 1949 Chevrolet Ambulance, Tank, Army Jeep, Large Field Cannon, Small Cannon, Searchlight, Skyray Jet, and Cutlass Jet. **200 250 350**

3198 LAND AND AIR SET: (1958) 4-inch series. Set contains 1949 Chevrolet Ambulance, Tank, Army Jeep, Large Field Cannon, Small Cannon, Searchlight, Starfire Jet, and F-86 Sabre Jet. **200 250 350**

4110 HO SPORT SET: (1960) Set contains Chris-Craft Boat and Trailer, U-Haul Trailer, Ford Sunliner Convertible, and Cadillac. **75 100 125**

4200 SERVICE STATION SET: (1959) 3-inch series. Set contains grease rack, gas pump island, four road signs, 1955 Thunderbird, Army Jeep, 1954 MG, 1954 Jaguar, 1955 Ford Tanker Truck, two 1954 Ford Wagons, and 1949 Ford Pickup Truck. **200 275 395**

4200 SERVICE STATION SET: (1960) 3-inch series. Set contains grease rack, gas pump island, four road signs, 1949 Ford Pickup Truck, Army Jeep, 1955 Ford Tanker Truck, 1955 Thunderbird, two 1954 Ford Wagons, 1954 MG, and 1954 Jaguar. **200 275 395**

4205 CORRAL SET: (1963-1964) 6-inch series. Set contains 1960 Chevy El Camino, 1956 CJ5 Jeep, Horse Trailer, Stakeside Trailer, cowboy, horse, and bull. **150 200 235**

4210 LAND AND AIR SET: (1959) 4-inch series. Set contains Army Jeep, Army Tank, Army Searchlight, two Field Cannons, F-86 Jet, and Starfire Jet. **200 250 350**

4215 ARMY SET: (1963-1964) Combination 6-inch and 4-inch series. Set contains 1956 Ford Anti-Aircraft Gun Truck, 1956 Ford Radar Truck, Army Jeep (4"), Shooting Cannon (4") with six shells, and three large plastic infantry soldiers. **150 200 300**

4225 RACEWAY SET: (1960) 6-inch series. Set contains Refreshment Trailer, Race Car and Trailer, 1959 Ford Wagon, and 1960 Chevy El Camino. **150 225 250**

4240 PLAYTIME AIRPORT SET: (1959) 3-inch series. Set contains billboard with printed poster, Cutlass Jet, Skyray Jet, Starfire Jet, Panther Jet, Sikorsky Helicopter, 1957 Plymouth, 1957 Ford Convertible, 1955 Ford Tanker Truck, and Army Jeep. **250 325 375**

Left: *No. 3198 Land and Air Set (1958).* **Right:** *No. 5798 Car and Ramp Set (1956). S. Butler Collection.*

G E M

4250 PLAYTIME SPORTSMAN SET: (1959) 6-inch series. Set contains 1955 Packard, 1959 Ford Wagon, 1956 Austin-Healy, U-Haul Trailer, and Chris-Craft Boat and Trailer. **200 275 340**

4250 PLAYTIME SPORTSMAN SET: (1959) 6-inch series. Set contains 1959 Ford Wagon, 1959 Oldsmobile Convertible, 1954 MG, U-Haul Trailer, and Chris-Craft Boat and Trailer. **200 275 350**

4250 SPORTSMAN SET: (1960, 1963-1965) 6-inch series. Set contains 1959 Oldsmobile Convertible, 1954 MG, Race Car and Trailer, and Chris-Craft Boat and Trailer. **175 225 275**

4260 RACE TEAM SET: (1964) 6-inch series. Set contains 1932 Hot Rod, Race Car with Trailer, Maserati race car, Ferrari Lancia race car, and three plastic crew men. **175 225 275**

4300 FARM SET: (1959) 6-inch series. Set contains Farm Tractor with Disc Harrow, Fertilizer Spreader, 1947 Mack Truck with tin top, 1956 Jeep with Plow, Harrow Plow, and eight farm animals. **275 325 375**

4301 FARM SET: (1960) 6-inch series. Set contains Ford Farm Tractor, 1956 Ford Stakeside Truck, Farm Wagon, Disc Harrow, six plastic animals, five sections of fence, and two horses. Top of box is mylar. Also found with 1960 Chevrolet El Camino Truck in place of Ford Truck. **175 250 300**

4301 FARM SET: (1963) 6-inch series. Set contains 1960 Chevy El Camino, Ford Farm Tractor with Harrow, 1956 CJ5 Jeep with Plow, Farm Wagon with two horses, and six farm animals. **200 275 325**

4310 PAN AMERICAN AIRWAYS SET: (1958-1959) Set contains Convair 240 with red body and silver wings, blue-and-silver Boeing 707 jet, all-silver Constellation, Beechcraft Bonanza, Sikorsky Helicopter, 1955 Ford Tanker Truck (3-inch), plastic molded hanger building and gas pump, baggage truck, two baggage carts, loading ramp, and two pilot wings. **425 550 625**

4310 PAN AMERICAN AIRWAYS SET: (1958-1959) Set contains Convair 240, all-silver Boeing 707 jet, Stratocruiser, Beechcraft Bonanza, Sikorsky Helicopter, 1955 Ford Tanker Truck (3"), plastic molded hanger building and gas pump, baggage truck, two baggage carts, and loading ramp. **425 550 625**

Left: *No. 7200 Motors Set (1947).* **Right:** *No. 4250 Playtime Sportsman Set (1959). Strombecker Corporation archives.*

Two variations of the No. 4310 Pan American Airway Set (1958). Strombecker Corporation archives.

The No. 4215 Army Set (1964).

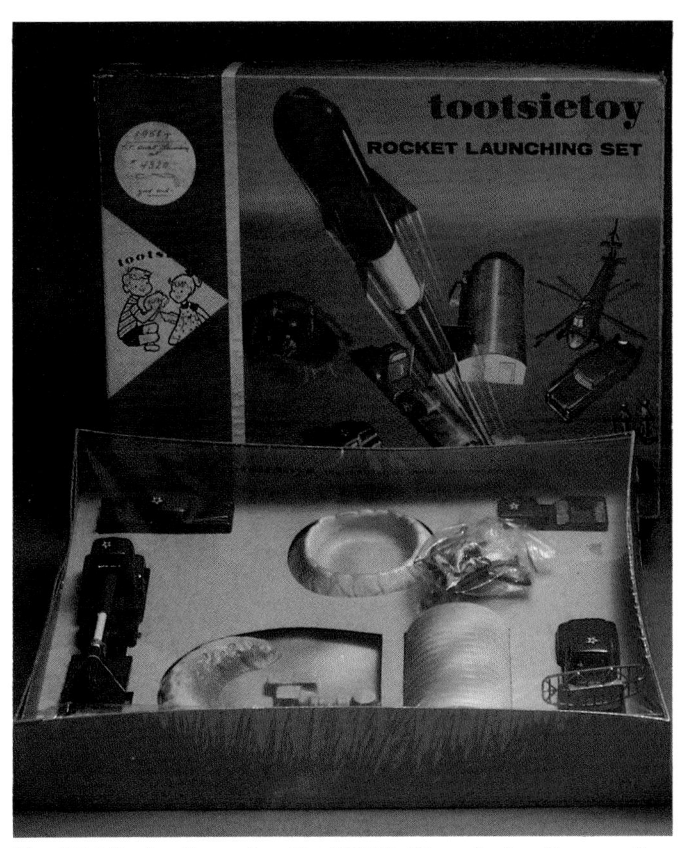

No. 4320 Rocket Launcher Set (1959). Strombecker Corporation archives.

G E M

4320 ROCKET LAUNCHER SET: (1959) Set contains 1955 International Tractor Truck with Missile Launcher Trailer and Rocket, Army Jeep (4"), 1954 Oldsmobile Army Staff Car (4"), 6" Ford Radar Truck, five rubber soldiers, molded plastic fox hole and bunker, and Sikorsky Helicopter. **275 350 400**

4330 CONSTRUCTION SET: (1959-1960, 1963) Set contains 1947 Mack Machinery Trailer Truck, 1947 Mack Dump Truck, Motor Grader, Bulldozer, and six roadway signs. **175 275 350**

4330 CONSTRUCTION SET: (1964-1966) 6-inch series. Set contains 1947 Mack Dump Truck, 1955 International Tractor Truck with Machinery Trailer, Caterpillar Bulldozer, Caterpillar Road Grader, and six road signs. **150 225 325**

4335 CAMPING SET: (1960) 6-inch series. Set contains Camper Trailer, Chris-Craft Boat and Trailer, 1959 Ford Wagon, 1959 Oldsmobile Convertible, 1956 CJ5 Jeep, two campers, tent, and tree. The top of the box is mylar. **200 275 325**

4335 CAMPING SET: (1963-1964) 6-inch series. Set contains Camping Trailer, Race Car with Trailer, U-Haul Trailer, Chris-Craft Boat and Trailer, 1959 Ford Wagon, 1959 Oldsmobile Convertible, and 1960 Chevy El Camino. **200 275 325**

4335 CAMPING SET: (1965) 6-inch series. Set contains Camper Trailer, Chris-Craft Boat and Trailer, 1962 Ford Wagon, 1959 Oldsmobile Convertible, 1956 CJ5 Jeep, two campers, tent, and tree. Top of the box is mylar. **200 275 325**

4340 CIVIL WAR SET: (1960) Set contains Civil War Wagon, Caisson, two Cannons, seven plastic horses, tent, eight Civil War soldiers, two trees, and two flags. Top of box is mylar. **100 150 175**

G E M

4350 CLASSIC ANTIQUE CAR SET: (1960, 1962) Set contains 1907 Stanley Steamer Runabout, 1906 Cadillac, 1912 Model T Ford, 1929 Model A Ford, and 1919 Stutz Bearcat. Top of box is mylar. **75 125 150**

4360 AMERICAN ROAD SET: (1964) Set contains two 1955 International Transport Trailer trucks with plastic trailer and loading ramp, six road signs, 1955 Scenicruiser Bus, two plastic boats, Hot Rod Model B (3"), and 1960 Ford Falcon (3"). **175 225 250**

4360 AMERICAN ROAD SET: (1964) Set contains 1958 International Boat Transport Trailer Truck with two plastic Boats, 1958 International Auto Transport Trailer Truck, Hot Rod Model B (3"), 1960 Studebaker Convertible (3"), 1955 Scenicruiser Bus, and six metal road signs. **175 225 250**

4398 U. S. ARMY COMBAT SET: (1958) Combination 4-inch and 6-inch series. Set contains 155 mm Mobile Howitzer, Cannon, 1949 Chevrolet Ambulance (4"), 1954 Oldsmobile Officer's Car (4"), Army Jeep (4"), six large polyurethane Soldiers, Starfire Jet, Panther Jet, Cutlass Jet, and 1956 Ford Convoy Truck (6"). **250 300 400**

4410 PLAYTIME VILLAGE SET: (1960) 6-inch series. Set contains 1947 Mack Tow Truck, 1956 Ford Stakeside with TOOTSIETOY tin top, 1956 Dodge Panel Truck, 1932 Hot Rod, 1954 Buick Wagon, 1954 Experimental Coupe, 1951 Buick

A No. 4410 Playtime Village Set (1960).

	G	E	M

Experimental XP300 Convertible, Skyray Jet, Cutlass Navy Jet, ten road signs, molded plastic gas station building and gas pump, and molded plastic airplane hangar. **350 500 650**

4500 TURNPIKE SET: (1958-1959) 6-inch series. Set contains one molded plastic Restaurant, 1947 Mack Van Trailer Truck, 1947 Mack Tanker Trailer Truck, 1955 Scenicruiser Bus, U-Haul Trailer, 1955 Packard, 1954 Buick Wagon, 1951 Buick Experimental XP300 Convertible, 1954 Experimental Coupe, and plastic roadway divider. **425 500 650**

4545 AMERICAN ROAD SET: (1963) Combination 3-inch and 6-inch series. Set contains 1959 Oldsmobile Convertible, 4" Race Car and Trailer, Camping Trailer, 1959 Ford Wagon, Chris-Craft Boat and Trailer, 1955 International Transport Trailer Truck with ramp, 1957 Plymouth (3"), 1956 Triumph TR-3 (3"), U-Haul Trailer, 1960 Chevy El Camino, and 1955 Scenicruiser Bus. **375 425 500**

4550 SERVICE STATION SET: (1963-1964) Combination of 4 inch and 6-inch series. Set contains three-piece fiberboard Service Station, two grease racks, two gas islands, two billboards, two signs, plastic play sheets, 1947 Mack Tow Truck, Civilian Jeep (4"), 1949 Ford Tanker Truck, 1962 Ford Fuel Truck, 1960 Chevy El Camino, 1956 Mercedes 190SL, 1955 Thunderbird (4"), 1953 Corvette (4"), 1956 Chevy Pickup Truck (4"), 1960 Rambler Wagon (4"), and 1960 Chrysler Convertible (4"). **400 500 600**

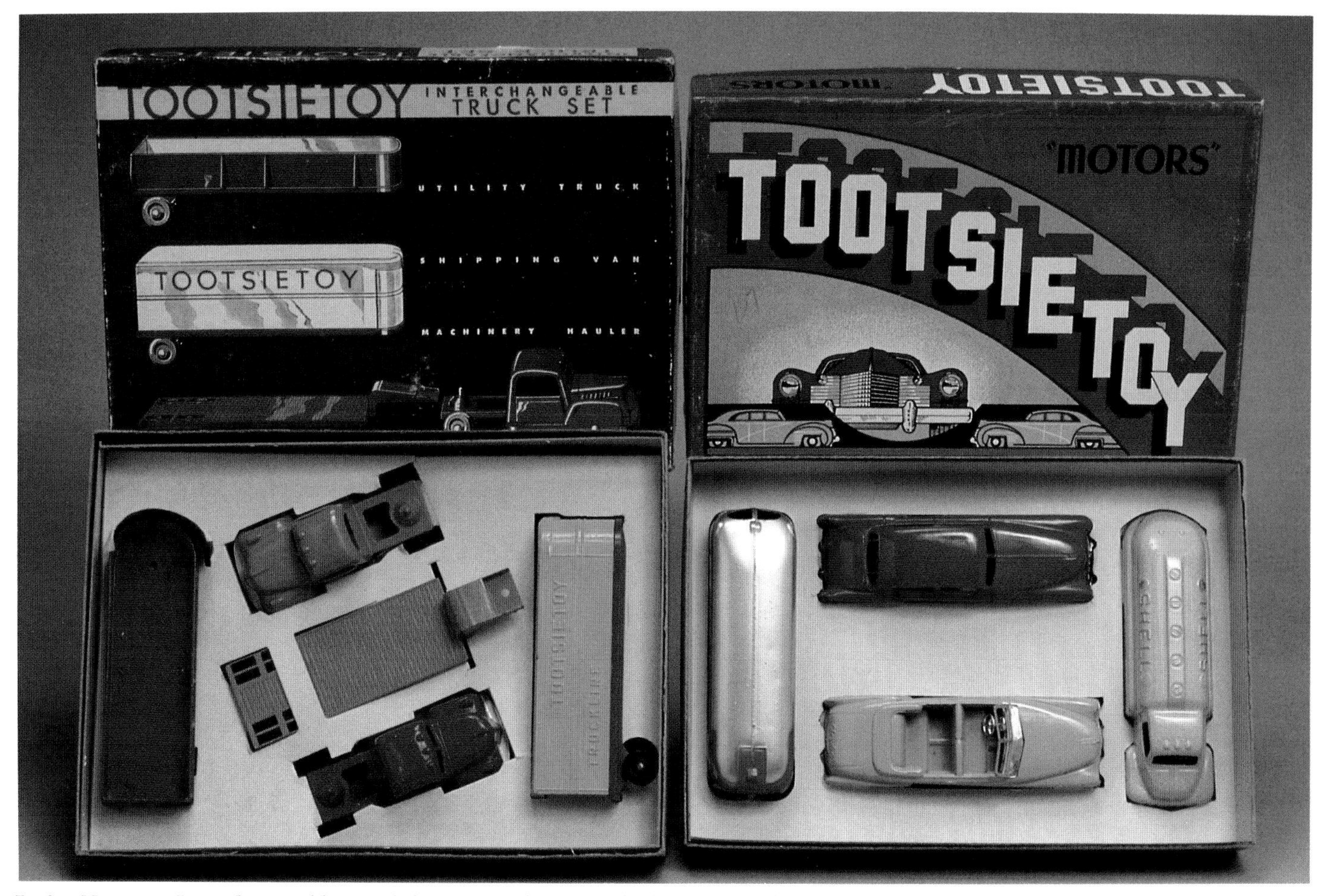

Left: *No. 4900 Interchangeable Truck Set (1955), S. Butler Collection.* **Right:** *No. 7250 Motors Set (1953).*

	G	E	M

4600 PLAYTIME SET: (1948) 3-inch series. Set contains Fire Pumper Truck, Fire Hose Truck, 1939 Four-Door Sedan, 1939 Coupe, 1937 International Wagon, Single-Seat Convertible, 1938 Federal Truck, 1937 GMC Tanker Truck, Ryan Navion, and Piper Cub. **300 375 450**

4600 TRUCK TERMINAL SET: (1958) Contents unknown. **NRS**

4700 HI-WAY SET: (1949) 6-inch series. Set contains 1947 Kaiser, 1947 GMC Bus, 1942 Rocket Roadster, and 1947 Diamond T Stakeside Truck. **275 325 350**

4700 JUMBO SET: (1948) 6-inch series. Set contains 1947 Kaiser, 1947 GMC Bus, 1942 Rocket Roadster, and 1947 Diamond T Stakeside Truck. **275 325 350**

4900 INTERCHANGEABLE TRUCK SET: (1949) Set contains 1947 Diamond T Tractor Truck, Van Trailer, Utility Trailer, and Machinery (low-boy) Trailer. **65 100 175**

4900 INTERCHANGEABLE TRUCK SET: (1950-1958) 6-inch series. Set contains two 1947 Diamond T Tractor Trucks, Van Trailer, Utility Trailer, and Machinery (low-boy) Trailer. **175 250 350**

	G	E	M

4900 INTERCHANGEABLE TRUCK SET: (1958) Set contains two 1947 Mack Tractor Trucks, Van Trailer, Utility Trailer, and Machinery (low-boy) Trailer. **175 225 350**

5000 MOTORS SET: (1942/1946) 3-inch series. Set contains Ford Wrecker, three 1939 Coupes, two Single-Seat Convertibles, two 1937 International Wagons, 1939 Sedan, 1940 Buick Phaeton Convertible, GMC Tanker Truck, Mack Hook and Ladder, Mack Pumper, Mack Hose Truck, Federal Truck, two U. S. Army Planes, and two DC-2s. **575 750 800**

5050 PLAYTIME SET: (1942/1946) 3-inch series. Set contains 1939 Coupe, 1939 Convertible, 1937 International Wagon, 1939 Sedan, 1940 Buick Convertible, GMC Tanker Truck, GMC Truck, Ford Wrecker, Lockheed Electra 10A, and U.S. Army Plane. **400 450 525**

5100 PLAYTIME SET: (1942/1946) Combination 4-inch and 6-inch series. Set contains Waco "Bomber", DC-4, Mack Hook and Ladder, Mack Hose Truck, Jumbo Wrecker (6"), Jumbo Bus (6"), Jumbo Sedan (6"), Jumbo Coupe (6"), Jumbo Roadster (6"), and Jumbo Pickup Truck (6"). **425 475 575**

5149 PLAYTIME MOTORS SET: (1952-1953) 3-inch series. Set contains Beechcraft Bonanza, 1949 American La-France Fire Truck, Army Jeep, 1949 Ford Sedan, 1937 GMC Tanker Truck, 1949 Chevrolet Panel Truck, 1949 Ford Pickup

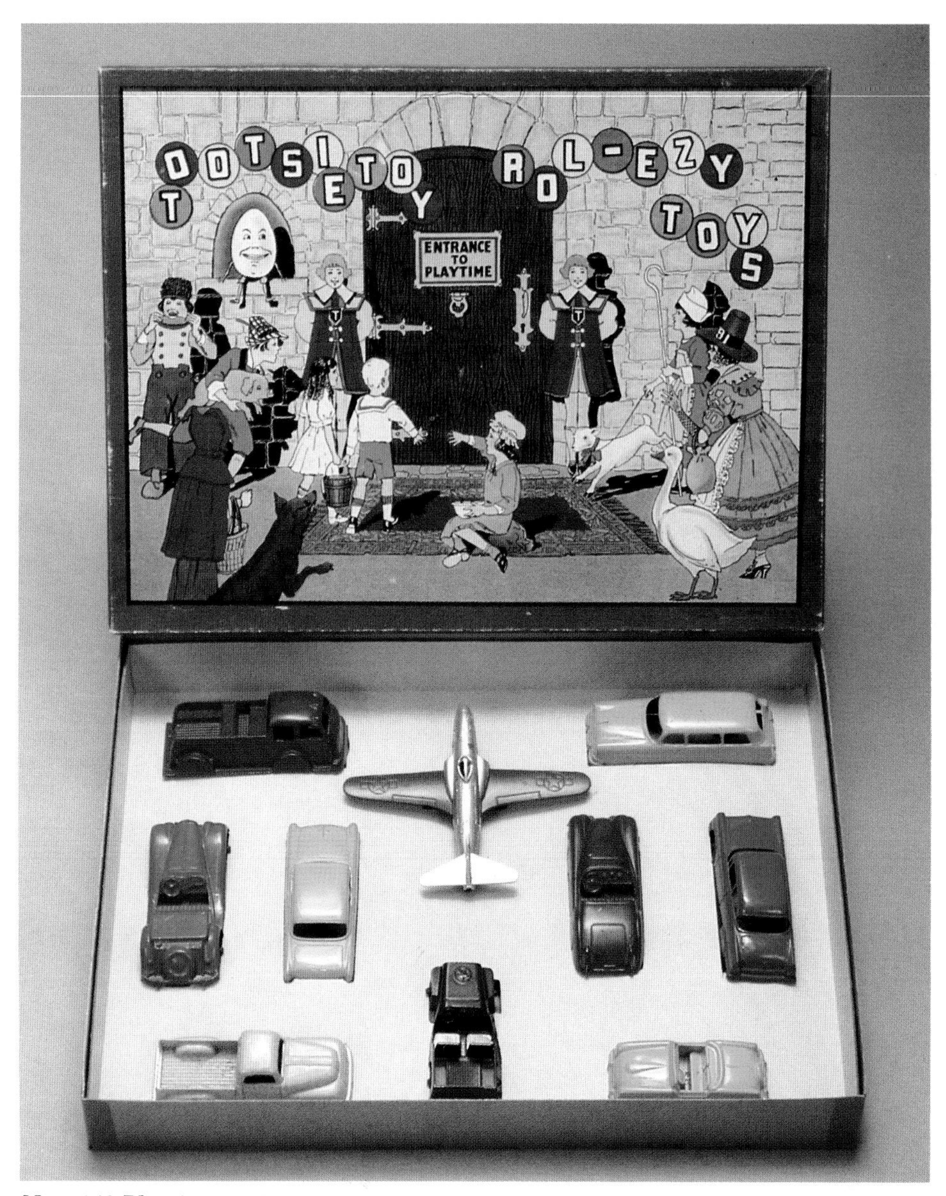

No. 5149 Playtime set (1955), J. Gibson Collection.

G E M

Truck, 1950 Plymouth Sedan, Indianapolis Race Car, and 1950 Chevrolet Fleetline. **225 300 375**

5149 PLAYTIME MOTORS SET: (1953) 3-inch series. Set contains F-86 Sabre Jet, 1949 American LaFrance Fire Truck, Army Jeep, 1949 Ford Sedan, 1937 GMC Tanker Truck, 1949 Chevrolet Panel Truck, 1949 Ford Pickup Truck, 1949 Ford Convertible, and Indianapolis Race Car. **225 300 375**

5149 PLAYTIME MOTORS SET: (1954) 3-inch series. Set contains Beechcraft Bonanza, 1949 Chevy Panel Truck, 1949 Ford Pickup Truck, Army Jeep, 1950 Chevrolet, 1949 Ford Sedan, Indianapolis Race Car, 1950 Plymouth, 1937 GMC Tanker Truck, and 1949 American LaFrance Fire Truck. **225 300 375**

5149 PLAYTIME MOTORS SET: (1955) 3-inch series contains P-80 Shooting Star Jet, Army Jeep, 1949 Ford Pickup Truck, 1949 American LaFrance Fire Truck, 1954 Nash Metropolitan, 1954 Ford Wagon, 1954 MG, 1955 Ford, 1954 Jaguar, and 1955 Chevrolet. J. Gibson Collection. **375 400 475**

5149 PLAYTIME MOTORS SET: (1955) 3-inch series. Set contains Bonanza Beechcraft Airplane, Army Jeep, 1954 Ford Wagon, American LaFrance Fire Truck, 1949 Jaguar, 1949 Ford Pickup Truck, 1954 MG, 1954 Nash Convertible, 1955 Ford Oil Truck, and 1955 Ford. **200 250 375**

5150 MOTORS SET: (1942/1946) 3-inch series. Set contains 1939 Coupe, 1939 Sedan, 1940 Buick Phaeton Convertible, 1939 Roadster, Federal Truck, GMC Tanker Truck, 1937 International Wagon, Mack Pumper, Mack Hook and Ladder, and Mack Hose Truck. **175 225 325**

5200 MOTORS SET: Date and contents unknown. **NRS**

No. 5211 Fire Department Set (1957). S. Butler Collection. Note the variations in silver-painted features on the fire trucks.

	G	E	M

5210 COMMERCIAL SET: (1942/1946) Combination 6-inch, 4-inch, and 3-inch series. Set contains Jumbo Wrecker, Jumbo Pickup, two Reo Tank Trucks, 1938 GMC Truck (3"), 1938 Station Wagon (4"), Mack Hook and Ladder Truck (4"), Waco Navy "Bomber," and two GMC Trucks (3").
250 350 450

5211 FIRE DEPARTMENT SET: (1953-1955) Combination 6-inch and 4-inch series. Set contains 1947 Diamond T Hook and Ladder Truck, 1947 Mack Pumper Truck, 1949 Mercury Fire Chief Car (4"), 1949 Chevrolet Ambulance (4"), Junior Fire Chief badge, axe and shovel, two fireman hats, and two extra ladders. **NRS**

5211 FIRE DEPARTMENT SET: (1953-1958) Combination 6-inch and 4-inch series. Set contains 1947 Mack Hook and Ladder Truck, 1947 Mack Pumper Truck, 1949 Chevrolet Ambulance (4"), 1949 Mercury Fire Chief Car (4"), Junior Fire Chief badge, axe, shovel, two fireman hats, and four ladders.
275 425 550

5220 ARMY SET: (1942/1946) 4-inch series. Set contains two U. S. Army Planes, Waco "Bomber", two miniature bombers, Tank, Armored Car, two Mack Supply Trucks, Graham Army Ambulance, and two Field Cannons. **450 650 800**

5400 JUMBO SET: (1942/1946) 6-inch series. Set contains Jumbo Tow Truck, Jumbo Four-Door Sedan, 1937 Reo Tank Truck, Jumbo Roadster, Jumbo Bus, Jumbo Coupe, Jumbo Pickup Truck, Mack Stakeside Trailer Truck, Waco "Bomber," and DC-4 Mainliner. **500 600 700**

5450 DIESEL FREIGHT TRAIN SET: Date and contents unknown. **NRS**

5500 FREIGHT TRAIN SET: (UK) Contents unknown.
NRS

5550 FREIGHT TRAIN SET: (1950-1953) Set contains gray and silver 4-6-2 Steam Engine with Santa Fe markings on the integral Tender; Boxcar painted orange over red with ATSF and SHIP AND TRAVEL SANTA FE ALL THE WAY on each side; Flatcar painted red over silver with three logs made out of dark stained dowels, marked with 1938 on the base of each side; Crane Car that uses the flatcar base painted green, silver, and red; Tank Car painted silver over red, marked 9358 in two places on each side; red Caboose marked TOOTSIETOY RR 4697 on each side. All pieces have two sets of black rubber tires. S. Butler Collection. **100 200 300**

5550 FREIGHT TRAIN SET: (1954) Set contains a 4-6-2 Steam Engine and Tender, Boxcar, Log Car, Tank Car, Crane Car, and Caboose. **175 225 275**

5600 FREIGHT TRAIN SET: (1942/1946) Contents unknown. **NRS**

5610 DIESEL FREIGHT TRAIN SET: (1955-1958) Set contains Union Pacific Diesel, Boxcar, Stock Car, Tank Car, Coal Car, and Caboose. **75 150 200**

5698 AIRPLANE SET: (1956) Set contains Panther Jet, Cutlass Navy Jet, Skyray Jet, Starfire Jet, and Beechcraft Bonanza. Box has prop-up top. J. Gibson Collection.
90 120 200

No. 5698 Airplane Set (1956). J. Gibson Collection.

	G	E	M

5698 AIRPLANE SET: (1956-1957) Set contains Panther Jet, Cutlass Navy Jet, Skyray Jet, Starfire Jet, F-86 Sabre Jet, and Beechcraft Bonanza. **90 175 275**

5698 AIRPLANE SET: (1958) Set contains Boeing Stratocruiser, Constellation, Beechcraft Bonanza, Sikorsky Helicopter, Boeing 707 Jet, pilot wings, 1955 Ford Oil Tanker (3"), ramp, baggage truck, and two baggage carts.
350 450 575

5700 NAVY FLEET SET: (1942/1946) Set contains two Carriers, two Submarines, two Destroyers, three Battleships, and three Cruisers. **125 165 225**

5700 AIRPLANE SET: (1958) Set contains Panther Jet, Cutlass Navy Jet, Skyray Jet, Starfire Jet, and Beechcraft Bonanza. J. Gibson Collection. Box has prop-up top.
90 120 200

5710 SERVICE STATION SET: (1958) 3-inch series. Set contains 1949 Ford Pickup Truck, Army Jeep, 1955 Ford Tanker Truck, 1954 MG, 1954 Jaguar, 1955 Thunderbird, two 1954 Ford Wagons, grease rack, gas pump island, and four road signs. J. Gibson Collection. **275 350 475**

5710 SERVICE STATION SET: (1960) 3-inch series. Set contains 1949 Ford Pickup Truck, Jeep, 1955 Ford Tanker Truck, 1949 Chevy Panel Truck, 1954 MG, 1954 Jaguar, 1949 American LaFrance Fire Truck, 1955 Ford, grease rack, gas pump island, and four road signs. J. Gibson Collection.
275 350 475

No. 5710 Service Station Set (1960). J. Gibson Collection.

G E M

5750 NAVY SET: (1942/1946) Set contains Submarine, Destroyer, Cruiser, Battleship, Carrier, and Transport.
75 100 150

5798 CAR AND RAMP SET: (1956-1958) 3-inch series. Set contains 1955 Ford Oil Truck, 1949 Ford Pickup Truck, 1955 Ford, 1954 Jaguar, American LaFrance Fire Truck, 1954 Ford Wagon, and grease rack. **200 275 375**

5798 CAR AND RAMP SET: (1960) 3-inch series. Set contains grease rack, 1949 Ford Pickup Truck, 1955 Thunderbird, 1955 Ford Oil Truck, 1954 Ford Wagon, 1954 MG, and 1955 Chevrolet Bel Air Sedan. J. Gibson Collection.
200 275 325

5798 CAR AND RAMP SET: (1956-1958) 3-inch series. Set contains 1955 Ford Oil Truck, 1949 Ford Pickup Truck, 1955 Ford Sedan, 1955 Chevrolet Sedan, 1955 Ford Thunderbird, grease rack, and 1949 Chevrolet Panel Truck. S. Butler Collection. **200 275 325**

5800 BATTERY OPERATED ELECTRIC TRAIN SET: (1966) Die-cast metal and polypropylene. HO scale battery-operated set contains Engine and Tender, two cars (Gondola/Boxcar), Caboose, ten curved-track sections, two straight-track sections, two-speed (forward/reverse) battery-operated transformer, wires and track clips, plastic telephone poles, crossing sign, and gate. Requires three 1½-volt D-cell batteries (not included). K. Jestes Collection. **65 85 125**

5800 BATTERY OPERATED ELECTRIC TRAIN SET: (1967-1969) Same as above but without telephone poles, crossing sign, and gate. **55 75 115**

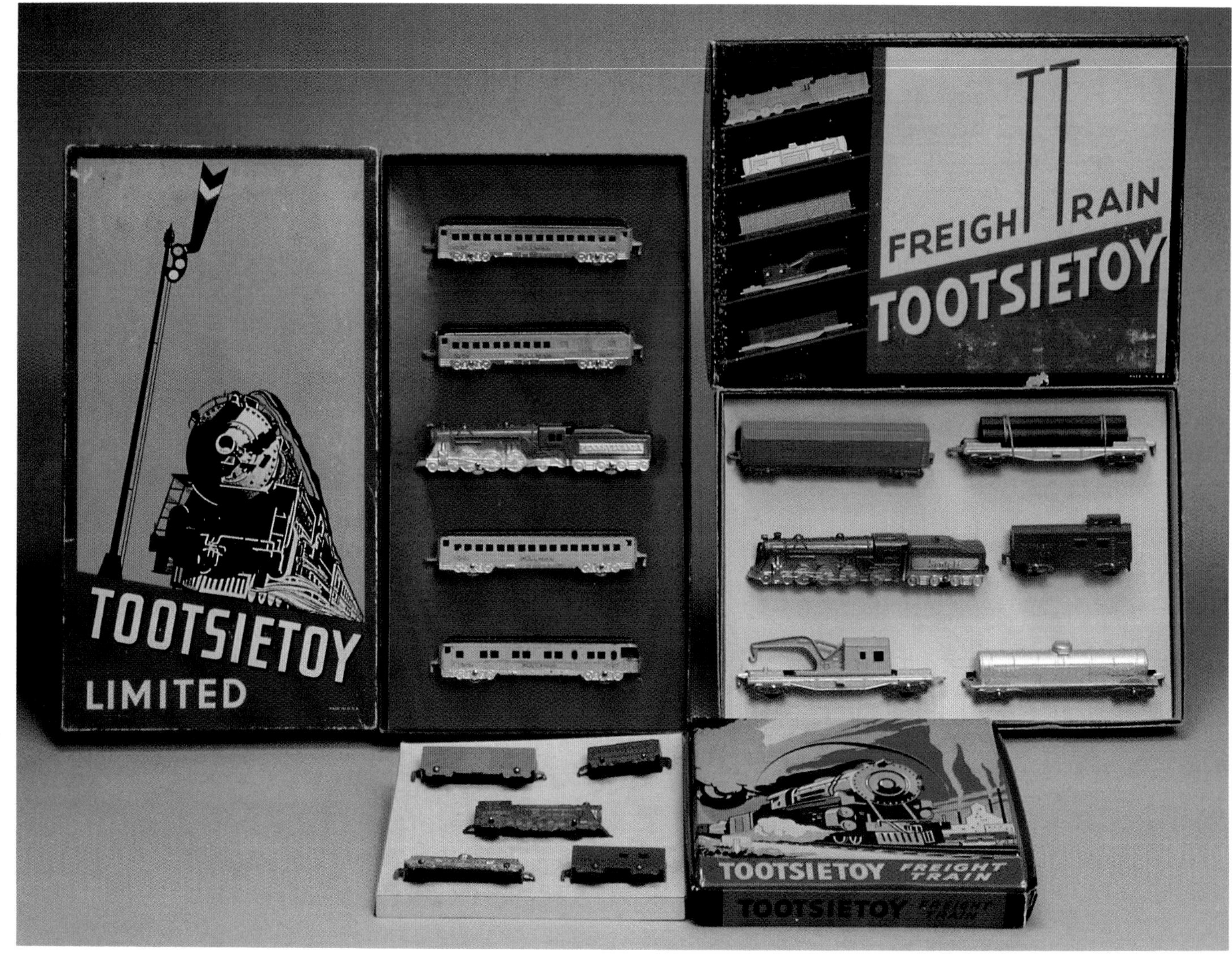

Top left: *No. 5850 Passenger Limited Set (1942/1946); right: No. 5550 Freight Set (1950).* **Bottom:** *No. 186 Fast Freight Set (1949). S. Butler Collection.*

	G	E	M

5810 TOOTSIETOY CARTOON TRAIN SET: (1966) Battery-operated die-cast metal and polypropylene set contains Engine and Tender, two Passenger Cars with removable figures, ten curved-track sections, two straight-track sections, and battery box. **50 75 100**

5810 BATTERY OPERATED TRAIN SET: (1967-1968) Die-cast metal and polypropylene set contains Engine and Tender with engineer, two Passenger Cars with removable figures, ten curved-track sections, two straight O-gauge track sections, track connector clips, and three-speed battery box for three 1½-volt D-cell batteries (not included). **65 100 125**

5850 PASSENGER LIMITED TRAIN SET: (1942/1946) Set contains gray and silver 4-6-2 Steam Engine with PENNSYLVANIA markings on the integral Tender; two Pullman passenger cars; Combination car; and Observation car. Each of the Pullman, Combination, and Observation cars are painted dark green, light green, and silver. All pieces have two sets of white rubber tires associated with prewar production. S. Butler Collection. **125 225 325**

5851 SANTA FE TRAIN SET: (1942/1946) Set contains Santa Fe engine, Baggage Car, two Pullman Cars, and Observation Car. **125 225 325**

5900 ELECTRIC TRAIN WITH TRANSFORMER: (1964) HO-scale set contains Engine and Tender, Gondola or Boxcar, and Caboose, eight curved track-sections, four straight-track sections, 4½-volt rheostat transformer, wire and track clip, two telegraph poles, four crossing signals, and two gates. Cars made of polypropylene and unbreakable die-cast metal, and feature easy coupling and weighted bodies. **85 125 150**

5900 ELECTRIC TRAIN SET: (1965-1966) Battery-operated set contains Engine and Tender, Gondola or Boxcar, and Caboose, ten curved-track sections, two straight-track sections, battery box, wire and track clip, two telegraph poles, four crossing signals, and two gates. **85 125 150**

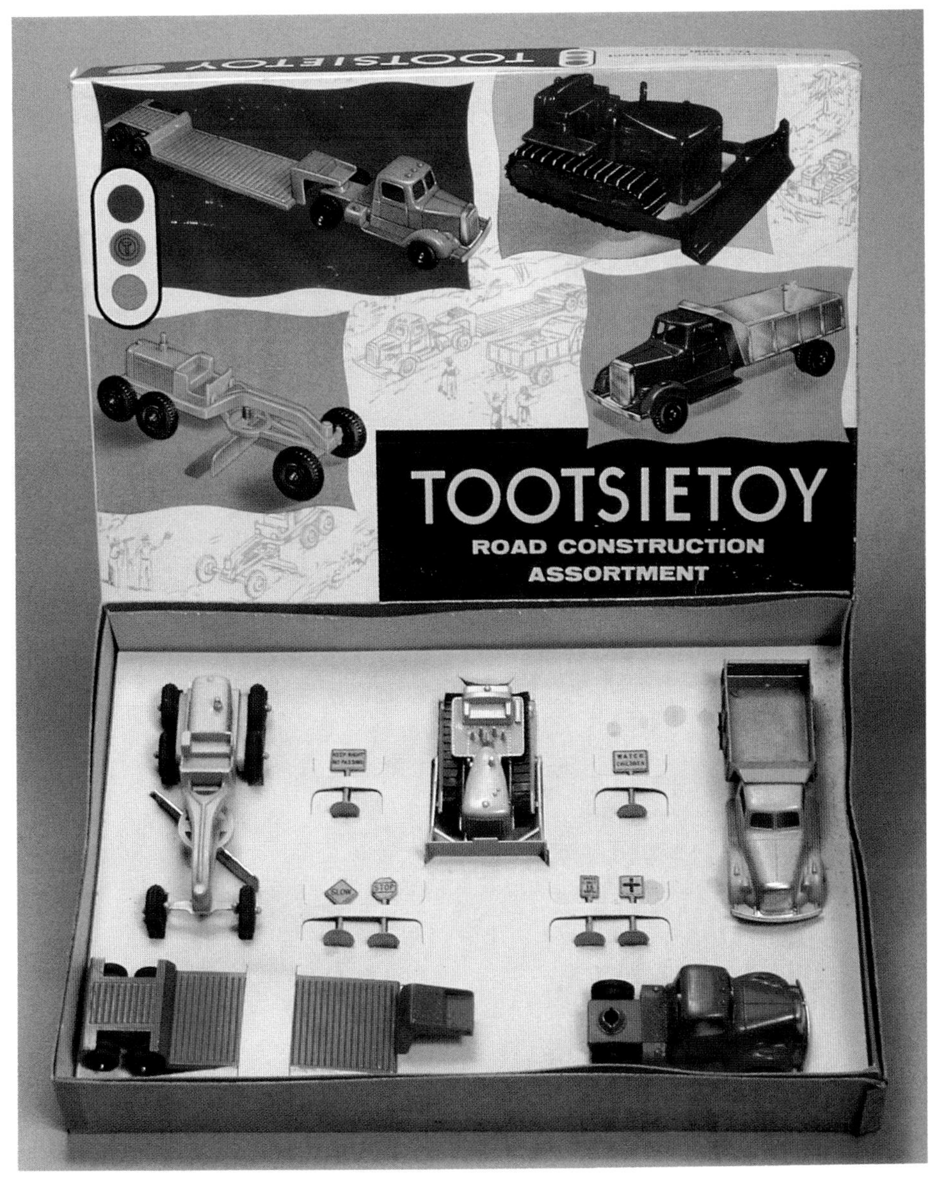

A No. 6000 Road Construction Set (1956).

G E M

5900 CONVOY SET: (1942/1946) Set contains six Destroyers, Tanker Ship, three passenger Transports, Battleship, and two Cruisers. **175 250 325**

6000 ROAD CONSTRUCTION SET: (1956-1958). Set contains Caterpillar Road Grader, Caterpillar Bulldozer, 1947 Mack Dump Truck, 1947 Mack Tractor Truck with Machinery Trailer, and six road signs. **175 250 325**

6100 SPEEDY AEROPLANE SET: (1942/1946) Set contains DC-2, two Lockheed Electra 10As, Army Transport, two U. S. Army Planes, two Aero-Dawn Seaplanes, two Waco "Bombers," Aero-Dawn, P-40 Fighter, Pilot wings pin. **400 600 800**

6150 AEROPLANE SET: (1942/1946) Set contains DC-2, DC-4, Waco "Bomber," Lockheed Electra 10A, U. S. Army Plane, and P-40 Fighter. **250 350 550**

6500 PAN AMERICAN AIRLINES AIRPORT SET: (1951-1953) Set contains Boeing Stratocruiser and Lockheed Constellation with Pan American markings, Convair 240, F-86 Sabre Jet, Ryan Navion, 1939 GMC Fuel Truck, PAA Master Pilot wings and Clipper Stewardess wings pins, two baggage carts, baggage truck, loading ramp. S. Butler Collection. **700 875 1000**

6500 PAN AMERICAN AIRLINES AIRPORT SET: (1951-1953) Set contains Boeing Stratocruiser and Lockheed Constellation with Pan American markings, Convair 240, F-86 Sabre Jet, Beechcraft Bonanza, 1939 GMC Fuel Truck, PAA Master Pilot wings and Clipper Stewardess wings pins, two baggage carts, baggage truck, loading ramp. **700 875 1000**

6500 PAN AMERICAN AIRPORT SET: (1953) Set contains Lockheed Constellation and Boeing Stratocruiser with Pan American markings, Convair 240, PAA Master Pilot wings and Clipper Stewardess wings pins, loading ramp, baggage truck, two baggage carts. **650 750 875**

Left: *No. 7000 Playtime Set (1952).* **Right:** *No. 7000 Playtime Set (1956). S. Butler Collection.*

	G	E	M

6500 PAN AMERICAN AIRWAY SET: (1958) Set contains Boeing 707, Boeing Stratocruiser, Convair 240, Beechcraft Bonanza, Sikorsky Helicopter, 1955 Ford Tanker Truck (3"), and molded plastic hanger. **425 500 550**

6800 FARM SET: (1958) 6-inch series. Set contains 1947 Mack Stakeside Truck with TOOTSIETOY tin top, 1956 Jeep with Plow, Disc Harrow, Ford Tractor, Fertilizer Spreader, Harrow Plow, and eight farm animals. **275 325 375**

7000 PLAYTIME SET: (1950) 6-inch series. Set contains P-38 Fighter, Convair 240, 1947 GMC Bus, 1949 Ford Tanker, Army Jeep, 1947 Diamond T Tow Truck, 1947 Diamond T Dump Truck, 1949 Buick Roadmaster, 1948 Cadillac, and 1946 International Tanker Truck. **475 575 650**

7000 PLAYTIME SET: (1950) 6-inch series. Set contains Convair 240, U. S. Coast Guard Amphibian, Army Jeep, 1949 Ford Tanker Truck, 1947 GMC Bus, 1947 Diamond T Dump Truck, 1947 Diamond T Tow Truck, 1949 Buick Roadmaster, 1948 Cadillac, and 1946 International Tanker Truck. **625 725 800**

7000 PLAYTIME SET: (1951) 6-inch series. Set contains Boeing Stratocruiser, F-86 Sabre Jet, 1950 Chrysler Convertible, 1947 Diamond T Tow Truck, Army Jeep, 1949 Ford Shell Tanker Truck, 1947 GMC Bus, 1947 Diamond T Dump Truck, 1948 Cadillac, and 1946 International Sinclair Tanker Truck. **575 675 750**

	G	E	M

7000 PLAYTIME SET: (1952) 6-inch series. Set contains Boeing Stratocruiser, Panther Jet (two-piece body), 1950 Chrysler Convertible (rare yellow color), 1947 Diamond T Tow Truck, 1947 Diamond T Stakeside Truck, 1947 Diamond T Dump Truck, 1947 GMC Bus, 1949 Ford Texaco Tank Truck, Army Jeep, 1948 Cadillac Sedan. S. Butler Collection. **575 675 750**

7000 PLAYTIME SET: (1952) 6-inch series. Set contains Boeing Stratocruiser, Starfire Jet, 1947 Diamond T Tow Truck, 1947 Diamond T Dump Truck, Army Jeep, 1947 GMC Bus, 1950 Chrysler Convertible, 1948 Cadillac, 1946 International Sinclair Tanker, and 1949 Ford Shell Tanker Truck. **575 675 750**

7000 PLAYTIME SET: (1953) 6-inch series. Set contains Boeing Stratocruiser, Convair 240, Army Jeep, 1947 Diamond T Stakeside Truck, 1947 Diamond T Dump Truck, 1948 Cadillac, 1946 International Sinclair Tanker Truck, 1953 Chrysler, 1952 Lincoln, and 1951 Buick Experimental Convertible. **525 625 700**

Left: *No. 7000 Playtime Set (1955).* **Right:** *No. 7600 Bild-A-Truck Set (1956). Strombecker Corporation archives.*

G E M

7000 PLAYTIME SET: (1954) 6-inch series. Set contains Convair 240, Boeing Stratocruiser, Army Jeep, 1947 Mack Truck, 1947 GMC Bus, 1948 Cadillac Sedan, 1953 Chrysler Sedan, 1952 Lincoln Hardtop, 1946 International Tanker Truck, and 1951 Buick Experimental. **500 600 675**

7000 PLAYTIME SET: (1955) 6-inch series. Set contains Panther Jet, F-86 Sabre Jet, 1947 GMC bus, Army Jeep, 1955 Packard, 1952 Lincoln, 1954 Cadillac, 1951 Buick Convertible, 1954 Buick Wagon, and 1947 Mack Truck. **450 525 650**

7000 PLAYTIME SET: (1955) 6-inch series. Set contains Panther Jet (two-piece body), F-86 Sabre Jet (two-piece body), 1947 Mack Truck, 1951 Buick Experimental, Army Jeep, 1947 GMC Bus, 1955 Chrysler Regent, 1955 Packard, 1954 Cadillac, and 1954 Buick Wagon. **NRS**

7000 PLAYTIME SET: (1956-1957) 6-inch series. Set contains 1947 Mack Tow Truck, 1952 Lincoln, 1954 Cadillac, 1951 Buick Experimental Convertible, 1955 Packard, 1954 Buick Wagon, 1947 Mack Truck, Panther Jet, Starfire Jet, and Army Jeep. S. Butler Collection. **375 475 550**

7049 PLAYTIME MOTORS SET: (1949) 4-inch series. Set contains 1941 Chrysler Convertible, 1941 International Panel Truck, 1947 Pickup Truck, Civilian Jeep, 1938 Buick Convertible, 1941 Buick, and 1937 International Wagon. **275 325 375**

G E M

7100 PLAYTIME DELUXE SET: (1947) 6-inch series. Set contains P-39 Fighter, 1947 Kaiser, 1942 Rocket Roadster, 1947 GMC Bus, 1937 Reo Texaco Tanker Truck, 1937 Reo Shell Tanker Truck, and 1947 Diamond T Stakeside Truck. **400 475 525**

7100 PLAYTIME DELUXE SET: (1942/1946) 6-inch series. Set contains Jumbo Pickup Truck, Jumbo Tow Truck, Jumbo Bus, Jumbo Convertible, Jumbo Coupe, Jumbo Sedan, Civilian Jeep, 1937 Reo Texaco Tanker Truck, and 1937 Reo Shell Tanker Truck. **400 450 550**

7100 PLAYTIME DELUXE SET: (1948) Combination 6-inch and 4-inch series. Set contains 1947 Buick Wagon (6"), 1947 Diamond T Dump Truck (6"), 1948 Diamond T Bottle Truck (6"), 1947 Diamond T Tow Truck (6"), P-80 Jet, 1938 Federal Truck (4"), 1937 International Wagon (4"), Midget Racer (4"), and 1937 Mack Fire Ladder Truck (4"). **425 500 550**

7200 MOTORS SET: (1947) 4-inch series. Set contains 1938 Buick Convertible, 1941 Chrysler Convertible, 1941 Buick Special, Civilian Jeep, 1937 International Wagon, and 1947 (Futuristic) Pickup Truck. **250 300 350**

7200 MOTORS SET: (1948) 4-inch series. Set contains two Midget Racers, Civilian Jeep, 1941 International Panel Truck, 1947 (Futuristic) Pickup Truck, 1941 Chrysler Convertible, 1938 Buick Convertible, and 1941 Buick Sedan. **275 325 375**

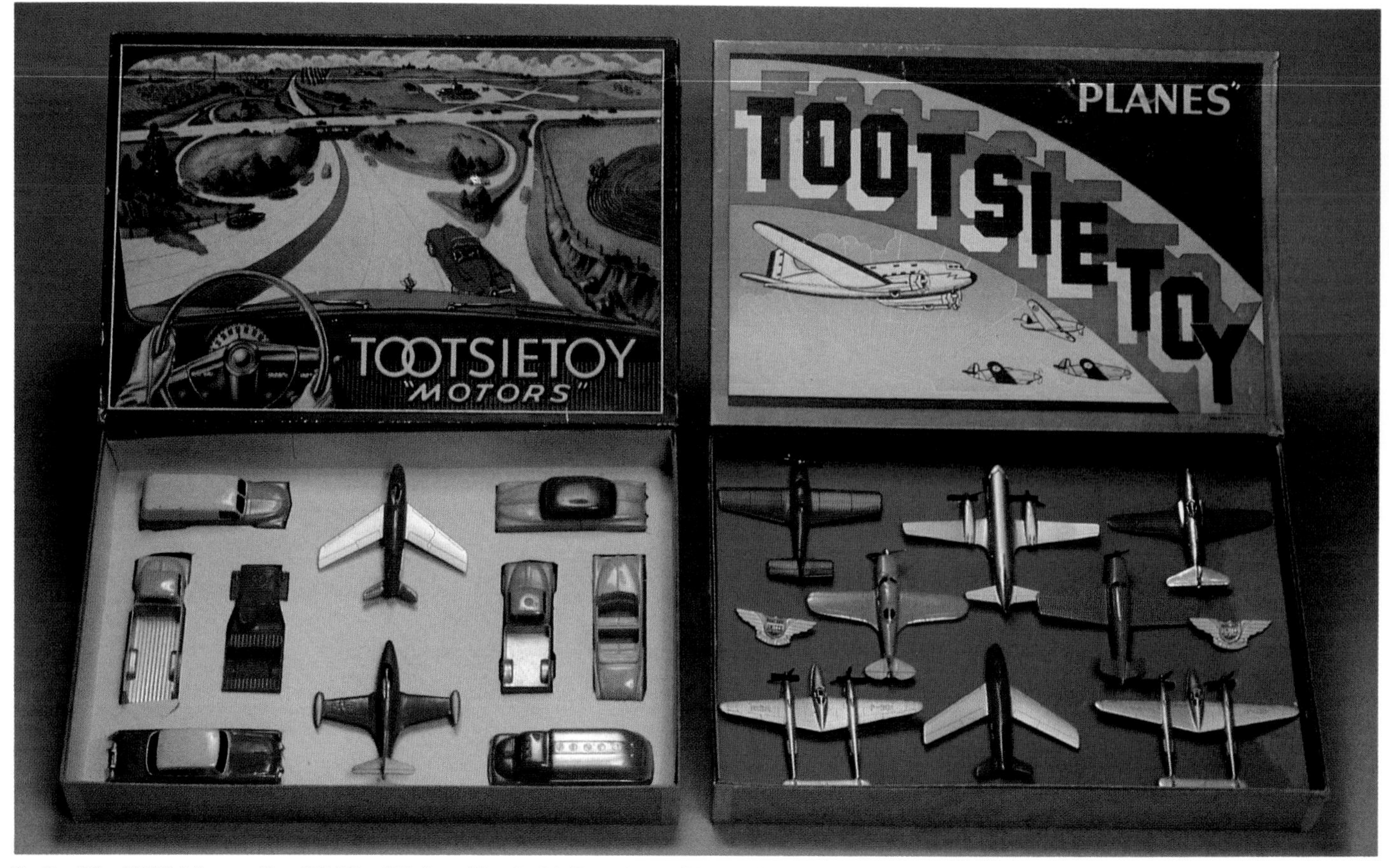

Left: *No. 7200 Motors Set (1953).* **Right:** *No. 7500 Tootsietoy Planes Set (1950). S. Butler Collection.*

G E M

7200 MOTORS SET: (1950) 4-inch series. Set contains P-38 Fighter, 1950 Pontiac Sedan, 1949 Ford Stakeside Truck, 1949 Oldsmobile Convertible, 1950 Dodge Pickup Truck, 1949 Chevy Panel Truck, Civilian Jeep, 1949 Mercury Sedan, and 1949 Ford Tanker Truck. **375 425 475**

7200 MOTORS SET: (1951-1952) 4-inch series. Set contains 1949 Ford Tanker Truck, 1949 Ford Stakeside Truck, 1949 Chevrolet Panel Truck, Civilian Jeep, 1950 Dodge Pickup Truck, 1949 Oldsmobile Convertible, 1950 Pontiac Sedan, 1949 Mercury Sedan, and Convair 240. **375 425 475**

7200 MOTORS SET: (1953) 4-inch series. Set contains Ryan Navion, Panther Jet (two-piece body), 1949 Ford Tanker Truck, Civilian Jeep, 1949 Ford Stakeside Truck, 1949 Chevrolet Panel Truck, 1950 Dodge Pickup Truck, 1949 Oldsmobile Convertible, 1950 Pontiac Sedan, and 1952 Mercury Sedan. **350 425 475**

7200 MOTORS SET: (1953-1954) 4-inch series. Set contains Panther Jet and F-86 Sabre Jet with two-piece bodies, 1949 Ford Tanker Truck, Civilian Jeep, 1949 Ford Stakeside Truck, 1949 Chevrolet Panel Truck, 1950 Dodge Pickup Truck, 1949 Oldsmobile Convertible, 1950 Pontiac Sedan, and 1952 Mercury Sedan. S. Butler Collection. **350 425 475**

7200 MOTORS SET: (1955) 4-inch series. Set contains Delta Jet, P-80 Jet (two-piece body), Civilian Jeep, 1949 Ford Truck, 1954 Oldsmobile, 1955 Thunderbird, 1954 Ford Wagon, 1950 Dodge Pickup Truck, 1953 Corvette, and 1949 Ford Oil Truck. **300 375 450**

G E M

7200 MOTORS SET: (1956) 4-inch series. Set contains Panther Jet, Starfire Jet, 1949 Ford Stakeside Truck, 1955 Thunderbird, 1954 Ford Wagon, 1954 Oldsmobile 98 Holiday, and 1956 Chevrolet Cameo Carrier. **250 300 400**

7200 MOTORS SET: (1956-1957) 4-inch series. Set contains 1954 Oldsmobile, 1949 Ford Truck, 1949 Ford Oil Truck, 1954 Ford Wagon, 1955 Thunderbird, 1953 Corvette, Civilian Jeep, 1950 Dodge Pickup Truck, and Service Station Rack. **275 325 425**

7250 MOTORS SET: (1950-1952) 6-inch series. Set contains 1948 Cadillac, 1946 International Standard Oil Tanker Truck, 1947 Diamond T Stakeside Truck, and 1947 GMC Bus. **175 250 275**

7250 MOTORS SET: (1953) 6-inch series. Set contains 1950 Chrysler Convertible, 1948 Cadillac Sedan (four-door), 1947 GMC Bus, and 1949 Ford Shell Tanker Truck. **175 275 350**

7250 MOTORS SET: (1953-1954) 6-inch series. Set contains 1950 Chrysler Convertible, 1948 Cadillac, 1946 International Oil Truck, and 1947 GMC Bus. **175 275 350**

7250 MOTORS SET: (1955) 6-inch series. Set contains 1952 Lincoln Capri, 1946 International Oil Truck, 1950 Chrysler Convertible, and 1947 GMC Bus. **175 275 350**

G E M

7250 MOTORS SET: (1956-1958) 6-inch series. Set contains 1954 Cadillac, 1951 Buick Experimental Convertible, 1955 Packard, 1954 Buick Wagon, and four road signs. **150 225 275**

7500 TOOTSIETOY PLANES SET: (1950) Set contains P-38 Fighter, F-86 Jet (two-piece body), P-80 Shooting Star Jet (two-piece body), U. S. Coast Guard Amphibian, Convair 240, Beechcraft Bonanza, Ryan Navion, Piper Cub, Future Pilot badge, and Jr. Stewardess badge. Ad in the April 1950 *Playthings* issue shows UNITED also on badges. **400 700 900**

7500 TOOTSIETOY PLANES SET: (1950) Same as above without U. S. Coast Guard Amphibian, but with two P-38 Fighters. S. Butler Collection. **400 700 800**

7600 BILD-A-TRUCK SET: (1954-1958) 6-inch series. Set contains two 1947 Mack Trailer Trucks, Stakeside Trailer with five removable stakes, Van Trailer, Tanker Trailer, six wood logs, two sets of tandem wheels, two sets of undercarriage trailer connections, and a PURE OIL sticker set. **300 350 450**

8000 PLAYTIME SET: (1949) 6-inch series. Set contains two 1948 Cadillacs, 1949 Buick Roadmaster, Army Jeep, 1946 International Sinclair Tanker Truck, 1949 Ford Texaco Tanker Truck, 1947 Diamond T Tow Truck, 1947 Diamond T Dump Truck, Beechcraft Bonanza, and Ryan Navion. **400 475 550**

Individually Boxed Items

A number of vehicles in the 6-inch series, like the 1955 Greyhound Scenicruiser, were sold in individual boxes. As stated in the first chapter, collectors find that having a Tootsietoy in its original box substantially increases its value depending on the condition of the box. Each box was given a special identification number: the earlier series were released in the fifties with a three-digit number; from 1959 to 1960, the later series were given four-digit numbers. Each box is illustrated with graphic depictions of the actual unit. Many of these toys were later sold in blister packaging after it was introduced in 1958. The values given are for boxed items in Good and Mint condition.

207 Auto Transport: See Chapter 7 and boxed set listings. **125 — 250**

245 1947 Mack Tow Truck: (1954-1958) See Chapter 3. **40 — 65**

249 1947 Mack Dump Truck: (1954-1958) See Chapter 3. **35 — 65**

285 Tootsietoy Army Jeep: (1953-1955) See Chapter 2. **25 — 45**

285 CJ5 Jeep: (1956-1958) See Chapter 2. **25 — 45**

289 Ford Tractor and Disc Harrow: (1951-1958) See Chapter 10 and boxed set listings. **125 — 195**

290 Ford Tractor, Shovel, and Wagon: (1953-1958) See Chapter 10 and boxed set listings. **125 — 225**

345 1954 Cadillac: (1956-1958) With tin chassis. See Chapter 2. **55 — 85**

G E M

349 1955 Packard: (1956-1958) With tin chassis. See Chapter 2. **55 — 80**

389 Ford Tractor with Scoop: (1956-1958) See Chapter 10. **65 — 95**

469 1947 Mack Pumper Truck: (1956-1958) See Chapter 3. **60 — 100**

489 1947 Mack Fire Ladder Truck: (1956-1958) See Chapter 7. **75 — 125**

569 1947 Mack and Log Trailer: (1955-1958) See Chapter 7. **60 — 115**

589 1947 Mack and Van Trailer: (1955-1958) See Chapter 7 for versions. **60 — 120**

669 1947 Mack and Oil Tanker: (1955-1958) See Chapter 7. **60 — 100**

679 Road Grader: (1956-1958) See Chapter 10. **40 — 55**

695 Bulldozer: (1956-1958) See Chapter 10. **45 — 70**

747 1947 Greyhound Bus: (1953-1955) See Chapter 3. **50 — 75**

769 Greyhound Scenicruiser: (1955-1958) See Chapter 3. **55 — 100**

869 1947 Mack Truck and Utility Trailer: (1955-1958) See Chapter 7. **90 — 130**

895 Pontiac Safari Wagon: (1956-1958) See Chapter 10. **150 — 200**

995 Mercedes Benz 300SL: (1956-1958) See Chapter 10. **175 — 300**

3600 Army Jeep with Cannon: (1959) 4-inch series. See Chapter 8. J. Gibson Collection. **60 — 90**

3700 Scenicruiser Bus: (1959) See Chapter 3. **55 — 90**

3710 Road Grader: (1959) See Chapter 10. **40 — 55**

3720 Sedan and U-haul Trailer: (1959) May be either a 1955 Packard or a 1954 Cadillac. See Chapter 2 for information on the vehicles, and Chapter 4 for the trailer. **60 — 100**

3730 Metro Truck: (1959) Blue Metro Van. See Chapter 3. **125 — 175**

3760 Log Truck and Trailer: (1959) 1959 Mack Trailer Truck, six wooden logs. See Chapter 7. **60 — 100**

3800 Utility Trailer and Truck: (1959) 1947 Mack Truck with Stakeside Trailer. See Chapter 7. **90 — 130**

3810 Tractor and Harrow: (1959) See Chapter 10. **60 — 85**

3820 Oil Tanker and Truck: (1959) 1955 Mack Truck with black-and-orange TOOTSIETOY Oil Tanker Trailer. See Chapter 7. **60 — 85**

3900 Tractor and Scoop: (1959-1960) Ford tractor. See Chapter 10. **85 — 125**

3905 Fire Ladder Trailer and Truck: (1959) 1947 Mack truck. See Chapter 7. **75 — 125**

3910 Bulldozer: (1959) See Chapter 10. **45 — 60**

		G	E	M
3915	**Van Trailer and Truck:** (1958) 1955 Mack truck in black and orange. See Chapter 7.	60	—	120
3920	**Auto Transport:** (1959-1960) 1955 International truck with transport trailer; loading ramp; three 3" vehicles. See Chapter 7.	80	—	160
3925	**Rocket Launcher:** (1959) U.S. Air Force 1955 International Rocket Launcher Trailer Truck with plastic rocket. See Chapter 8.			
	(A) As described above.	125	—	195
	(B) Same as (A) but in olive-drab Army color.	125	—	175
3930	**Sedan, Boat, and Trailer:** (1959-1960) 1954 Cadillac Sedan with Chris-Craft boat. See Chapter 4.	70	—	100
3930	**Car and Boat Trailer:** (1959-1960) 1959 Ford Wagon with Chris-Craft boat. See Chapter 4.	50	—	95
3945	**Cement Mixer:** (1959) 1955 Mack Truck. See Chapter 3.	50	—	95
3960	**Atomic Tank:** (1959) Army tank. See Chapter 8.	80	—	125
4025	**Buck Rogers Space Ships:** (1953) See Chapter 10.			NRS

Cellophane Packaging

A brief history of blister packaging was given in Chapter 1. The first form of this type of packaging by Dowst in 1956 did not actually use a "blister pack;" it utilized individual plastic or cellophane bags that could be hung on long protruding pins from a metal display rack. The bags were designed to hold various vehicles with small accessories such as road signs, hand tools, and badges. The clear cellophane or plastic bag was stapled at the top to a colorfully designed piece of cardboard. A punched-out hole in the cardboard allowed the package to be slipped onto the long metal pins of the display rack. The 1956 No. 9000 Tootsietoy Display Rack held up to eighty-four individual packages. The packaging of any of the larger 6-inch series in this manner was limited, and no trailer trucks were packaged in this manner. Many of the toys in S. Butler's collection that are packaged this way have two-tone paint. Listed below are the known cellophane packaged toys to date. See the appropriate chapters for vehicle descriptions. The values given are for unopened packages in Mint condition only.

3-inch series

	G	E	M
1949 Ford Pickup Truck with road sign	—	—	35
1949 American LaFrance Fire Truck	—	—	35
1949 Chevy Panel Truck	—	—	30
1954 Jaguar with road signs	—	—	30
1954 MG with road signs	—	—	35
1954 Ford Ranch Wagon with road signs	—	—	35
1955 Ford Tanker Truck	—	—	30
1955 Ford with road signs	—	—	35
1955 Chevrolet with road signs	—	—	35
1955 Thunderbird with road signs	—	—	35

4-inch series

	G	E	M
Army Jeep (1956-1958)	—	—	35
1949 Ford Stakeside Truck	—	—	35
1949 Ford Stakeside Truck with hand tools	—	—	40
1949 Ford Tanker Truck	—	—	35
1949 Ford Tanker Truck with hand tools	—	—	40
1949 Mercury Fire Chief Car, badge, fire hat	—	—	60
1949 Mercury Sedan	—	—	40
1949 Mercury Sedan with road signs	—	—	45
1950 Dodge Pickup Truck	—	—	40
1950 Dodge Pickup Truck with hand tools	—	—	50
1950 Pontiac Fire Chief Car, badge, fire hat	—	—	60
1950 Pontiac Sedan with road signs	—	—	50
1953 Corvette	—	—	40
1953 Corvette with road signs	—	—	50
1954 Ford Station Wagon	—	—	40
1954 Ford Station Wagon with road signs	—	—	50
1954 Ford Station Wagon, police badge, gun	—	—	60
1954 Oldsmobile Holiday 98	—	—	40
1954 Oldsmobile Holiday 98 with road signs	—	—	50
1955 Thunderbird	—	—	40
1955 Thunderbird with road signs	—	—	50

Airplanes

	G	E	M
Beechcraft Bonanza	—	—	30
Cutlass Jet	—	—	30
F-86 Sabre Jet	—	—	30
Panther Jet	—	—	30
Starfire Jet	—	—	30
Skyray Jet	—	—	30

6-inch series

	G	E	M
1956 Army Jeep, soldier, bugle, and gun	—	—	60

"Skin" or Blister Packaging

The next form of packaging, often referred to as "skin" packaging in the catalogues, started in 1958 and became a standard packaging method by 1959. Referred to as blister packaging by many collectors, it consists of a piece of cardboard on which a toy is placed, and heavy plastic skin-tight wrapping placed over the item and that forms to its shape when heated. A hole in the top of the cardboard allowed these items to be hung on metal pins for visibility. At some point in time all of the 6-inch units, Pull Trailer sets, Farm sets, and Tractor Trailer sets were produced and sold in blister packs. A majority of the 4-inch and 3-inch series were only packaged this way if they contained more than one piece.

The blister packs were designed with their own colorful display graphics. Like boxes used for sets, the art styles used on this form of packaging went through at least four different design changes during its history. One of the major changes occurred when the Dowst Manufacturing Company became the Strombecker Corporation; the cardboard inside the package was completely redesigned. Blister packs with the Dowst name can be expected to bring a slightly higher value than those with the Strombecker name.

The cardboard was produced in a number of different sizes. The 4-inch by 7-inch card was mainly used to hold a single 4-inch vehicle or two 3-inch vehicles, though some 6-inch vehicles may be found on cards of this size. The 7-inch by

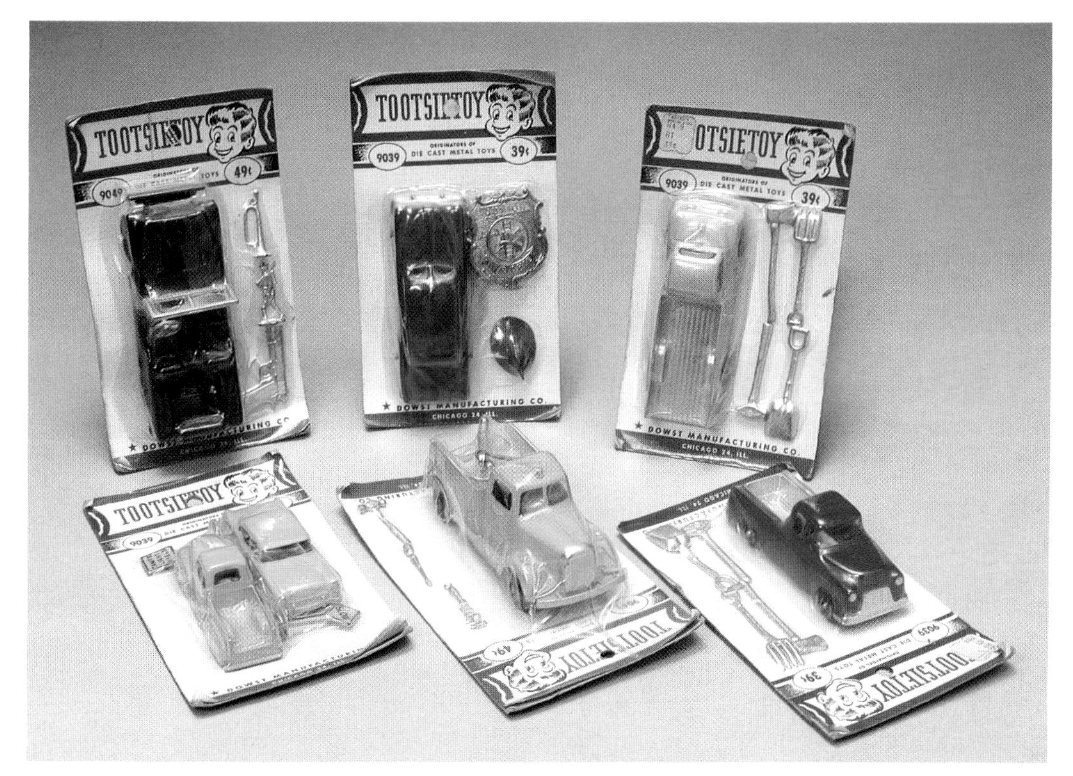

An assortment of the first series of blister packs. S. Butler Collection.

10¾-inch card was used for the 6-inch and 4-inch series and always contained at least two or three units—more if they were mixed with smaller items and accessories. The 4-inch by 10-inch blister card was used for the large Tractor Trailer trucks and some of the 6-inch vehicles with small Pull Trailers.

The values assigned to these listings are for samples in blister packs that are found in Mint, unopened condition only. Most of the 6-inch and 4-inch toys packaged this way came with the desirable two-tone paint scheme with painted features. **Note**: Information on many of these blister packs: C. Jones and K. Jestes Collections.

Early Blister Packs

The first series of blister-packaged toys were issued in 1958 as dealer sets No. 9039 and No. 9049.

No.	Item	G	E	M
9039	1949 Ford Stakeside Truck (4″) with four hand tools.	—	—	**45**
9039	1950 Pontiac Fire Chief Car (4″) with badge, fire hat.	—	—	**70**
9039	1949 Ford Pickup Truck (3″) and 1955 Chevy (3″) with two road signs.	—	—	**60**
9039	1956 Chevy Cameo Pickup Truck (4″), four hand tools.	—	—	**50**
9049	1947 Mack Tow Truck (6″) with three hand tools.	—	—	**65**
9049	1956 Army Jeep (6″) with soldier, bugle, and gun.	—	—	**70**

6-inch series in Blister Packs

No.	Item	G	E	M
1350	CJ5 Jeep, 1960-1962.	—	—	**30**
2005	Hot Rod, driver, racer, trailer; 1966-1967.	—	—	**75**
2010	MG Convertible, driver, boat, trailer; 1966-1967.	—	—	**85**
2015	MG Convertible, driver, U-Haul trailer; 1966-1967.	—	—	**75**
2300	1932 Hot Rod; 1960-1969.	—	—	**40**
2300	1954 Experimental Coupe; 1961-1967.	—	—	**45**
2300	1956 Dodge Panel Truck; 1960-1961.	—	—	**50**
2300	1960 El Camino; 1961.	—	—	**35**
2300	1940 Ford Convertible; 1962-1964.	—	—	**45**
2300	1956 Jeep, molded windshield; 1962-1964.	—	—	**30**
2300	1959 Ford Wagon; 1960-1967.	—	—	**30**
2300	1959 Oldsmobile Convertible; 1960-1968.	—	—	**30**
2300	1962 Ford Wagon; 1962-1968.	—	—	**30**
2350	1956 Dodge Panel Truck; 1962-1964.	—	—	**50**
2350	1960 El Camino; 1962-1963.	—	—	**35**
2350	1962 Ford Econoline Pickup Truck; 1962-1963.	—	—	**40**
2350	1962 Ford Tanker Truck; 1962-1963.	—	—	**40**
2415	Austin-Healy Sports Car kit; 1961.	—	—	**125**
2418	Civil War Cannon; 1960.	—	—	**35**
2420	1947 Mack Tow Truck; 1960-1964.	—	—	**55**
2450	Maserati Race Car; 1962-1964.	—	—	**30**
2453	Ferrari Race Car; 1964.	—	—	**30**
2505	Road Grader; 1963-1964.	—	—	**40**
2515	Civil War Caisson, horses; 1960.	—	—	**50**
2525	CJ5 Jeep; 1959.	—	—	**30**
2525	CJ5 Jeep with Plow; 1960-1961.	—	—	**55**
2550	1947 Mack Dump Truck; 1961, 1963-1964.	—	—	**40**

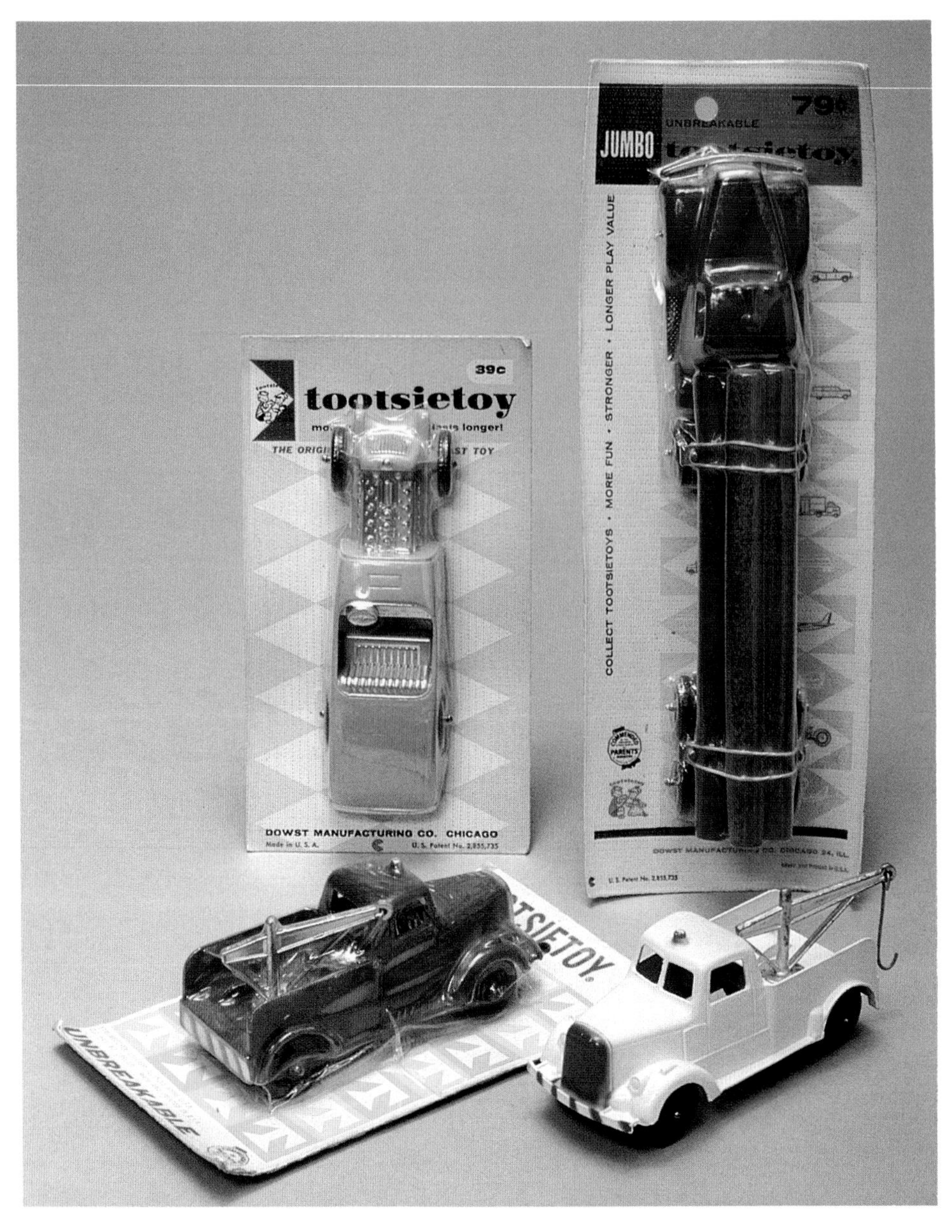

An assortment of Dowst blister packs. S. Butler Collection.

No.	Description	G	E	M
2700	1955 Scenicruiser Bus; 1959, 1960-1961, 1963.	—	—	80
2720	1959 Oldsmobile Convertible, U-Haul Trailer; 1960-1961, 1963.	—	—	65
2760	1947 Mack Logger Trailer Truck; 1961, 1963.	—	—	75
2760	1955 Mack Logger Trailer Truck; 1960.	—	—	70
2810	Ford Tractor, Disc Harrow; 1950-1969.	—	—	85
2815	Greyhound Scenicruiser Bus; 1964-1969.	—	—	85
2820	1959 Chevrolet Mobil Oil Tanker; 1966.	—	—	150
2820	1955 Mack Mobil Oil Tanker; 1960-1961, 1963-1965, 1967-1969.	—	—	115
2820	1947 Mack "Tootsietoy" Oil Tanker; 1959.	—	—	80
2825	1962 Ford Wagon, U-Haul Trailer, Barrel Load; 1962-1968.	—	—	55
2825	1962 Ford Wagon, U-Haul Trailer, Tire Load; 1962-1968.	—	—	55
2830	1947 Mack Logger Trailer Truck; 1964-1965.	—	—	85
2830	1955 Mack Logger Trailer Truck; 1967-1968.	—	—	85
2830	1959 Chevrolet Logger Trailer Truck; 1966.	—	—	125
2901	1955 Mack Utility Trailer Truck, four farm animals; 1960-1961, 1963.	—	—	60
2905	1959 Chevrolet Hook and Ladder Truck; 1966.	—	—	150
2905	1947 Mack Hook and Ladder Truck; 1959-1961, 1963-1965, 1967.	—	—	115
2905	1955 Mack Hook and Ladder Truck; 1968.	—	—	115
2907	1956 Maserati Race Cars, pit crew of three; 1962-1963.	—	—	65

No.	Description	G	E	M
2908	1947 Mack Tow Truck, 1940 Ford Convertible; 1963-1965.	—	—	95
2910	Caterpillar Bulldozer; 1960-1967.	—	—	55
2911	Hi-Way Repair Set: Road Grader, 4" Chevrolet El Camino Pickup Truck, 4" Army Jeep; 1962-1967.	—	—	90
2912	1962 Ford Pickup Truck, Pull Trailer, cowboy, bull; 1963-1965.			NRS
2914	Gas Station Set: CJ5 Jeep, 1962 Ford Oil Truck, plastic gas island; 1963-1966.	—	—	75
2916	Police Chase Set: 1962 Ford Wagon, 1932 Hot Rod, .45 miniature revolver; 1964-1966.	—	—	90
2917	1959 Chevrolet Boat Transport Set: two plastic boats; 1965-1966.	—	—	125
2917	1955 Mack Boat Transport Set: two plastic boats; 1967.	—	—	100
2917	1955 International Boat Transport Set: two plastic boats; 1962-1964, 1968.	—	—	80
2920	1959 Chevrolet Auto Transport Set: loading ramp, 1956 Triumph (3"), 1960 Ford Falcon (3"); 1965-1966.	—	—	130
2920	1955 Mack Auto Transport Set: loading ramp, 1956 Triumph (3"), Hot Rod Model B (3"); 1967.	—	—	100
2920	1955 International Auto Transport Set: loading ramp, 3" 1956 Triumph (3"), 1960 Ford Falcon (3"); 1960, 1962-1963, 1968.	—	—	90
2920	1955 International Auto Transport Set: loading ramp, 1955 Ford (3"), 1954 Jaguar (3"); 1964.	—	—	100
2920	1955 International Auto Transport, 1949 American LaFrance Fire Truck, 1955 Ford, 1957 Jaguar; 1959.	—	—	130
2921	Radar Set; 1964-1965.			NRS
2923	Artillery Set; 1964-1965.			NRS
2925	Missile Launcher; 1959-1960, 1963-1964.	—	—	175
2930	Playtime Set; 1959, 1962-1964.			NRS
2938	1960 El Camino, Camper Top, Boat; 1962-1965.	—	—	60
2940	1959 Ford Wagon, Chris-Craft Boat, Trailer; 1959, 1964-65.	—	—	75
2940	1959 Oldsmobile Convertible, Chris-Craft Boat, Trailer; 1968.	—	—	75
2941	Boeing 707 Jet, loading ramp, baggage truck, two baggage carts; 1960-1961, 1964-1966.	—	—	55
2942	1959 Oldsmobile Convertible, Horse Trailer; 1960-1961.	—	—	70
2943	1959 Ford Wagon, Camping Trailer; 1960-1967.	—	—	55
2944	1955 International Moving Van; 1960-1961, 1964-1965, 1967.	—	—	50
2944	1959 Chevrolet Moving Van; 1966.	—	—	75
2945	1955 Mack Concrete Mixer; 1960-1961, 1964-1969.	—	—	50
2946	Covered Wagon; 1960-1961.	—	—	45
2947	Civil War Cannon and Caisson; 1960, 1961.	—	—	60
2949	1960 El Camino, Refreshment Trailer; 1961, 1963.	—	—	90
2950	1960 El Camino, Race Car, 4" Vehicles, Trailer; 1961-1965.	—	—	80
2952	1962 Ford Wagon, Race Car, Trailer; 1962-1968.	—	—	65
2968	Hi-Way Set: 1962 Ford Pickup Truck, 1960 El Camino, two road signs; 1965-1966.	—	—	80
1955	International Flatbed Truck, 3" Army Jeep and three soldiers (UK).	—	—	95
1962	Ford Wagon, Camping Trailer; 1962-1968.	—	—	50
1962	Ford Wagon, Boat, and Trailer; 1962-1968.	—	—	70
	U.S. Space Ship; three 5" variations; 1958 or 1959.	—	—	75

4-inch series

No.	Description	G	E	M
2310	1954 Ford Wagon, police badge, whistle; 1959-1960.	—	—	45
2320	1949 Mercury Fire Chief Car, badge, fire hat; 1959-1960.	—	—	60
2330	1956 Chevrolet Pickup Truck, tools; 1959.			35
2400	Military Field Cannon; six plastic shells; 1959.	—	—	25
2903	Race Car Set; 1964-1966.	—	—	65
2906	1955 Thunderbird, 1953 Corvette, 1956 Chevy Pickup Truck, repair ramp; 1963.	—	—	125
2935	Army Jeep, Field Cannon, four soldiers; 1959, 1964.	—	—	55
2935	Army Jeep, Cannon, three Soldiers; 1960, 1963.	—	—	45
1969	Ford LTD, U-Haul Trailer, six pieces furniture; 1970.	—	—	45
	Panther Jet; 1959-1969.	—	—	20
	P-80 Shooting Star Jet; 1959-1969.	—	—	20
	Cutlass Jet; 1959-1969.	—	—	20
	Skyray Jet; 1959-1969.	—	—	20

3-inch series

Description	G	E	M
1954 Ford Ranch Wagon, road sign; 1959-1960.	—	—	30
1954 MG, road sign; 1959-1960.	—	—	30
1954 Jaguar, road sign; 1959-1960.	—	—	30
1955 Thunderbird, road sign; 1959-1960.	—	—	30
1957 Plymouth, 1957 Ford Pickup Truck, road sign; 1959-1961.	—	—	50
Six vehicles: 1960 Ford Falcon, 1957 Ford Pickup Truck, 1960 Studebaker Convertible, 1954 Volkswagen, 1960 Ford Ranch Wagon, Hot Rod, two road signs; 1960.	—	—	150

Accessory and Bonus Items

With many of the boxed sets, the company included accessories or bonus pieces to enhance their play value. Some accessories were included with cellophane packaged vehicles, and the practice continued into the blister pack line as well as in later sets produced up through 1969. A number of these items are listed here. The values are for individual accessories in Excellent (E) condition.

Item	E
Airplane Loading Ramp. Green metal. Included in set Nos. 5698 and 6500 and in assorted blister packs.	3
Baggage cart. Green or blue metal. Included in set Nos. 5698, 6500, 1689, 1740, and assorted blister packs.	1
Baggage Truck. Yellow or red metal. Included in set Nos. 5698, 6500, 1689, 1740, and in blister packs.	1
Bugle. Metal.	5

E

Construction Hand Tools. Silver metal. Axe, hammer, pipe wrench, and screwdriver included in a number of gift sets, cellophane, and blister packs. **.50 each**

Deputy Sheriff Badge. **5**

Farm Animals. White plastic. Set contains horses, pigs, goat, cows, and chickens. **1**

Fireman's Hat. All-metal. **5**

Fire Ladder, 4-inch series. Metal. **6**

Fire Ladder, 6-inch series. Metal. **8**

Foot Soldier. Shown in 1941 catalog as No. 4545 but included in a blister pack with a 1956 6" Army Set. Silver (metal); 1" in length. **5**

Future Pilot Wings. Red, white, blue, and silver or gold. Included in various airplane gift sets. **10**

Gas Pump Island. Red metal. Included in set No. 1743, 4550, 4200, 5710, Midget Service Station No. 1693, and Super Service Set No. 1815, and in assorted blister packs. **50**

Grease Rack. For 3" vehicles. **25**

Junior Fire Chief Badge. Silver. Included in set Nos. 1810, 1743, 1691, 5211, and others. **10**

Junior G-Man Badge. **5**

Jr. Stewardess Wings, UNITED AIRLINES. Silver or gold with white, red, blue, and black. Included in various airplane sets. **10**

Modern Soldiers, assorted. **2**

Overhead Light Poles. Silver metal. Included in sets Nos. 1815, 1743, 1693, and Midget Service Station. **6/pair**

Police Whistle. Red and blue plastic. Included with 4" Ford Wagon and badge. **1**

Police Gun. Silver. Included with 4" Oldsmobile and badge and in 6" Jeep blister pack. **2**

Top: *Gas Pump Island.* **Left:** *Ten assorted Road Signs.* **Middle and right:** *Miniature game and candy toy pieces.*

E

Road Block Barriers, Water Tank, Tool Cart, Generator, Covered Wagon, Open Hauler. All six items are a silver-gray plastic and were included in set No. 1730. **2**

Road Signs. Yellow and black metal. Included with a number of gift sets, cellophane, and blister packs. Ten different types known to exist. **2**

Service Station Rack. For 4" vehicles. **35**

Special Police Badge. Silver. Included in set No. 1702 and in blister packs with a 4" Ford Wagon/Oldsmobile. **3**

405 Tootsietoy Badge Assortment. Includes badges marked Deputy Sheriff, Junior G-Man, Special Police, and Junior Fire Chief. **100**

CHAPTER 12

Tootsietoys of the Late Sixties

During the sixties, Strombecker introduced a number of vehicle lines referred to in the first chapter as Postwar Second Generation Series. These lines, as they were issued, include Road Racing Sets, the Midget Series, the Collector Series, the Super Tootsietoys Series, the Hitch-Ups Series, and the Playmate Series, as well as several Platform Display Sets and Vehicle Cases. Extensive use of plastic is evident in some of these lines.

Three other series included in the Postwar Second Generation chart in Chapter 1 were discussed in Chapter 10, since they are primarily metal lines. The toys covered in this chapter were issued in a wide range of quality and price and are generally not yet as collectible as other Tootsietoys. Cast-in information on the underside of each vehicle appears last in each listing.

The Midget Series

The first of the new production lines in the sixties was the Midget Series, introduced with the Midget Toy Assortment. The small vehicles with metal bodies and polypropylene wheels are approximately 2 inches in length and painted in either red, yellow, silver, light blue, medium blue, green, or purple (the fire trucks were produced in red only).

The listings cover the period of production from 1966 through 1969. Many of the Midget vehicles have no specific production information in the catalogues. A number of catalogues from the late sixties show the same boxed assortments of vehicles available to the dealer, but the gift sets offered contained a number of vehicles not shown in any assortment. This makes it difficult to assign a production year to each vehicle. In Mint or Like New condition, they can be found for less than two dollars each.

Strombecker issued its Midget Tootsietoy vehicles in "viewer packs", blister packs, and the new open-front Jam-Pac™ set boxes. Some of the gift sets also contained accessory items to enhance their play value. The sets are listed by catalogue number, contents, and values for a sealed set in Good and Mint condition. Additional information on accessories can be found in Chapter 11.

The Midget vehicles are as follows:

American LaFrance Pumper Truck
Ba-ja Runabout
Cadillac Eldorado
Cheetah
Chevy Corvette
Chevy Pickup Truck
Chris-Craft Boat and Trailer
CJ5 Jeep
Earth Mover (Pan)
Ferrari Formula 1 Racer
Fiat Abarth
1940 Ford Coupe
Ford GT
Ford Mustang
Ford Tanker Truck
Ford Thunderbird
Ford Tow Truck
Formula D Jaguar
Hot Rod Truck
Hot Rod (two-seater)
Indy Race car
Jeepster
Jeep Pickup Truck
Jeep Tanker Truck
Jeep Tow Truck
Jeep Delivery Truck
1939 Mercedes
Mercedes Convertible
Midget Auto Racer and Trailer
MG
Monza
Oldsmobile Toronado
Roadster
Shuttle Truck
Skip Loader
Utility Trailer
Volkswagen
Wedge Dragster

G E M

1404 SERVICE STATION SET: (1967-1968) Set contains Ford Tanker Truck, Ford Tow Truck, Jeep, gas island with two pumps, and two overhead lights. 5 — 10

1404 FIRE STATION SET: (1967-1968) Set contains American LaFrance Pumper Truck, Emergency Jeep, Oldsmobile Fire Chief Car, and badge. 4 — 8

1404 SPORTS SET: (1967-1968) Set contains Jeep, Chevy Pickup Truck, Formula D Jaguar, Boat Trailer, and Boat. 4 — 8

1687 GRAND PRIX SET: (1968-1969) Set contains Cheetah, Ferrari Formula 1 Racer, two Honda Motorcycles, Trailer, Ford J Car, and Porsche. 5 — 10

1689 AIRPORT SET: (1967) Set contains Beechcraft Bonanza, Luggage Transport with baggage carrier, service

G E M

ramp, Jeep, Ford Tanker Truck, El Camino Pickup Truck, and Jeep Truck. 12 — 25

1689 AIRPORT SET: (1968) Set contains F-86 Sabre Jet, Luggage Transport with baggage carrier, Ford Tanker Truck in two pieces, Jeep, El Camino Pickup Truck, and Jeep Truck. 12 — 25

1689 AIRPORT SET: (1969) Set contains Shooting Star Jet, Ford Tanker Truck, Jeep Truck, and Jeepster. 7 — 15

1693 AUTO SERVICE SET: (1969) Set contains Ford Tow Truck, Ford Tanker Truck, Ford GT, 1940 Ford Coupe, CJ5 Jeep, Volkswagen, two lights, and pump island. 15 — 30

1694 CAR FLEET SET: (1967-1968) Set contains Chris-Craft Boat with Trailer, Midget Racer with Trailer, Jeep Truck, Oldsmobile Toronado, Ferrari Formula 1 Racer, Formula D Jaguar, Hot Rod Truck, and Ford Mustang. 12 — 25

1694 CAR FLEET SET: (1969) Set contains Ford Mustang, Formula D Jaguar, Hot Rod Truck, Volkswagen, Chevy Pickup Truck, Ferrari Formula 1 Racer, and Boat and Trailer. 12 — 25

1700 TRANSPORTATION SET: (1966) Set contains Beechcraft Bonanza, Skyray Jet, Jeep Truck, Jeep, Chris-Craft Boat and Trailer, Locomotive, Tender, Boxcar, and Caboose. 12 — 25

1700 TRAVEL SET: (1967) Set contains Locomotive and Tender, Boxcar, Caboose, Beechcraft Bonanza, Jeep, Chris-Craft Boat and Trailer, Ford Tow Truck, Ford Mustang, Oldsmobile Toronado. 12 — 25

1700 TRANSPORTATION SET: (1968) Set contains Shooting Star Jet, Chris-Craft Boat and Trailer, Locomotive, Tender, Gondola, Caboose, Jeep Truck, Volkswagen, and game spinner. Back of box contains "Traffic Jam" game board. 12 — 25

1703 AMERICAN ROAD SET: (1967) Set contains Utility Trailer, Chris-Craft Boat and Trailer, Midget Racer and Trailer, El Camino Pickup Truck, Hot Rod Truck, Formula D Racer, Ford Tow Truck, Jeep, Ford Tanker Truck, Oldsmobile Toronado, Volkswagen, Mercedes Convertible, Monza, and Ford Mustang. 12 — 15

1703 CROSS COUNTRY SET: (1968-1969) Set contains Ford Tow Truck, Midget Racer and Trailer, Chris-Craft Boat and Trailer, Volkswagen, Formula D Jaguar, Ford GT, El Camino Pickup Truck, Ford Mustang, Fiat Abarth, 1939 Mercedes, and game spinner. Back of box contains "Route 66" game board. 12 — 25

1703 TRAVEL SET: (1966) Set contains two 3" Ford Pickup Trucks, three Jeeps, Midget Racer and Trailer, Chris-Craft Boat and Trailer, Ferrari Formula 1 Racer, Hot Rod Truck, Jeep Truck, Utility Trailer, two Volkswagens, and Formula D Jaguar. 7 — 15

1740 TRAVEL SET: (1966) Set contains Locomotive and Tender, Boxcar, Caboose, Beechcraft Bonanza, Starfire Jet, Jeep, Jeep Truck, Jeep Tow Truck, Ramp, Hot Rod Truck,

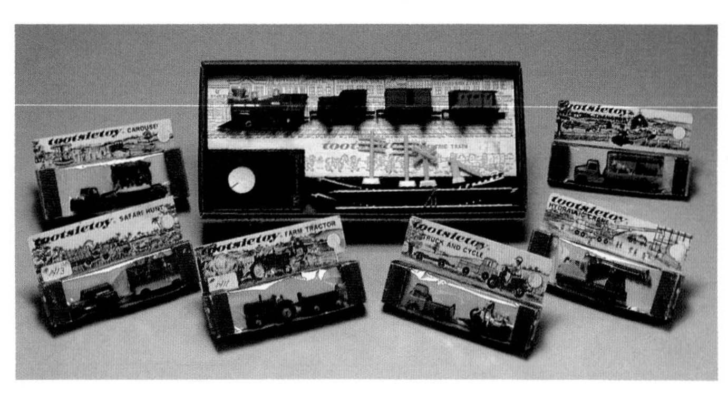

Top: *No. 5800 HO Battery Operated Train Set, described in Chapter 11.* **Bottom:** *An assortment of boxed Collector Series toys. K. Jestes Collection.*

G E M

Formula D Jaguar, Chris-Craft Boat and Trailer, 4" Ford Tanker Truck, gas island, and two overhead lights. 18 — 35

1740 AMERICAN TRAVELER SET: (1967) Set contains Locomotive and Tender, Boxcar, Caboose, Panther Jet, Ford Mustang, Volkswagen, Jeep, Jeep Tow Truck, Midget Racer and Trailer, Formula D Jaguar, Chris-Craft Boat and Trailer, Oldsmobile Toronado, El Camino Pickup Truck, and two road signs. 12 — 25

1740 AMERICAN TRAVELER SET: (1968) Set contains Locomotive and Tender, Boxcar, Caboose, Beechcraft Bonanza, baggage carrier with tractor, Honda Motorcycle, Chris-Craft Boat and Trailer, Hot Rod Truck, Formula D Jaguar, Ford GT, Indy Racer, MG, and Ford Mustang. 12 — 25

2301 MIDGET CAR WITH RACER AND TRAILER: (1966) Set contains Jeep, Midget Racer, and Trailer. — — 5

2302 MIDGET CAR WITH UTILITY TRAILER: (1966) Set contains Jeep and Utility Trailer. — — 5

2303 MIDGET CAR WITH BOAT AND TRAILER: (1966) Set contains Jeep Truck, Chris-Craft Boat, and Trailer. — — 5

2304 MIDGET CAR SET: (1966) Set contains Indy Racer and Volkswagen. — — 5

2834 TOOTSIETOY JAM-PAC™ FLEET: (1969) Set contains three-pump gas pump island, Volkswagen, CJ5 Jeep, Jeep Truck, American LaFrance Pumper Truck, Oldsmobile Toronado, Formula D Jaguar, Ford Mustang, and Jeep Delivery Truck. 16 — 35

2835 TOOTSIETOY JAM-PAC MIDGETS: (1966) Set contains two Volkswagens, CJ5 Jeep, two Ferrari Formula 1 Racers, two Jeep Trucks, two Formula D Jaguars, and Hot Rod truck. 10 — 20

2835 TOOTSIETOY JAM-PAC: (1967-1968) Set contains Volkswagen, CJ5 Jeep, Earth Mover, Jeep Truck, Formula D Jaguar, Ford Tow Truck, Ford Tanker Truck, American LaFrance Pumper Truck, Hot Rod Truck, Chevy Pickup Truck, Ferrari Formula 1 Racer, and Oldsmobile Toronado. 12 — 25

G E M

2835 TOOTSIETOY JAM-PAC: (1969) Set contains Hot Rod Truck, Formula D Jaguar, Volkswagen, Earth Mover, Shuttle Truck, Earth Mover Dump Truck, Chevy Pickup Truck, CJ5 Jeep, Oldsmobile Toronado, and Cadillac Eldorado. **10 — 20**

2840 MIDGET TRAVEL SET: (1966) Set contains Jeep with Chris-Craft Boat and Trailer, two Jeep Trucks, Volkswagen, Formula D Jaguar, Utility Trailer, and Hot Rod Truck. **5 — 10**

2842 MIDGET AIRPORT SET: (1966) Set contains Beechcraft Bonanza, Skyray Jet, Jeep Tanker Truck, Jeep Truck, Jeep Tow Truck, Volkswagen, and Utility Trailer. **10 — 20**

2843 MIDGET GAS STATION SET: (1966) Set contains Jeep Tanker Truck, Jeep Tow Truck, Indy Racer, Hot Rod Truck, Volkswagen, Formula D Jaguar, gas island, and two overhead lights. **7 — 15**

The Collector Series

In 1966 Strombecker advertised the new Collector Series, a small line of sets using items from the Midget line. The idea behind the new "collector" series was so well-accepted that in 1967 another line of vehicles was introduced as the Turnpike Collector Series. The term "Turnpike" was dropped the following year, however, and collectors now refer to this series as the Collector Series. For the most part these new cars, trucks, and construction and farm equipment pieces are made of die-cast metal with some plastic parts.

This series may be the biggest "sleeper" from a collector's standpoint, since they will probably increase in value and be in greater demand over the years. Their quality matches that of the similarly-sized Matchbox toys of the same era, although these toys have not yet garnered the same attention. The Collector Series includes two well-made and well-detailed American LaFrance fire trucks, an aerial ladder truck and a snorkel fire truck. Both of these items will probably become the most desired pieces of this Series, which includes ten vehicles with pull trailers, construction vehicles, a dump truck, a cement truck, and farm equipment.

The tractor trailer units were produced with both a Ford and Chevy cab unit. The cabs were painted in red, blue, or green with trailers painted in red, silver, metallic blue, and dark blue. At least twelve different tractor trailer units can be found through 1969. A point to remember is that these units are very small—less than half the size of the trailer trucks featured in Chapter 7. In mint condition they will be found in a visual box, a blister pack, or a gift set. The "visual packages" have full-color illustrations and clear mylar windows. They were designed to be stacked or hung on pegboard.

The listings include those units made through 1969, though Strombecker continued to produced some of the pieces into the seventies. In cases where there are duplicate numbers, the numbers refer to the dealer assortments, with no secondary numbers assigned to the items in each assortment. The sizes provided represent the total length if more than one piece is included as a unit. **Note:** The values given are for complete, sealed sets in Good and Mint condition.

G E M

1420 CARS AND TRAILERS: (1967) 4½" in total length. Display pack contains Ford Mustang, Chris-Craft Boat, and Trailer. **3 — 6**

1420 CARS AND TRAILERS: (1967) 4½" in total length. Display pack contains Jeep Pickup Truck with U-Haul Trailer. **3 — 7**

1420 CARS AND TRAILERS: (1967) 4½" in total length. Display pack contains CJ5 Jeep, Midget Racer, and Trailer. **3 — 6**

1430 CARS AND TRAILERS: (1968-1969) 4½" in total length. Display pack contains Ford Mustang with Chris-Craft Boat, and Trailer. **3 — 6**

1430 CARS AND TRAILERS: (1968-1969) 4½" in total length. Display pack contains CJ5 Jeep, Midget Racer, and Trailer. **3 — 6**

1431 HIGHWAY TRUCKS: (1967-1969) 4¼" in total length. Display pack contains Ford or Chevy Van Transport Trailer Truck with Trailer. **3 — 7**

1431 HIGHWAY TRUCKS: (1967-1969) 4¼" in total length. Display pack contains Ford or Chevy Flatbed Trailer Truck with Trailer, three natural-finish logs. **3 — 7**

1431 HIGHWAY TRUCKS: (1967-1969) 4¼" in total length. Display pack contains Ford or Chevy Tanker Trailer Truck with MOBIL sticker on sides of tanker. **3 — 7**

1432 FIRE TRUCKS: (1967-1969) 4⅛" in total length. Display pack contains American LaFrance Snorkel Fire Truck. **5 — 10**

1432 FIRE TRUCKS: (1967-1969) 4⅛" in total length. Display pack contains American LaFrance Ladder Truck. **5 — 10**

1433 CONSTRUCTION EQUIPMENT: (1967-1969) 3" long. Display pack contains Hendrickson Dump Truck. **2 — 5**

1433 CONSTRUCTION EQUIPMENT: (1967-1969) 3" long. Display pack contains Hendrickson Cement Truck. **2 — 5**

1450 AUTO TRANSPORT: (1967) 4¼" in total length. Display pack contains Ford or Chevy Auto Transport Carrier with two Triumph cars. **5 — 10**

1451 FARM TRACTOR AND UTILITY WAGON: (1968-1969) 4¼" in total length. Display pack or box contains Tractor and Wagon. **5 — 10**

1452 HEAVY DUTY HYDRAULIC CRANE: (1968-1969) 4" long. Display pack or box contains MOBIL Crane with telescoping boom and rotating cab. **5 — 10**

1455 LIVESTOCK TRANSPORT: (1967) 4¼" in total length. Display pack contains Ford or Chevy Trailer Truck; two horses, and two cattle; Trailer. **4 — 8**

1456 HONDA MOTORCYCLE WITH TRUCK: (1968-1969) 4½" in total length. Display pack or box contains Jeep Truck, Trailer, and chrome Honda Motorcycle. **3 — 7**

	G	E	M
1457 HEAVY DUTY POWER SHOVEL: (1968-1969) 4″ long. Display pack or box contains "Mobil" Shovel with operating boom and rotating cab.	5	—	10
1460 AUTO TRANSPORT: (1968-1969) 5″ in total length. Display pack or box contains Ford or Chevy Transport Trailer with cars.	7	—	15
1463 SAFARI HUNT: (1968-1969) 5¼″ in total length. Display pack or box contains Jeep Panel Truck, plastic animal cage Trailer, giraffe, elephant, and hippopotamus.	3	—	15
1464 CAROUSEL AND TRANSPORT UNIT: (1968) Display pack contains Ford or Chevy Flatbed Trailer Truck, plastic Carousel.	7	—	15
1465 LIVESTOCK TRANSPORTS: (1968-1969) Display pack or box contains Ford or Chevy Livestock Transport Trailer Truck, two horses and two cows.	4	—	8
1466 ROAD BUILDER: (1969) Visual package contains Long-nose Tractor Truck, Flatbed Trailer and Michigan Earth Mover.	2	—	4
1467 HOUSEBOAT AND TRANSPORTER: (1969) 4¼″ in total length. Visual package contains Ford or Chevy Flatbed Trailer Truck, House Boat (1969).	5	—	10
1468 CAR AND CABIN CRUISER: (1969) 5½″ in total length. Visual package contains Eldorado Custom Cadillac, Boat Trailer, plastic Cabin Cruiser.	5	—	10
1469 TRUCK AND HORSE TRAILER: (1969) 4½″ in total length. Visual package contains Jeepster, Stakeside Trailer, four horses.	5	—	10

The Collector Series also featured number of gift sets which primarily contained vehicles from the Collector Series with the addition of some Midget vehicles. Some sets contain accessory items, including game boards on the back of their "viewer" boxes. Please note: the values provided are based on sealed sets in Good and Mint condition. Additional information on accessories can be found in Chapter 11.

	G	E	M
1686 FARM EQUIPMENT SET: (1968-1969) Set contains Farm Tractor, Disc Harrow, Plow, and Utility Wagon.	10	—	20
1688 STATE FAIR SET: (1968) Set contains Jeep Truck, Jeep, Trailer and Carousel, Stake Trailer, and three animals.	10	—	20
1688 STATE FAIR SET: (1969) Set contains Jeep Truck, Jeep, Horse Trailer and four horses, Stake Trailer, giraffe, hippo, and elephant.	12	—	25
1690 TRUCK FLEET SET: (1967) Set contains Ford Log Truck, Semi-Trailer, Jeep Pickup Truck, Jeep Truck, and Utility Trailer.	10	—	20
1690 TRUCK FLEET SET: (1969) Set contains Ford Log Truck with three logs, Ford Semi-Trailer, Jeep, Jeep Truck, and six barrels.	12	—	25
1691 FIRE FIGHTING SET: (1967) Set contains American LaFrance Snorkel Truck, American LaFrance Ladder Truck, American LaFrance Pumper, Mustang Fire Chief Car, and badge.	12	—	25
1691 FIRE FIGHTING SET: (1969) Set contains American LaFrance Ladder Truck, American LaFrance Pumper, Jeep, Panel Truck, Fire Chief Car, and badge.	10	—	20
1692 CONSTRUCTION SET: (1967-1969) Set contains Cement Truck, Loader, Earth Mover, Ford Tractor Trailer Truck, and Jeep Pickup Truck.	10	—	20
1693 SERVICE STATION SET: (1967-1968) Set contains Ford Tanker Truck, Ford Tow Truck, Volkswagen, service station island, two overhead lights.	10	—	20
1701 SERVICE STATION SET: (1966-1967) Set contains Ford Tanker Truck, Ford Tractor Trailer Truck, Ford Oil Truck, Ford Tow Truck, service station island, ramp, two overhead lights, three cars, Utility Trailer, racer, trailer.	12	—	25
1702 TRAFFIC CONTROL SET: (1968-1969) Set contains Ford GT, Hot Rod Truck, Sikorsky S-58 and Hiller 12c Helicopters, Transport Truck with two miniature cars, Honda Motorcycle, badge, and game spinner. Back of box contains "Stop and Go" game board.	75	—	195
1730 POWER CONSTRUCTION SET: (1968-1969) Set contains Crane Truck, Hydraulic Truck, Cement Truck, Dump Truck, Earth Mover, Hauler, Jeep, El Camino Pickup Truck, construction tools, road barriers, water tank, tool cart, generator, wagon, and game spinner. Back of box contains "Needle In The Hay Stack" game board.	17	—	35
1742 TURNPIKE SET: (1967) Set contains Ford Auto Transport with two cars, Ford Trailer Truck, Ford Gasoline Truck, Ford Log Truck, El Camino Pickup Truck, Jeep Truck, Ford Tow Truck, Ford Oil Tanker, Mustang, Boat and Trailer, four road signs, ramp, service station island, and two overhead lights.	12	—	25
1743 CITY PLAYTIME SET: (1967-1969) Set contains American LaFrance Snorkel Fire Truck, Ladder Fire Truck, Pumper Truck, Fire Chief Car and badge, Ford Oil Tanker, Ford Tow Truck, service station island, two overhead lights, Formula D Jaguar, Oldsmobile Toronado, 1939 Mercedes, Hot Rod Truck, Ford Mustang, Jeep Truck, Monza, Boat and Trailer, and game spinner. Back of box contains "Gran Prix" game board.	17	—	35
2920 AUTO TRANSPORT: (1969) 8¾″ long. Transport features metal Hendrickson Tractor Truck, polypropylene Transporter Trailer with let-down ramp, and three Midget cars.	10	—	20
2930 DOUBLE BOTTOM-DUMPER TRUCK: (1969) 8¼″ long. Two die-cast Bottom-Dumper Transport units pulled by Hendrickson Tractor Truck. Dumper features three-position lever for dumping of the transport.	7	—	15

The Hitch-Ups Series

A whole new line of vehicles was introduced in 1969 called the Hitch-Ups®; each item contained a pull trailer for dif-

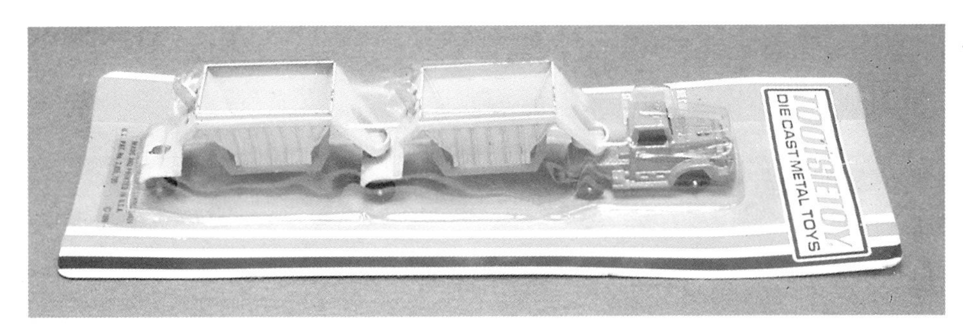

A No. 2930 Double Bottom-Dumper Truck, (1969).

G E M

ferent types of recreation vehicles. The line used more plastic and featured larger tires and axles; it became the main line of vehicles to be offered as the company entered into the seventies. Six different units were made in 1969 but have not generated much interest. Most used units are being resold at less than the original selling price. Prices provided are for items in Good and Mint condition.

2522 TOOTSIETOY K-9 HITCH-UP: (1969) 7½″ in total length. Pickup Truck with Trailer, eight miniature dogs, and clear cover which fits over the trailer. **5 — 10**

2523 TOOTSIETOY HONDA HITCH-UP: (1969) 7″ in total length. Jeep Truck with Trailer; two Honda Motorcycles. **5 — 11**

2524 TOOTSIETOY CABIN CRUISER HITCH-UP: (1969) 7″ in total length. Jeep truck with Boat Trailer, plastic Cabin Cruiser. **5 — 10**

2525 TOOTSIETOY U-HAUL HITCH-UP: (1969) 7½″ in total length. Jeep Truck with U-Haul Trailer; six pieces of furniture. **5 — 10**

2526 JUNGLE CAGE HITCH-UP: (1969) 7¼″ in total length. Jeep Truck, Trailer with cage; one lion or tiger. **6 — 12**

2527 TOOTSIETOY BEACH BUGGY HITCH-UP: (1969) 7″ in total length. Sandpiper Beach Buggy with removable top and two surfboards; Pickup Truck. **4 — 8**

1745 TOOTSIETOY "HITCH-UPS" SET: (1969) Set contains two Jeep Truck, Truck, Cabin Cruiser and Trailer, Beach Buggy with two surfboards, and Trailer with two Motorcycles. **7 — 15**

Road Racing Sets

Dowst Manufacturing bought the Becker division of road-racing sets from Strombeck/Becker in 1961 because of the growing popularity of electric racing sets. The Dowst management decided to change the company's name to Strombecker to capitalize on the worldwide recognition of Strombeck/Becker road racing sets. Production of Strombecker's sets did not continue after 1966. Extra racing cars were offered in blister packs, and have been known to sell for $60 to $70 each in mint condition.

5100 ROAD RACING SET: (1963-1965) Battery-operated set contains two die-cast metal Corvair Monzas, figure-eight track sections, and button controls. **NRS**

G E M

5200 ROAD RACING SET: (1963) Set contains two die-cast metal Corvair Monzas, figure-eight track sections, power pack, and two rheostat controls. **NRS**

5175 AMERICAN ROAD RACING SET: (1964-1966) Set contains two 1/64 scale racing cars: a Falcon racing car and Corvair Monza Speedster; sufficient track to form 125″ figure-eight circuit; two rheostat controls; 4½-volt power pack; bridge; track supports; control tower; decals; and instructions. **NRS**

Playmates

In 1967, Strombecker introduced a totally different line of toys intended to compete with other manufacturers' toddler toys. The Playmate Line was made of both metal and polyethylene and painted with non-toxic paints, and the toys were promoted as being safer, stronger, and longer lasting. This very colorful line contains a variety of trucks, carts, tractors, and a Choo-Choo train that was used in the initial development of nine different boxed units and a combination gift set. Each unit includes a variety of little people and accessories designed for preschool children. Package design includes full-color illustrations with a visual display on the front and the toy in actual use with scenery and a poem on the back.

By 1969, this line had grown to nineteen different units, some incorporating various forms of action. It is recognized that these toys are of no interest yet to most collectors. In fairness to those that have an interest in the company itself, and to cover completely all toys produced under the Tootsietoy name, we feel it is important to include these listings. The value of these toys is unknown; however, some partial pieces have been observed at very reasonable prices, ranging from fifty cents to one dollar. Boxed units that are complete will probably range from $5 to $15 each, depending on the size of the unit.

2018 KENNY'S KENNEL: (1967-1969) 4″ long. Truck with canopy, kennel keeper, and dog. **NRS**

2018 CHARLEY CORNHUSKER: (1967-1969) 4″ long. Truck with stake fence back; farmer and animal. **NRS**

2018 DONNY'S DELIVERY: (1967-1969) 4″ long. Delivery Truck with canopy, delivery boy, and five pieces of clothing. **NRS**

2019 FARMER JONES: (1967-1969) 6″ long. Truck, Trailer, farmer, and vegetables. **NRS**

G E M

2019 HOKY SMOKY: (1967-1969) 6" long. Truck, Trailer, fire chief, and Dalmatian. **NRS**

2019 MICKEY MILK: (1967-1969) 6" long. Milk Delivery Truck, Trailer, delivery man, and milk can. **NRS**

2020 CHOO-CHOO: (1967-1969) 12" long. Die-cast metal and polyethylene; four-piece hook-together set; Train, Tender, Passenger Car, and Caboose. **NRS**

2024 TOMMY TRACTOR: (1967-1968) 6" long. Tractor, two carts, farmer, and two vegetables. **NRS**

2024 TOMMY TRACTOR: (1969) 6" long. Tractor and farm cart. **NRS**

2025 PETER PILOT: (1969) 7" long. Airplane with fold-up wings and hitch in back; Jeep. **NRS**

2026 RONNIE RACER: (1969) 6½" long. Car and Pickup Truck. **NRS**

2050 FUNNY JUNGLE: (1968-1969) 7½" long. Cage with flip-top roof, metal Trailer, and Jeep; tigers, bears, and monkeys with movable parts; hunter with no movable parts. **NRS**

2051 HICKORY, DICKORY, DOCK: (1968-1969) 7½" long. Plastic clock affixed to die-cast metal base; three-piece set is pulled by die-cast metal car. **NRS**

2052 TOOTSIETOY TUG: (1968-1969) 7½" long. Five-piece set includes Boat, die-cast metal Car, Trailer, captain, and first mate. **NRS**

2054 FERRIS WHEEL: (1968-1969) 7½" long. Seven-piece set based on the fable of the "Three Little Pigs"; plastic wheel sits on die-cast base, towed by die-cast metal car. **NRS**

2078 TOOTSIETOY COUNTRY FOLK: (1967-1969) 16" long. Set includes Tractor, cart, vegetable, ranch hand, Stake Truck, either horse or cow; Pickup Truck, farmer, Utility Wagon, barnyard animal. **NRS**

2078 CITY FRIENDS: (1967-1969) 16" long. Set contains delivery boy; Clothing Truck with five pieces of laundry; Pick-up Truck with milkman, cart, and Grade "A" milk can; dog catcher, Kennel Truck, one dog. **NRS**

2085 CAR CARRIER: (1968-1969) 14" long. Preschool-type Car Carrier with three die-cast metal Cars and four drivers; heavy-duty plastic Trailer with tailgate that raises and lowers. **NRS**

2088 COUNTING TRUCK: (1968-1969) 13" long. Abacus-styled toy has same cab and driver as Car Carrier above; heavy-duty plastic Trailer with three rows of happy-faced apples, lemons, and oranges resting on vertical steel rods. The numbers one to ten are featured below each column of fruit. **NRS**

2090 MOTHER GOOSE: (1968-1969) 13" long. Six-piece set includes hand-decorated Mother Goose, Peter riding on her back, Peter's wife in take-apart pumpkin shell, Old Lady in lacing-up shoe. Plastic characters are mounted on die-cast metal bases. **NRS**

Platform Display Sets

In 1968 and 1969 Strombecker featured three special Platform Display Sets, each containing a building and a number of vehicles from the Collectors Series.

G E M

1805 FAIR ACRES FARM: (1968-1969) Set contains two-story barn, fenced corral, two horses, two pigs, two cows, one chicken, Farm Tractor, Disc Harrow, Plow, Utility Wagon, Jeep Truck, Pickup Truck, Overland Jeep, and Skip Loader. **NRS**

1810 FIRE STATION: (1968-1969) Set contains two-story fire station, Snorkel Truck, Pumper Truck, Panel Truck, Fire Chief Car, Emergency Jeep, Aerial Ladder Truck, Fire Chief badge, emergency net, two ladders, fire axes, and stretcher. **NRS**

1815 SUPER SERVICE STATION: (1968-1969) Set contains three-level service station, two grease racks, gas pump island, two overhead lights, MOBIL Gas Tanker Trailer Truck, Tow Truck, Jeep, Oil Truck, and four Cars. **NRS**

Super Tootsietoys Series

Strombecker introduced the Super Tootsietoys in 1964. This line of large vehicles consisted of trucks as well as a farm tractor, a racer, a boat trailer and boat, all with die-cast metal cabs and chassis, steel axles, and polypropylene bodies, grilles, and bumpers. Most of the units are 8 inches in length; the farm tractor is the smallest at slightly under 7 inches. They are packaged in a "picture frame" box, open on the front and wrapped in clear film. Current values in Good and Excellent for some of these items are listed below.

1300 SUPER TOW TRUCK: (1966-1968) 8½" long. Ford or GMC Truck with red cab has white rear tow assembly with windup winch and tow hook. **14 20 —**

1305 SUPER DUMP TRUCK: (1966-1968) 9⅜" long. Blue Ford or GMC Truck with yellow operating rear dump. **14 20 —**

1310 SUPER PICK-UP TRUCK: (1966-1968) 8" long. Ford Pickup Truck painted red and yellow. **12 18 —**

1315 SUPER INDIANAPOLIS "500" RACER: (1966-1968) 7½" long. Dark blue and white Racer with oversized driver's head in the cockpit; driver referred to as "Terrible Tommy" in the 1966 catalogue; 96 on front hood; rear engine with exposed motor; roll bar; spoked wheels and racing tires; wind screen; tail pipes. **NRS**

1320 SUPER TRACTOR: (1966) 6¾" long. Modern farm tractor. **NRS**

1325 SUPER U-HAUL TRUCK: (1966) 8½" long. Ford closed-body, orange and silver Truck with U-Haul markings on sides and front. **NRS**

1335 SUPER STAKE TRUCK: (1966) 8" long. Ford or GMC stake-body Truck with removable rear gate. **14 20 —**

1340 PICK-UP TRUCK, BOAT, AND TRAILER: (1966) 16" in total length. Ford Pickup Truck with "super-size" 8"

The Super Series U-Haul Truck. D. Campbell Collection.

G E M

die-cast metal boat trailer and speedboat-styled polypropylene 7" Cabin Cruiser. **NRS**

1345 SUPER CAMPER: (1966) 8½" long. Ford Pickup Truck with rear, removable truck Camper. **15 25 —**

1350 CHERRY PICKER: (1966) 8" long. Ford Pickup Truck with cherry picker snorkel mounted in truck bed; picker moves up and down. **NRS**

1352 KENNEL TRUCK: (1967) 8" long. Ford Pickup Tuck with clear plastic dome over truck bed; bed partitioned to hold four different canines included. **NRS**

1355 TRENCHER SHOVEL TRUCK: (1966-1967) 8" long. Ford or GMC Flatbed Truck with trencher mounted in truck bed; working mechanical trencher swivels and scoops. **NRS**

1360 SUPER SANDWHEEL TRUCK: (1966-1967) 8½" long. Ford or GMC Flatbed Truck with working sandwheel mounted to the rear truck bed. **NRS**

1755 SUPER TOOTSIETOY PLAYTIME SET: (1967) Set contains one each of Nos. 1340, 1355, and 1360. **NRS**

2926 SUPER TOW TRUCK: (1964-1965) 8½" long. Ford or GMC Truck with rear tow assembly; cab painted red; white rear tow assembly; wind-up working winch. **14 20 —**

2927 SUPER U-HAUL TRUCK: (1964-1965) 8½" long. Orange and white Ford closed-body Truck with U-Haul markings on sides. **NRS**

G E M

2928 SUPER TRACTOR: (1964-1965) 6¾" long. Modern farm tractor. **NRS**

2929 PICKUP TRUCK, BOAT, AND TRAILER: (1965) See No. 1340 for description. **NRS**

2930 SUPER STAKE TRUCK: (1965) See 1335 for description. **14 20 —**

2931 SUPER DUMP TRUCK: (1964-1965) 9⅜" long. Blue Ford or GMC Truck with yellow operating rear dump unit. **14 20 —**

2932 SUPER PICK-UP TRUCK: (1964-1965) 8" long. Ford Pickup Truck painted red and yellow. **12 18 —**

2933 SUPER INDY "500" RACER: (1964-1965) 7½" long. Dark blue and white Racer with 96 on the hood; rear engine with exposed motor; oversized driver's head in open cockpit. **NRS**

2934 SUPER CAMPER: (1965) See No. 1345 for description. **15 25 —**

2937 CHERRY PICKER: (1965) See No. 1350 for description. **NRS**

2939 TRENCHER SHOVEL TRUCK: (1965) See No. 1355 for description. **NRS**

2953 SUPER PICK-UP TRUCK WITH PULL TRAILER: (1965) Ford Truck painted red with orange Trailer. **NRS**

Midget Series assortment.

G E M

2954 SUPER SANDWHEEL TRUCK: (1965) See No. 1360 for description. **NRS**

4555 SUPER TOOTSIETOY PLAYTIME SET: (1965-1966) Set contain one each of Nos. 1340, 1355, and 1360. **NRS**

By 1968 only four of these units were being produced: the Indy Racer, the Pickup Truck, the Tow Truck, and the Super Dump Truck. No units were offered in 1969.

Vinyl Carrying Cases

Two types of carrying cases with cars were introduced in 1969. They were made of vinyl and carried vehicles from the Midget Series.

1715 VINYL CAR CARRYING CASE: (1969) 7″ by 9½″ case with plastic inner tray having separate spaces for fifteen cars. Case comes with eight cars. CAR CASE and MINIATURE CAR COLLECTION on the front of the case; CAR DISPLAY CASE on the left side. **NRS**

G E M

1780 SERVICE STATION CARRYING CASE: (1969) 2½″ by 5″ by 12″ plastic service station with pull-out ramp to second story; folds into carrying case with handle. Garage doors lift up. Case comes with ten cars; illustrated with gas pumps, oil racks, and roadways. TOOTSIETOY SUPER SERVICE, Champion logo, and "the original die-cast METAL toy" on the front. **NRS**

Wall Display Cases

1710 12-CAR WALL DISPLAY CASE: (1969) 9½″ by 11″ visual display case to be mounted on wall or stacked on shelf; twelve miniature die-cast metal cars; for home or store use. TOOTSIETOY DIE CAST METAL CARS. **NRS**

1720 20-CAR WALL DISPLAY CASE: (1969) 11½″ by 14¼″ display case; twenty miniature metal cars. TOOTSIETOY DIE CAST METAL CARS. **NRS**

CHAPTER 13

Mexican "tutsitoys"

In the early sixties, Strombecker developed a joint venture with Antonio and Eduardo Guraieb of Mexico to manufacture selected discontinued Tootsietoy vehicles for the Mexican market. The molds for those items were sold to Strombecker de Mexico with the stipulation that samples of their toys be sent to Strombecker in Chicago. The molds were not altered in any way by the Mexican manufacturer, and therefore many of the toys that they produced have the same cast-in identification markings underneath as the pieces that had been produced by Strombecker in Chicago. To the best of my knowledge, the molds sold to the Mexican manufacturer included toys from the 6-inch, 4-inch, and 3-inch series, airplanes, the 1955 International and Mack trailer trucks, bulldozers and scrapers, farm tractors, the gas pump island, pull trailers, and the 7-inch Mercedes Benz. Production of these Mexican Tootsietoys continued as late as 1987.

Collectors have expressed concern about the these Mexican Tootsietoys. How could they distinguish between a vehicle made in Chicago and one in Mexico? Were the materials the same? Indeed, a large quantity of different vehicles were made in Mexico and sold in that company's own blister packages and boxes.

After visiting the Strombecker facility in 1992, examining samples sent from Mexico, and discussing this with company officials, it seems that there *are* a few telltale ways to distinguish the American from the Mexican versions once they are out of their boxes. The best way is by studying the tires: the depth of the tire tread on Mexican Tootsietoys is considerably less, and the tread does not extend across the width of the tire. In addition, Mexican tires have a talcum-powdered look, probably the result of the manufacturing process, and do not have "TOOTSIETOY" cast into the sidewalls, as do most of their American counterparts. Wooden tires were also used on some of the tractor truck units.

Other telltale marks include decals: the tractor trailer truck and the 6-inch tanker truck have "Pemex" stickers on the side, easily identifying them as Mexican (Pemex is a Mexican oil company). Many toys are painted in unusual colors not associated with the U.S. Tootsietoys, such as pink, light turquoise, or violet!

If a unit is found in its original box or blister pack, identification is considerably easier! The yellow and red colors on the packaging, the spelling of "tutsitoy," and the phrase "Made in Mexico" eliminate any doubt.

The following is a list of known units manufactured in Mexico. No values are available.

Tractor Trailer Trucks

1955 International with Low-boy Trailer and 3″ Hot Rod Model B
1955 International Moving Van (Auto Express)
1955 International PEMEX tanker, C. Jones Collection.
1955 International with Utility Trailer
1955 Mack Hook and Ladder Fire Truck

6-inch series

Caterpillar Scraper
Caterpillar Bulldozer
Farm Tractor
Farm Tractor with Disc Harrow
Mercedes Benz (7″)
Greyhound Scenicruiser Bus
1940 Ford Convertible
1947 Mack Dump Truck
1947 Mack Stakeside Truck
1947 Mack Tow Truck
1954 MG
1955 Mack Cement Truck
1956 Dodge Ambulance Panel Truck
1956 Dodge Panel Truck
1956 Jeep
1959 Ford Wagon
1959 Oldsmobile Convertible
1960 Chevy El Camino
1962 Ford (C-600) PEMEX Oil Tanker Truck, C. Jones Collection.
1962 Ford Pickup Truck

Airplanes

Beechcraft Bonanza
Boeing 707 Jet
F-86 Jet
Cutlass Jet
Skyray Jet
Starfire Jet
Panther Jet
Plane Assortment Gift Set

A dealer's boxed assortment of 6-inch cars and trucks. Strombecker Corporation archives.

3-inch series

Hot Rod
World War II Jeep
1949 Ford Pickup Truck
1954 Jaguar
1954 Ford Wagon Ambulance
1954 MG
1955 Ford Tanker Truck
1957 Ford Convertible
1957 Jaguar

Pull Trailer Set

1954 MG with Boat and Trailer (6-inch series)
1956 Jeep with Camping Trailer (6-inch series)

Gift Sets

AUTO SERVICIO SET. Set contains 1955 International Pemex tanker trailer truck, 1947 Mack Tow Truck, two 1954 MGs (3-inch), 1957 Ford Convertible (3-inch), and gas pump island.

An assortment of blister packs and boxed toys. Strombecker Corporation archives.

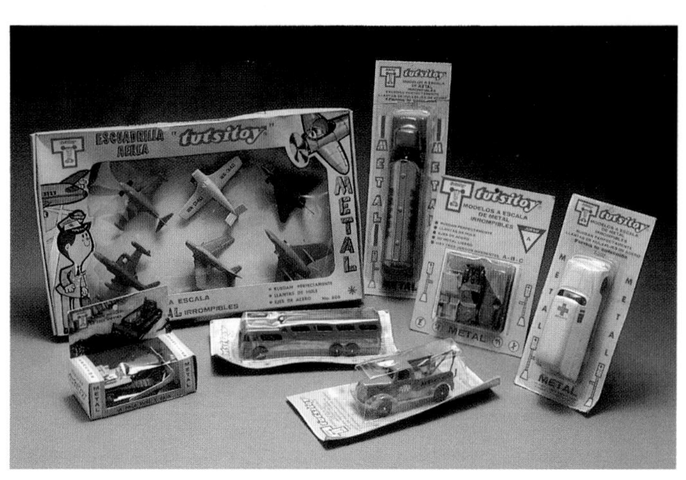

An assortment of blister packs and an airplane gift set. Strombecker Corporation archives.

Appendix
Using Tootsietoys on Train Layouts

Collectors who may be slightly nostalgic (as I am) *and* who also have an operating train layout usually have a few Tootsietoy vehicles decorating their layouts. While there are numerous examples of good quality, excellently detailed vehicles from other manufacturers, most of them were not produced during the years when the popular trains achieved their greatest following and which today probably enjoy an even greater popularity. Tootsietoys were produced during those eras, and thereby add authenticity to the layouts.

Because of the wide variety produced by Tootsietoy, there are a number of options in vehicle size to choose from. Your choice should be based on your own tastes and preferences as well as on your desire to achieve a scale look to your layout. The A.C. Gilbert Company of New Haven, Connecticut, actually used Tootsietoys on a number of their American Flyer cars. The U.S. Navy Jeep Transport Car is one of the most sought after train cars by collectors. It featured two World War II Jeeps in the military olive-drab color. Three different vehicles were used from 1941 through 1961, the Armored Car, the Midget Racer, and the World War II Jeep from the 4-inch series.

In addition to these train car units, A.C. Gilbert used a number of other Tootsietoy vehicles in their catalogue advertisements. In 1946 and 1947, the four-door Jumbo Torpedo Sedan was featured with the No. 584 Bell Danger Signal and the No. 582 Automatic Blinker Signal. In 1948 and 1949, the same advertisement was shown for the No. 582 Automatic Blinker Signal only. In 1950 a new train layout was featured on page 16 of their catalogue, and among the small assortment of vehicles used on this layout was the 4-inch 1949 Mercury Four-Door Sedan. Information was provided by H. Timmes.

The following comparison chart lists various Tootsietoy vehicles that go well with O, O27, S, G, and HO gauge trains. See Chapter 10 for the descriptions of other HO-scale vehicles made by Strombecker.

Comparison Chart of Tootsietoys and Train Scales

	3" Cars	3" Trucks	4" Cars	4" Trucks	6" Cars Early Series	6" Cars Later Series	6" Trucks	Tractor Trucks
O & O27	Under Scale	Under Scale	Acceptable	Varies	Acceptable	Over Scale	Varies	Acceptable
O, O27 Flat Cars and Car Carriers	MPC*	MPC	Acceptable	Acceptable	Over Scale	Over Scale	Varies	Acceptable
O, O27 Accessories and Buildings	Under Scale	Under Scale	Acceptable	Varies	Acceptable	Over Scale	Varies	Acceptable
S Gauge	Under Scale	Under Scale	Acceptable	Acceptable	Over Scale	Over Scale	Over Scale	Acceptable
S Gauge Flat Cars and Car Carriers	Under Scale	Under Scale	Acceptable	Acceptable	Over Scale	Over Scale	Over Scale	Over Scale
S Gauge Accessories and Buildings	Under Scale	Under Scale	Acceptable	Acceptable	Over Scale	Over Scale	Over Scale	Acceptable
G Gauge	Under Scale	Under Scale	Under Scale	Under Scale	Under Scale	Acceptable	Under Scale	Under Scale
G Gauge Flat Cars and Car Carriers	Under Scale	Under Scale	Under Scale	Under Scale	Under Scale	Acceptable	Varies	Under Scale

* MPC is the common terminology used in train collecting for the Lionel produced from 1970 to 1985.

Always Look For The Name On Every Toy

tootsietoys

The Original Die Cast All Metal Toys... Since 1893

1954

MANUFACTURED BY

DOWST MANUFACTURING CO.

CHICAGO 24, ILLINOIS

Bibliography

Angelucci, Enzo. *World Encyclopedia of Civil Aircraft.* New York: Crown Publishers, 1982.

Antique Toy World. Chicago: Antique Toy World Magazine. Dale Kelley, ed. Various issues.

Dammann, George H. *Illustratrated History of Ford.* Florida: Crestline Publishing Co., 1971, rev. ed.

Flink, James J. *The Car Culture.* Cambridge: MIT Press, 1975.

Georgano, G. N., ed. *Complete Encyclopedia of Motor Cars: 1885-to the Present.* New York: E. P. Dutton & Co., 1968.

Hertz, Louis H. *The Complete Book of Building and Collecting Model Automobiles.* New York: Crown Publishers, Inc., New York, 1970.

Jane's Encyclopedia of Aviation. New York: Crown Publishers, Inc., 1989.

Langworth, Richard M., Chris Pools, and the Auto Editors of Consumer Guide. *Great American Automobiles of the 50's.* Lincolnwood, IL: Publication International, Ltd., 1989.

Lewis, Albert L. and Walter A. Musciano. *Automobiles of the World.* New York: Simon and Schuster, 1977.

Lunz, Lois. "Let's Visit the Strombeck-Becker Manufacturing Co." *The Hobby Merchandiser.* Reprint, n.p.: July 1953.

Playthings. New York: Geyer-McAllister Publication Co., Inc. Numerous issues.

Ruiz, Marco. *One Hundred Years of the Automobile: 1886-1986.* New York: W.H. Smith Publishers, Gallery Books, 1985.

Ward, Ian. "The World of Automobiles." *Illustrated Encyclopedia of the Motorcar.* Vol. 1, 3, 7, 9, 11, and 12. New York: Columbia House, n.d.

Weal, Elke C. *Combat Aircraft of World War II.* New York: Macmillan Co., 1977.

World Book Encyclopedia. Chicago: Field Enterprises Educational Corporation: 1967, Vol. A: 924, s.v. "Automobile."

Index

This is an index to the listings of postwar Tootsietoys. Vehicles within each grouping are first ordered alphabetically by model type, then by model year. Since model car collectors verbally identify a vehicle by its model year and then make (e.g., 1956 Ford Tanker Truck), the model year has remained before the model in this index. To list them in chronological order would have interspersed the various makes, making finding a particular vehicle more involved.

In Chapter 11, Postwar First Generation boxed sets are listed in order of the set number. A summary listing of airplane, military, train, and vehicle sets, with their numbers, is provided for your convenience on page 102. By consulting it you can readily find the description of a specific set in Chapter 11. Individually packaged items are listed on pages 121–126. Sets and series issued in the late sixties are listed in Chapter 12. Other sets and items which are part of series are listed under those series: Classic Antique, Collector, Hitch-Ups, Midget, Platform Display, Playmates, Pocket, Road Racing, and Super Tootsietoys.
(**Note:** (PW) refers to Prewar reissue.)